£33.14 net

F

2

A Garland Series

Accounting History and the

A thirty-eight-volume facsimile series

)evelopment of a Profession

Edited by Richard P. Brief, NEW YORK UNIVERSITY

Collected Papers on Accounting and Accounting Education

VOLUME 2
History, Education, and Management Accounting

David Solomons

GARLAND PUBLISHING, INC.
NEW YORK & LONDON
1984

For a complete list of the titles in this series
see the final pages of this volume.

The papers in this volume are reprinted
with permission of the journals, editors and publishers
listed in the table of contents.

Library of Congress Cataloging in Publication Data

Solomons, David.
Collected papers on accounting and accounting education.

(Accounting history and the development of a profession)
Includes bibliographical references.
Articles which originally appeared in various
publications between 1948 and 1982.
Contents: v. 1. Theory and standards—v. 2. History,
education, and management accounting.
1. Accounting—Addresses, essays, lectures.
2. Accounting—Study and teaching—Addresses, essays,
lectures. I. Title. II. Series.
HF5635.S6894 1984 657 83-49444
ISBN 0-8240-6311-2 (v. 1 : alk. paper)
ISBN 0-8240-6312-0 (v. 2 : alk. paper)

The volumes in this series are printed on
acid-free, 250-year-life paper.

Printed in the United States of America

To Jonathan

Contents

Introduction

Volume I of this collection was devoted to papers spanning the 35 years 1948–1983 on topics that can loosely be called accounting theory and accounting standard setting. I have always had an interest in accounting theory; but two related events—my appointment to the chairmanship of an American Accounting Association committee on the standard setting process in 1970 and my appointment by the American Institute of CPAs to the Wheat Committee in 1971—motivated me to become interested in financial accounting standards, and that interest has grown ever since. Yet most of my first two decades as an academic—my first in Britain and my second in America—were devoted to management accounting and its history.

I explained in the introduction to volume I how I became an academic almost by chance, and how my civilian career in academe started at the London School of Economics with my time divided between teaching and practice. My first non-trivial piece of writing, "Cost Accounting and the Use of Space and Equipment," might not have been written if I had not continued for a while, while teaching, to work for one day a week as an accountant; for it was on one of my office days that I was having lunch in the cafeteria of the D. H. Evans department store in London's Oxford Street when I observed that the allocation of space between the self-service cafeteria and the full-service restaurant was adjusted by positioning moveable screens. That led me to think about the whole problem of resource allocation in a way that would now be handled easily by mathematical programming but which then seemed novel.

My paper was one of the first to be presented (in 1947) to Ronald Edwards's LSE seminar on industrial administration. Usually the speakers at those weekly meetings (and some of the participants) were industrial leaders of eminence, and the series continued for years, even after Edwards had left academe and had himself become an important figure in British industry. So it was quite a distinction for a junior lecturer to be asked to make a presentation to such a group. Edwards's influence on my work during my years at LSE was strong and direct; but he was only one of an outstanding group of colleagues who made LSE an exciting place to work in during those post-war years. Their influence can be seen in much of my writing both at that time and since.

The fact that my paper was published, in the spring of 1948, in *The Accountant* says something about the state of academic accounting in Britain at that time. *The Accountant* was (and is) a weekly periodical strongly professional in its orientation. My paper was distinctly academic. Yet there was no academic journal in Britain at that time that would have provided a more appropriate outlet, and the possibility of publishing in America never occurred to me. Had I been better informed about coming events or less impatient to get into print, I might have waited for the first issue of *Accounting Research,* which appeared in November 1948. That journal was published by the Cambridge University Press for the Incorporated Accountants' Research Committee. It was edited by F. Sewell Bray and Leo T. Little, both of them associated with the Society of Incorporated Accountants, and during its brief life of ten years it did much to raise the level of academic work in accounting in Britain. When the Society of Incorporated Accountants was absorbed by the Institute of Chartered Accountants in England and Wales in 1957, *Accounting Research* was discontinued as a separate publication. The last issue appeared in October, 1958, and it was then incorporated in *Accountancy,* which by that time had become the Institute's monthly journal. Once more, and for the next twelve years, there was no British academic accounting journal.

Though my paper on the use of space and equipment had already appeared when the first issue of *Accounting Research* was published, that issue did contain a related article, by E. B. Palmer, one of my first generation post-war LSE students, entitled "The Use of Departmental Accounts, in Particular as a Guide to the Allocation of Floor-Space."

My essay on the historical development of costing grew out of a book that was never published. Edwards, George Thirlby and I started work in 1949 or thereabouts on a book that was to contain the LSE gospel on cost and management accounting. My historical essay, reprinted in this volume, was to be the introduction to that book. But the partnership broke up, and my essay became instead the introduction to a book of readings, *Studies in Costing,* that I edited and published in 1953. As I explained in the introduction to volume I, this was, to my knowledge, only the second book of readings put together for accounting students (the first was *Studies in Accounting,* edited by William Baxter). Such books are now legion; but I believe mine was the first in the management accounting field.

Though all accounting educators naturally have an interest in accounting education, they do not all write about it. What first stimulated me to do so was my departure from London in 1955 to become the University of Bristol's first professor of accounting. There I was required to deliver an inaugural lecture, and the opportunity that gave me to express some of my frustrations over the state of accounting education in Britain was irresistible. "Accounting Education for New Responsibilities" was the result—the words "for new responsibilities" were added to the title at Arnold Plant's suggestion. Plant had been my teacher during my undergraduate days at LSE, had been largely responsible for enabling me to get a teaching appointment there after the war, and was a supportive colleague throughout my stay at the School.

I referred earlier to my dissatisfaction with the state of British accounting education. Those frustrations played an important part in my decision in 1959 to leave Bristol and to accept an appointment at the Wharton School of the University of Pennsylvania. Only a year or so later, my gloomy estimate of the prospects for improvement in Britain was amply vindicated by the publication of an Institute of Chartered Accountants committee report—the Parker Report—which expressed almost total satisfaction with the then existing state of affairs. Writing my 1961 piece for *Accountancy* attacking that report gave me more satisfaction, I think, than anything else I have written.

Whether that article had anything to do with the invitation I received—and accepted—eleven years later from the six major professional bodies of accountants in the U. K. to return and conduct a long-range inquiry into their education and training arrangements I do not know. I spent 1972/73 in London working on the inquiry and 1973/74 writing the report, mostly in the U.S. It was published, with the title *Prospectus for a Profession,* in 1974. My 1977 and 1981 papers and one of my 1980 addresses to the English Institute's centenary conference reflect some of that work. I wish I could say that *Prospectus*—it is better known in the U. K. as the Solomons Report—had left a deep mark on British accounting education, but I cannot. At the most, it caused a few ripples. It was politely received by the six bodies that had commissioned the study. They then turned their backs on it and went their several ways. One day, perhaps, it will be rediscovered and put to use.

Not long after I moved to Philadelphia, the Financial Executives Research Foundation approached the Wharton School with a request that we make a study of the problem of control in divisionalized companies. My department chairman at that time, Rufus Wixon, asked me to undertake that task, and the result was the publication by the Foundation, in 1965, of my book, *Divisional Performance: Measurement and Control.* The book was reissued by Richard D. Irwin in 1968 and was reprinted by Markus Wiener Publishing Inc. in 1983. Work on *Divisional Performance* gave me an entrée into some twenty-five divisionalized companies and enabled me to study a number of management accounting problems at first hand. My two papers on conflict (1966 and 1971) and my 1968 paper in *Public Reporting by Conglomerates* reflect that experience.

My 1971 paper on intracorporate conflict in international business is also a reflection of the year (1963/64) that I spent in Switzerland teaching at IMEDE. That year was particularly rich in international experiences, for my studies for that paper and other travel took me into every country of western Europe except Scandinavia, Luxemburg and Portugal. And the students in that IMEDE class came from all over the world. But I have been unusually fortunate in the opportunities I have had, not only then but throughout my professional career, to see the international dimension of accounting. I have had the advantage of having made my home and of working on both sides of the Atlantic; and some of my other travels—New Zealand, British Columbia, Quebec, Ontario, Ireland, Austria—show up in these volumes. To know only one country is not to know it well, for judgment, like measurement, always implies comparison. But at this point a humbling thought breaks in. I have always envied people—like my wife—who are fluent in more than one language. I have no such skill. What right do I have to talk about "the international dimension"?

David Solomons
Philadelphia, PA
November 1983

Accounting History

The Historical Development of Costing*

by David Solomons

So much has been written about the early history of double-entry book-keeping that every schoolboy now knows that it took its rise in the highly developed civilization of Northern Italy in the fourteenth and fifteenth centuries, that it was used by many merchants of the time both in Italy and in the Netherlands and Southern Germany, where the mercantile influence of the Italians was very strong; that it was not, however, until the end of the fifteenth century that the technique of the art was systematically set down by the mathematician-monk, Luca Paciolo, and published in Venice in 1494 as part of a book on mathematics; and that from then on, texts on the subject appeared in Germany, the Low Countries, France and England.

In none of these early texts is there so much as a mention of any economic activity other than buying and selling. The merchant was king, and for him alone were book-keeping texts written. The fact is, of course, that to the extent that manufacturing processes were in the hands of small craftsmen closely controlled by the rules of their guilds, there was little scope for anything worthy of the name of industrial accounting; and while it is conceivable that monastic and other large landed estates might have developed book-keeping methods which could separate the results of different activities, they do not in fact seem to have done so. The main purpose of their records was accountability of bailiff to master, not the comparison of costs and revenues, the fixing of selling prices and the ascertainment of profit and loss.

With the enclosure of land and the growing importance in industry of capitalists who gave out materials to be worked on by artisans in their own homes, new problems emerged. There was, for instance, the need for effective methods of controlling stocks of materials in the hands of outworkers, of linking amounts earned by the workers with the amounts paid to them, and separation of the financial results achieved by the capitalist on each of his separate activities.[1]

*First published in *Studies in Costing*, 1952.

[1]It should be noted that merchants' accounts had coped with somewhat similar problems from early times, *e.g.*, the control of stocks in the hands of consignees and the striking of profits on separate ventures and consignments. See B. S. Yamey on "Scientific Book-keeping and the Rise of Capitalism" in *The Economic History Review*, Second Series, Vol. 1, Nos. 2 and 3, 1949, pp. 111-112.

It was only when, in the course of the great growth of capitalistic production which we call the Industrial Revolution, the domestic system was replaced by the factory system and the employment of costly machines and equipment was made possible, that there was added to the already existing costing problems, which were almost exclusively concerned with the cost of labour and materials, those difficult questions concerning the treatment of overheads which we are still some way from having disposed of satisfactorily.

An adequate account of the evolution of book-keeping into a tool of industrial management has yet to be written. Certainly nothing as brief as this essay can hope to fill the gap. What it can hope to do, however, is to sketch the main lines of development, so that the studies which it is the main purpose of this book to present (or, rather, to re-present) can be better seen in perspective as the end-products of a great deal of earlier thought.

That earlier thought divides rather clearly into two parts. The first part, covering the period from the early fourteenth century down to the third quarter of the nineteenth is largely, though by no means only, concerned with bringing the records of industrial activity within the compass of double-entry book-keeping, and of extending the scope of that system to cover transactions, such as the transfer of materials from process to process *within* a business, which its early practitioners had never had in view. By 1875 or thereabouts, that technical problem had been completely solved. The second part of the story, which spans the three-quarters of a century down to our own day, is concerned, not with a rather narrow technical problem in book-keeping, but with the broader issue of making the accounting records mean something, of making them flexible and capable of providing information which would be significant not for one purpose (say, the measurment of profit or loss) or two (say, in addition, the fixing of selling prices) but for any of the purposes which, in modern business, figures may be called upon to serve. In the earlier period, there is really a single line of development which it is not too difficult to trace. In the later period, however, the trail divides, so that it is easy to go off on a false scent. We are, of course, still too close to this period to be able to distinguish with certainty the paths which lead to open country from those which are blind alleys. But the attempt, nevertheless, must be made.

The Beginning of the Story

Mrs. de Roover, in her fascinating study of the accounting records of the Antwerp printer, Christopher Plantin,[2] puts the earliest use of accounting in industry as at the beginning of the fourteenth century, in Italy.

[2] "Cost Accounting in the 16th Century"; *The Accounting Review*, Vol. 12, No. 3, September, 1937, pp. 226–237. Reprinted in this volume, pp. 50–68.

We have a fairly detailed picture of its state of development there two centuries later from her husband, Raymond de Roover, who has given us an account of the business organisation set up by members of the Medici family in Florence in the sixteenth century for the manufacture of woollen cloth.[3] The firm of Raffaello di Francesco de' Medici & Co., one of a succession of Medici partnerships, was founded in 1531 and was liquidated three years later. It bought wool, put it out for processing, sometimes through factors, to artisans working in their own homes, and sold the finished cloth, mostly in the Levant. Probably only a few processes such as wool sorting, cleansing (but not washing), combing and carding were carried on in the firm's own workshop. The firm's books, of which there were eight, were kept by double-entry. There was a waste book, to record transactions in chronological order as they occurred, and in considerable detail; a journal, which reproduced from the waste book in an abridged form particulars of purchases and sales; a general ledger with both personal and impersonal accounts; a subsidiary wages ledger (which was represented in the general ledger by a control account) containing accounts for most of the factors and artisans who worked for the firm—the most independent ones, such as the dyers, had their accounts in the general ledger; a cash book; and three special journals, recording the materials given out to and the amounts earned by the artisans, the figures of earnings being posted to one or other of the two ledgers.

Reference has already been made to the fact that neither Paciolo nor his successors for two centuries attempted to apply their book-keeping technique to industrial problems, nor, as de Roover points out, did they refer to the use of subsidiary books. It is clear, therefore, from the Medici records, that at this time, practice was well ahead of theory. The book-keeping system of the Medici, writes de Roover, "was not yet a cost-finding system, but it came very close to being one. The account books give enough indication to permit one to assume that the Medici had a good knowledge of their approximate cost and used this information in pricing their finished cloth."[4] It is worth noting that the problem of overheads hardly obtruded itself, for such expenses represented only about 10 per cent. of total cost.

If we could be certain that the Plantin records were typical, we should have to conclude that the gap between practice and precept in the mid-sixteenth century was even greater than is suggested by the Medici accounts. Yet what Plantin was doing in Antwerp must have been widely practised in Venice and elsewhere in Italy, for we know

[3]"A Florentine Firm of Cloth Manufacturers"; *Speculum*, Vol. 16, No. 1, January, 1941, pp. 1-33. We cannot assume, of course, that what was done by the Medicis was necessarily widely practiced by other manufacturers of the time.

[4]Raymond de Roover; *loc. cit.*, p. 28.

that young men from merchant families in the Low Countries were often sent to Italy to learn commercial practices. Plantin's methods would have done credit to a printer of his size three and more centuries later, for he kept separate job accounts for each book printed, he had stock accounts in value and quantity for each kind of paper used, and he kept a plant ledger. His system really was a double-entry cost-finding system of extraordinary maturity. But readers have only to turn on a few pages to Mrs. de Roover's article to read about that for themselves.

During the next two centuries, little evidence of progress in industrial accounting has come down to us. Yet progress must have been made; for in England, James Dodson, in 1750, works out a remarkably clear illustration of a shoe-maker's accounts[5]. He has an account for the stock of leather, which is debited with purchases in value and quantity (the quantity units being hides and skins) and credited with transfers to accounts for soles and heels and upper leathers when the hides and skins are cut. These accounts are in turn credited with the quantities and values of the parts (pairs of soles and heels and upper leathers) put out to artisans for making up into shoes, and a personal account for each artisan is debited. On the return of the finished work, the artisan is credited with the agreed value of the shoes, which value is debited to a finished stock account for shoes, this account having quantity columns to distinguish the main types. The artisans' accounts are balanced, subject to small differences carried forward, by a debit for cash paid in settlement for the work done. Finally, the finished stock account is credited with cash and credit sales, a debit balance is carried down for the stock unsold, and the account thus shows the trading profit.[6]

As a matter of subsidiary interest, Dodson recommends the use of separate books for different kinds of transactions, *e.g.*, a workman's ledger, a cash sales book and so on. This kind of segregation of different transactions was by no means a commonplace feature of accounting systems of his time.

When Hugh Crispin, Dodson's shoe-maker, cuts his 20 hides into soles and heels and his 50 skins into upper leathers and quarters he gets numbers of sets of different sizes. To each size he attaches a different

[5]In *The Accountant, or The Method of Book-keeping, Deduced from Clear Principles and Illustrated by a Variety of Examples*, by James Dodson, Teacher of the Mathematics, London, 1750. Dodson was at one time employed by the Earl of Macclesfield in connection with his estates.

Extracts from the accounts in Dodson's book, and from a number of other English and French works referred to below are reprinted in a series of articles by Professor R. S. Edwards entitled "Early literature and development of cost accounting in Great Britain" in *The Accountant*, Vol. 97 (1937, July-December), pp. 193, 225, 253, 283, 313 and 343, and in his *A survey of French contributions to the study of cost accounting during the 19th century*, published for the Accounting Research Association by Gee & Co. (London), May, 1937.

[6]For extracts from these accounts, see Edwards, *The Accountant*, Vol. 97, pp. 227-8.

value, such that the total value of the parts cut exactly equals the cost of the hides and skins used up. It would be interesting to know how the value for each size was arrived at. On this point, however, which would be of some importance in costing the different sizes of shoe made, he throws no light.

Dodson is dealing with what we would now call "batch costing". An early description of process costing in England is given by Wardhaugh Thompson in 1777.[7] He takes a simplified example of the manufacture of "thread-hosiery" from flax, and shows how the cost of the finished product can be built up in a series of double-entry accounts, kept in quantities and values, process by process.[8] Thus, there is shown a flow of values from the flax stock account through accounts for spinning, bleaching, dyeing, weaving, trimming, finally to emerge as "brown thread hose (dress'd)" at "about 2s. 7d. per pair."

Robert Hamilton devoted a chapter of his *Introduction to Merchandise*[9] to "tradesmen's," *i.e.*, manufacturers' accounts, and made some very sensible suggestions as to the kind of subsidiary books which it would be useful to keep. Thus he recommends the use of "a book of materials, where the quantities purchased and consumed are entered in separate parts or on opposite pages," "a book of work, where the quantities of materials delivered to journeymen, the quantities of wrought goods received in return, the dates of the delivery and return, the value of the materials and wages; and the value of the wrought goods are entered in separate columns," and "a book of wages, which contains the names of the journeymen and other servants employed, the work they are employed at, the number of days, and rate per day, if they be paid by days-wages, or the quantities of work done, and rate, when paid by the piece." He also advised that the ledger should contain separate accounts for different kinds of expense, such as "materials, wages, upholding of machinery, rents, excise, incident charges, etc." And in the closing paragraphs of his chapter,[10] he shows great understanding of one of the central problems of process costing:—

> "When a person is engaged in several branches of manufacture, whether on different materials, or on the same materials through several successive stages, he should keep his books in such a manner as to exhibit the gain or loss on each.
>
> "Take the example of a linen manufacturer who purchases or imports rough

[7]In *The Accountant's Oracle; or Key to Science. Being a Compleat Practical System of Book-keeping. Together with the Nature and Use of Banking Business; and a plain accurate and concise method for manufacturers to keep their Books by Double Entry*. By Wardhaugh Thompson, many years an Accountant in London. York, 1777. Extracts from this book are given by Edwards, *loc. cit.*, pp. 229-231.

[8]Thompson. *Op. cit.*, Vol. 2, pp. 243-253.

[9]Edinburgh, 1788, pp. 486-488. Part IV of the book is on "Italian Book-keeping" and Part V on "Practical Book-keeping". Hamilton was Professor of Philosophy in the Marischal College, Aberdeen.

[10]*Op. cit.*, Pt. 5, Chap. 5, pp. 487-488.

flax, dresses it by his own servants, and sells such kinds as do not suit his purpose; delivers the rest to be spun, and receives the yarn from the spinners; weaves part in his own work-house by journeymen, and delivers the rest to other weavers; gives out the linen to be bleached, and receives and sellls it when white.

"If all these branches of business were necessarily connected, and the manufacturer had no other choice than to purchase the rough flax, and carry on the successive operations, it would be sufficient to keep his books in a form that should exhibit the gain or loss on the whole; but if he has an opportunity of beginning or desisting at any stage of the manufacture, his books should exhibit the gain or loss on each operation separately. He may purchase dressed flax or yarn; he may sell the linen before it be bleached; and, since he chooses to unite the several trades of flax-dresser, spinner, weaver, and bleacher, it is proper he should have a separate view of the success of each. This is the leading principle by which his books should be regulated."

The Early Nineteenth Century in England

Both Dodson and Thompson are recording transactions with persons external to the firm, *i.e.*, with outworkers, suppliers and customers; and Hamilton does not actually give an illustration of a set of manufacturers' accounts. There is no question yet, therefore, of any of these writers showing how to record an internal flow of values from process to process *within* the firm. That was to come, naturally, only with the development of the factory system, in the nineteenth century. Still, there was no justification for the sweeping assertion by F. W. Cronhelm in the preface to his book, *Double Entry by Single*,[11] that "from the pale of the Italian System, Retailers and Manufacturers have ever been excluded." Yet he is probably fairly reflecting the opinion of his day when he says that "it is a common prejudice that, from the very nature of his business, and the numerous processes through which his goods pass, the Manufacturer is unable to keep his Accounts on the same systematic principles as those of the Wholesale Dealer or the Merchant,"[12] and this certainly suggests that at the beginning of the nineteenth century in England systematic records for manufacturing transactions were by no means in common use. Unfortunately, although Cronhelm claimed that his own "New Method enables [manufacturers] to obtain that PROOF of their Books which has hitherto been deemed impracticable"[13] his achievement falls far short of his promises. His illustration of a manufacturer's books is drawn for a woollen cloth manufacturer, but the only feature of them which might distinguish them from those of a merchant is a warehouse ledger divided into three sections, one for raw wool, one for work-in-progress and one for finished manufacture. This ledger is kept in *quantities only*. Each section is columnar in form,

[11]London, 1818, p. viii.
[12]*Op. cit.*, p. 125.
[13]*Op. cit.*, p. viii.

separate columns being kept for different grades of wool and cloth. The section of the ledger devoted to wool stocks is kept in units of *weight*. When a certain weight of wool is put into process, the weight is credited to the wool account, and the "manufactory" is debited with the *number* of pieces of cloth which the wool "ought to produce, according to those rules and proportions which are established in all regular and well managed concerns."[14] The "merchandise" or finished stock section of the warehouse ledger is, of course, also kept in numbers of pieces.

Cronhelm ascertains the profit or loss for the business monthly in a "Merchandise Account," which is really a detailed trading account written up from day to day, being debited with the opening inventory, purchases and expenses and credited with sales and closing inventory. Except for the frequency of the balancing, there is nothing at all advanced in all this. We can certainly agree with Littleton that Cronhelm's illustration of manufacturers' accounts was "deficient."[15]

As the country which led the Industrial Revolution in Europe, England might have been expected to lead the way in industrial accounting during the early nineteenth century. Yet to judge from the literature which has come down to us, this was a period of sterility compared with the stream of advanced thinking which came out of France. One English writer of this period, like the earliest writers on book-keeping an eminent mathematician, must, however, claim our attention. This is Charles Babbage, Lucasian Professor of Mathematics in the University of Cambridge from 1828 to 1839. In two famous paragraphs of his book *On the Economy of Machinery and Manufactures*[16] he puts forward a case for the devotion of time and attention to costing which has hardly been improved since, and I cannot resist the temptation to quote it in full:—

> "The great competition introduced by machinery, and the application of the principle of the subdivision of labour, render it necessary for each producer to be continually on the watch, to discover improved methods by which the cost of the article he manufactures may be reduced; and, with this view, it is of great importance to know the precise expense of every process, as well as of the wear and tear of machinery which is due to it. The same information is desirable for those by whom the manufactured goods are distributed and sold; because it enables them to give reasonable answers or explanations to the objections of inquirers, and also affords them a better chance of suggesting to the manufacturer changes in the fashion of his goods, which may be suitable either to the tastes or to the finances of his customers. To the statesman such knowledge is still more

[14] Cronhelm, *op. cit.*, p. 45. We have here, perhaps, an early use of standards in bookkeeping.

[15] A. C. Littleton: *Accounting Evolution to 1900;* New York, 1933; p. 334.

[16] London, 1832. The quotation which follows is from Chap. 21. "On the Cost of Each Separate Process in a Manufacture," page 203, paragraphs 253 and 254.

important; for without it he must trust entirely to others, and can form no judgment worthy of confidence, of the effect any tax may produce, or of the injury the manufacturer or the country may suffer by its imposition.

"One of the first advantages which suggests itself as likely to arise from a correct analysis of the expense of the several processes of any manufacture, is the indication which it would furnish of the course in which improvement should be directed. If a method could be contrived of diminishing by one-fourth the time required for fixing on the heads of pins, the expense of making them would be reduced about 13 per cent.; whilst a reduction of one-half the time employed in spinning the coil of wire out of which the heads are cut, would scarcely make any sensible difference in the cost of manufacturing of the whole article. It is therefore obvious, that the attention would be much more advantageously directed to shortening the former than the latter process."

Babbage did not give any guidance in his book as to how industrialists were to achieve these admirable objectives, though he does refer later to the necessity, in any but the smallest factory, "to establish an accountant's department, with clerks to pay the workmen, and to see that they arrive at their stated times; and this department must be in communication with the agents who purchase the raw produce, and with those who sell the manufactured article."[17] Whether contemporary accountants were commonly able to provide the cost information which Babbage so clearly saw to be desirable must be open to doubt.

The French Contribution to Industrial Accounting

This rather barren period in British accounting coincided, oddly enough, with a period of considerable advance in French thought on industrial, and more especially, agricultural accounting. One has only to compare Cronhelm's work in England with that of Anselme Payen[18] in France, published a year earlier, to see the difference in quality. As illustrations, Payen takes three quite different types of business, a carriage-maker, a glue manufacturer and a producer of (apparently) certain chemical products. The records distinguish between "accounts in money" which we might call the financial accounts, "accounts in kind," which are broadly what we would call cost accounts, and materials accounts, which show the movement of materials in quantities. The accounts in money and the accounts in kind are not formally linked together, though the figures in the two sets of accounts can be easily shown to agree. The costs which are taken account of include the depreciation of utensils and furnaces, rent and interest. Payen's system, while stopping short of the neat tie-up between cost and financial accounts which was achieved by the end of the nineteenth century, was

[17]*Op. cit.*, p. 216, paragraph 268.

[18]*Essai sur la Tenue des Livres d'un Manufacturier:* Paris, 1817. Payen was himself a manufacturer.

a considerable step on the way towards it. In view of the fact that it has already been discussed at some length by other writers, however, I do not propose to devote more space to it here.[19]

There is about the work of the Frenchman, Godard, whose treatment of industrial accounting appeared in 1827,[20] in some respects a remarkable air of modernity. Godard was a glass manufacturer who had, he says, been much occupied with accountancy in a long administrative career, and he certainly describes process costing with great skill. He discusses the depreciation and maintenance of buildings and plant, he recognizes the problem of pricing out materials which have been purchased at varying prices—he favours a single average price for the year for each material—and he includes interest on capital among the expenses in his profit and loss account. He also describes a system of perpetual inventory. He is writing, as the eighteenth-century writers in England were not, about *factory* accounting.

Louis Mézières, some 30 years later, brings us several steps along the road to modern job costing. His book on *Industrial and Manufacturing Accounts*,[21] which had run into five editions by 1862, was written primarily for technical schools, and he claimed to be the first to concern himself with an elementary text on industrial accounting. "The factories," he says, " have long cried out for a book-keeping system more appropriate to the needs of industry," and he addresses himself not only to students but to industrialists.

As a method of accounting for materials, he illustrates a form of stock record showing, on a single page, with one line for each type of material used, the quantity in stock at the beginning of the month, the quantity and value received, the quantity and value issued *to jobs completed during the month*, and a balance in quantity only. Particulars of materials received are obtained from a purchases recapitulation which he illustrates, and materials issued are also summarized to give the figures needed for the stock record. Next, labour, in days of work, is analysed, by means of a monthly summary of workman's time, over the jobs worked on each month. In the cost ledger, each job has its account, in which is recorded the materials and labour used on it. The cost ledger is said to be written up from notes made by the foreman. Whenever he issues material to a workman he notes the job on which it is to be used,

[19]Payen's work is discussed at length by Littleton, in *Accounting Evolution to 1900*, pp. 323-333: and Edwards gives extracts from it in his *Survey of French Contributions to the Study of Cost Accounting during the 19th Century*, pp. 1-7.

[20]M. Godard, *Traité Général et Sommaire de la Comptabilité Commerciale*, Paris, 1827. Section III is devoted to manufacturers' accounts. Edwards gives extracts in his *Survey*, pp. 9-17.

[21]*Comptabilité Industrielle et Manufacturiére;* Paris, 5th edition, 1862. I have not been able to ascertain when the book first appeared. Mézières was the accountant of and also taught accounting at the Technical College at Châlons.

and also how workmen's time is to be charged. The foreman's notes are made from day to day, and are summarized before entry in the cost ledger, since in each job account there is only one entry for each type of material and one entry for each workman engaged on the job. The costs recorded against the job are added to the profit on it to give the selling price. Finally Mézières has a "Work Executed" Book, which shows in chronological order, on the left-hand page, particulars of completed work and the selling price charged or to be charged. Articles sold during the month are extended into the money column, the total of which must agree with that of the sales column of the (analysed) journal: the item is shown as sold by having the journal folio entered against it. Articles made for stock and unsold at the end of the month are extended into one of the columns on the right-hand page—there is one column for each month of the year—which thus shows for each month the total finished stock on hand, at selling price.

Mézière's system has certain serious shortcomings. He has no record of work in progress, and he admits that his raw material stock balances include materials in process. He appears not to recognize the existence of overhead expenses, for no mention is made of them. Moreover, by using constant purchase prices throughout his illustrations, he evades entirely the problem of valuing issues of material bought at fluctuating prices. Yet for all this, he shows a clear grasp of the kind of records which a job cost system demands. He adds nothing to the theory of costing, but in its practice he displays considerable facility.

Payen, Godard and Mézières are only three of several French writers who, during the first 60 years or so of the nineteenth century, carried forward the study of industrial accounting at a time when, as the premier industrial country of the time, England might have expected to lead the way. She did, as a matter of fact, take over the lead again for a short time towards the end of the century, but by that time America was beginning to lay claim to the pre-eminent position both in industry and in industrial accounting which she has since attained. These latter-day development must shortly claim our attention. But before turning to them, it is worth while pausing to notice how earlier writers on agricultural accounting had dealt with what were essentially costing problems.

Farm Accounting in the Eighteenth and Nineteenth Centuries

One of the earliest and most delightful works in English to deal with farm accounts was *The Gentleman Accomptant: or an Essay to Unfold the Mystery of Accompts* by "a Person of Honour."[22] The author directs his

[22]London, 1714: the author has since been identified as the Hon. Roger North, youngest son of the fourth Lord North and author of *Lives of the Norths*. See Murray, *Chapters in the History of Book-keeping*, Glasgow, 1930, p. 261.

reader to open separate accounts for husbandry and for pasture, as well as for a separate farm which is supposed to be under the management of a bailiff. He further shows how, "if a Gentleman will condescend to traffick with Butchers, etc.," it is easy to sub-divide the accounts still further, and he opens a separate account for a flock of sheep. Each activity is debited with the opening value of live or dead stock, is charged with its expenses, credited with sales or the value of produce taken by the household, and also with the closing value of the stock. The balance is transferred to Profit and Loss Account. In his account for personal chattels, he writes off £100 "by Profit and Loss, failure of values." In the accounts for husbandry, sheep, etc., however, opening and closing stocks are maintained at constant amounts, so that no question of depreciation arises.

At the end of his book, the "Person of Honour" devotes a passage to what he calls "Tabular Arithmetick, which serves for short Views of Accompts and Estimates." He first explains the application of the tabular idea to a rent-roll which, like a modern columnar rent-roll, will show the position of each tenant with regard to arrears. He then illustrates "a Tabular Register of Labourers," which, in more modern terminology, is a weekly diary or time sheet for the staff of labourers, there being a vertical column for each of the six working days, and a line for each labourer.[23] The performance of each labourer each day is thus systematically recorded. "The knowledge that such an Accompt as this is kept," says the author, "is sufficient to keep Men to true Reckoning, lest they lose their Credit and their Work"; and he explains that it will also help the master in making bargains with the men, for he will then know what they can do in a given time.[24]

Robert Hamilton's *Introduction to Merchandise*, which was referred to above, contains a chapter on farm accounts[25] in which a number of useful subsidiary books are recommended for use. He proposes to have a Corn-Book, which is a stock book for different kinds of grain, being ruled with columns for wheat, barley, etc., and recording quantities received from the barn and quantities disposed of by sale, consumption or milling. He also has a Journal of Work, "where the labour performed each day is entered, specifying the field and the number of men and horses employed." Third, he has a Field-Book, "where several pages are allotted for each field, and ruled with two columns, for extending the sum of the expenses, and the produce. The register of the same field, in successive years, is continued from page to page that the success of the different manures, rotations, and methods of treatment, may be easily compared, and a judgment formed of the whole, when continued for a

[23]Extracts from *The Gentleman Accomptant*, including the register of labourers, are reprinted by Edwards in *The Accountant*, Vol. 97, p. 226.

[24]*The Gentleman Accomptant*, p. 208-9.

[25]Pt. 5, Chap. 7, pp. 401-495.

sufficient length of time."[26] He explains how to arrive at the average cost of a yoking, and the cost per acre for reaping, in a commendably clear and practical manner. All this shows a growing appreciation of the value of accounting records in directly productive activities, such as had long been shown in relation to purely merchanting businesses.

Hamilton's treatment of farm accounting, while admirable as far as it goes, is very incomplete. Within the next 40 years, thought on this subject in France seems to have made substantial progress, as the work of de Cazaux, Godard and a host of later writers testifies. De Cazaux's book[27] was first published in 1824, and an expanded version of it appeared in 1825 as Book III of his *Eléments d'Economie Privée et Publique*. It shows a remarkable mastery of the principles of agricultural accounting. Although in its original form, it is quite short, it would take too long to summarize all the interesting things it contains; but some of them must be mentioned. Thus, de Cazaux sees the desirability of distinguishing profits on cultivation from speculative profits from holding produce after it has been raised. Long-maturing investments, like vine-yards and woods, are to be charged with 5 per cent. per annum compound interest whilst maturing, and credited with the value of the produce obtained, so that it can easily be seen whether the annual return on the investment is more or less than 5 per cent.[28] Depreciation of equipment, buildings and improvements is taken account of, by writing off the cost over the expected lives of the assets (at different rates even for different parts of the same asset, according to the durability of the part), with an adjustment if it should be found that the actual asset life differs from expectations. The depreciation is charged proportionately to each of the activities which the assets serve.

As for the records, de Cazaux recommends that an account be opened for each field, each crop, each herd or flock and each fixed asset. Each field account is opened with a debit for its capital value at the beginning of the year, this being put at 20 times its rental value (*i.e.*, the capitalization rate is put at 5 per cent.). It is then debited with the

[26]The specimen which he gives of this book is reprinted by Edwards, *loc. cit.*, p. 254.

[27]*De la Comptabilité dans une Entreprise Industrielle et specialement dans une Exploitation Rurale*, by L. F. G. de Cazaux; Toulouse, 1824.

[28]Cf. Robert Hamilton, *op. cit.*, pp. 490–491: "If a sum of money, suppose £500, be expended to improve the farm, which the proprietor does not expect to draw back in less than 10 years, the whole sum, at the end of the first year, is considered as part of the stock on the farm; but at the end of the second, when one tenth part, or £50, was expected to be drawn back, the remainder only, or £450, should be considered as part of the stock; and this allowance is gradually diminished £50 each year, till it be exhausted. If no returns be expected for several years, the allowance is not diminished till the time when benefit was expected. This, however, should be regulated by the hopes entertained when the money was expended, and not by the success of the improvements; and then the balance of the farm-accompt, in the successive years, will show how far the improvements have exceeded or fallen short of expectation."

costs of cultivation including a due proportion of any general costs such as depreciation of equipment. The value of its crop is credited to the field and debited to the crop account, which is in turn credited with its realized price when sold, or its value when used as forage for animals. The animals are charged with the value of forage fed to them. And so on. But this does not exhaust de Cazaux's subtlety; for crops which increase the fertility of the soil are to be further credited with the value of a quantity of manure equal to two-thirds of the weight of dry fodder produced when they are cropped, and this value increment is to be debited to the field account. The converse treatment is given to crops which use up fertility. Finally, all accounts are credited with the closing inventory valuation, so as to show final profits or losses.

Perhaps enough has been said to suggest how mature de Cazaux's work was. But he was not content with accounting after the event and in the 1825 edition of his book, he goes on to consider budgeting. I shall return to this aspect of his work later.

De Cazaux was followed by a number of other French writers on agricultural accounting and costing who, during the next 40 years or so, maintained an impressive level of thought on the subject, a level which is the more extraordinary in view of the generally backward state of French agriculture at this time. Godard, whose work on industrial accounting has already been referred to,[29] deals also with farm accounts. The general approach used by de Cazaux is worked out in even greater detail, the farm results being presented in a tabular "Comparative Table of Expenses and Produce for the Financial Year"[30] having separate sections for husbandry, livestock and experimental cultivations.

In 1841 Armand Malo won a prize of 1,000 francs offered by the Minister of Africulture and Commerce for "a good elementary work on agricultural accounting, designed to teach this science to the more intelligent children from the primary schools." Malo's book[31] is mainly of interest for the subsidiary books which he describes. In spite of the excellent work of his predecessors, he can still write: "We cannot deplore too much the faults of internal organization which unfortunately paralyse the existence of the greater part of our farms. . . . The word '*Comptabilité*' is itself almost unknown in agriculture. This is a truth painful to state, but who could dispute it?" Continuing the tradition, A. Monginot[32] developed the use of columnar records and

[29]Traité Général et Sommaire de la Comptabilité Commerciale; 1827.

[30]This table is reproduced by Edwards in *A Survey of French Contributions etc.* pp. 16–17.

[31]*Elements de Comptabilité Rurale;* Paris, 1841. For extracts, see Edwards, *op. cit.*, pp. 22–23. Malo is described as "ancien élève de l'Institut de Grignon, professeur de comptabilité à l'École Royale des Haras du Pin."

[32]*Nouvelles Ètudes sur la Comptabilité Commerciale, Industrielle et Agricole;* Paris, 1854. For extracts, see Edwards, *op. cit.*, pp. 24–29. Monginot was "Professeur de Comptabilité, Expert près les Cour et Tribunaux de Paris."

adapted them to the needs of farm accounting. Saintoin-Leroy[33] charged out *all* expenses very carefully to all departments of the farm, so as to show a net profit or loss on each separate activity. The animals are credited with the value of manure produced; this is first debited to a manure account and then charged out to the crops on which it is used. There is very little in modern farm costing which these nineteenth century writers did not anticipate. Even the complaints, over the years, of neglect by farmers to make use of accounting have a familar modern ring.

English Costing in the Mid-Nineteenth Century

It is interesting to compare the standard of these French works with what was available in England in the middle of the century. For farmers, there appeared in 1851, *An Improved System of Farm-Book-Keeping.*[34] The author saw that it was not enough to ascertain the total profit or loss on the farm for the year, for "no comparative judgment can be found of the value of different modes of culture, or different kinds of stock, without keeping a separate account of each, in order to see how the profit or loss arises, and to enable the farmer to determine on the propriety of continuing or abandoning the one or the other."[35] To this end accounts are opened in the ledger and posted from the cash account. Much of the book is devoted to specimen rulings for the various accounts, which make the ledger more a record of operations than a mere book of account. The explanations of the accounting aspects of the system, however, are very defective, whatever its agricultural virtues may have been, and there is none of the subtlety which marks the French works on the subject.

Little seems to have been published in England in this period which could be dignified by the name of industrial accounting. There is a book on book-keeping for tanneries,[36] in which considerable attention is paid to stock records so as to provide a basis for the valuation of stocks of both hides and leather. But there is nowhere in the book anything that can be called leather costing. Even 30 years later, it was possible for a book on brewers' book-keeping to be written,[37] complete with an illustration of a Brewing Book, showing the quantity of materials used

[33] *Manuel de Comptabilité Agricole Pratique;* Paris, 1861. 2nd edition, 1863. Saintoin-Leroy was Administrateur-Trésorier du Comice Agricole d'Orléans.

[34] By "The Author of 'British Husbandry,'" Longmans, London, 1851.

[35] *Op. cit.*, p. 4.

[36] *A System of Book-keeping drawn up for and expressly adapted to the Tanning Trade*, by Joseph Sawyer; 1st edition, London, 1851, 2nd edition, 1862. Sawyer describes himself as a "mercantile and public accountant, and arbitrator."

[37] *Amsdon's Guide to Brewers' Book-keeping*, by Edward Amsdon, Brewers' Accountant, London, 1881.

for each gyle and the barrels produced from them, but without any hint that it might be useful to the brewer to know the cost of each gyle, much less any directions as to how such information might be ascertained.

It may well be that English practice at this time had once more run ahead of theory. We need first-hand studies of the industrial accounts of the period to enable us to judge what practical men were doing, and to compare it with the impression of feebleness which is conveyed by contemporary accounting literature. Certainly all the signs point to a lack of interest among industrialists in the application of accounting to industrial processes—at least in England,[38] the leading industrial country of the period. But it was not long before the pressure of events was to bring about a change.

The Costing Renaissance

The last three decades of the nineteenth century were marked by what can only be described as a costing renaissance in the English speaking world. In the 1880's and 1890's a growing number of writers on costing explained "new" ideas. Yet to a great extent they were only rediscovering ideas that were becoming of great practical importance for the first time but which could certainly have been found, though perhaps in an undeveloped state, in earlier works.

The impact of the new writing on industrialists was, however, not dramatic. There is plenty of evidence that even at the turn of the century anything that could be called a costing system was still to be found only exceptionally both in British and American industry: the typical situation was for a manufacturer to compute product costs on some rough and ready basis, while distribution costs were largely ignored altogether. Alexander Hamilton Church (of whom more will be said later) writes in 1900: " . . . the majority of firms of any size have some sort of cost method, however rough and home-made, which enables them to tell how much labour and what value of material have been expended on any particular job. Between this elementary stage and the next there is a very wide gap which is bridged over by comparatively few firms even in the go-ahead United States."[39] And a year later he writes: "No board would think of carrying on operations

[38] I cannot claim sufficient acquaintance with the literature in Germany to say how matters stood there. Edouard Löw, an accounting officer (Rechnungsrat) in the Ministry of Trade, Industry and Public Works, writing in 1860, gives a short account of German developments to date in his *Theorie des Rechnungswesens*. German writers were certainly very active, for he lists 44 books on farm accounting published between 1787 and 1860, seven on mining and ironworks accounts between 1822 and 1854, and 17 on accounts for factories and handicrafts between 1805 and 1858.

[39] *Engineering Magazine*, Vol. 20, No. 3, December, 1900: "The Meaning of Commercial Organisation," p. 394.

without a set of commercial books arranged by an accountant in whom they had confidence, yet the equally important technical records are nearly always treated in an amateur spirit. . . . So far is this attitude carried that many otherwise experienced business men really and conscientiously do not believe that shop accounts are of any use at all."[40] E. J. Smith, a pioneer of uniform costing in Great Britian, wrote in 1899, after referring to a number of industries of which he had had experience: "Speaking for these and of these, I have no hesitation in saying that the one evil in each and all which has most impressed me is the marvellous absence of really useful and practical knowledge as to the cost of the article produced."[41] It would be easy to bring much further evidence in the same sense.

Reasons for the Growing Interest in Costing

It is from this time, however, that we can begin to detect a growing interest among practical business men in the industrial uses of accounting. Doubtless the increasing scale and complexity of business and the administrative problems which resulted had much to do with this. In the iron industry, for example, the size of business and the degree of integration had ceased to be limited by the availability of water power. The coal mining industry had similarly developed; the sinking of deep shafts, construction of galleries, ventilation and pumping equipment and transport all called for large capital investment. The textile industries had been transformed by the introduction of power machinery. Thus the importance of buildings, plant, equipment and supervision, *i.e.*, of overhead costs, had rapidly increased in relation to the prime costs of materials and labour. Larger bodies of labour had to be paid and controlled, complex processes to be organized and administered. Moreover, the development of railways, with their enormous volume of fixed equipment, had brought the problem of overheads to the fore. These factors doubtless played a part in the development of cost accounting. And their effect was reinforced around the end of the century by the steady absorption of small businesses by large, giving rise to a demand for means of controlling operations by managers and directors divorced from their actual execution.

Perhaps the most important factor, however, leading to a growth of interest in costing, was the increasing difficulty of price fixing in the engineering industry. As the industry grew and as it became more competitive, so the interest in cost accounting developed. This interest is marked by references to the subject in the trade and professional journals in the second half of the century. For example, in 1869 a

[40] "The Proper Distribution of Establishment Charges," in the *Engineering Magazine*, July, 1901, pp. 510–11.

[41] *The New Trades Combination Movement*, p. 21.

leading article in *The Engineer* pointed out that an "estimate right within 20 per cent. of the actual cost is . . . regarded as a very good estimate, and one reflecting much credit on the engineer and all concerned." And the same article goes on to say that " it is not to negligence, however, that we are inclined to ascribe the thoroughly unsatisfactory state in which the practice of estimating now is, but rather to incapacity. There is no good treatise on the subject...."[42] A year later, a correspondent in the same journal wanted to know of a "good system of getting out cost price,"[43] and subsequent correspondence showed a very real and practical interest in the subject. An editorial on "Practical Prime Costs" in *Engineering* in 1891 remarked: "The present-day conditions of the engineering and manufacturing trades, as regards keenness of competition and consequent narrowness of profit, render this subject of an increased importance." Up to 20 years ago, it said, conditions had been different. "Selling prices could generally be fixed at figures leaving good margins, and a 'rough and ready' cost of a certain article or piece of work, upon which could generally be fixed a fancy profit, with a liberal contingency allowance, was as a rule found all that was required. . . . It is during the past 15 or 20 years that prime costing has been developed to the elaborate systems in operation in many of our large and well-managed firms."[44]

Here, then, was a practical reason, a reason that would appeal to business men, for the quickening interest in cost accounting. Writing in 1904 John Mann[45] went so far as to say that "Records of costing doubtless originated in the need of data required in estimating, especially in engineering and kindred trades where the work is specially contracted for, and where there is no scale of market prices."[46] While it is going too far to say that costing originated in this way it was, no doubt, the growing recognition that careful records of past experience might improve price estimating in this type of industry that persuaded business men that it was worth spending money on.

The Ascertainment of "Actual" Cost

During this period (1875–1900) the typical costing system (where such a thing existed at all) in the engineering industry relied on the foreman for details of time spent by workmen on each job, and often for details of materials used also. A check on total wages was kept by the use of a

[42] *The Engineer*, London, September 3, 1869, p. 166.
[43] *The Engineer*, November 25, 1870, p. 363.
[44] *Engineering*, London, December 4, 1891, pp. 665–6.
[45] Sir John Mann, K.B.E., C.A. died in 1955 at the age of 92.
[46] *Encyclopaedia of Accounting*, Vol. 2, p. 260, on "Cost Records or Factory Accounting."

time book kept at the works gate by a timekeeper to record employees' arrival and departure times: or sometimes this was done by giving each worker a disc with his works number, the disc being taken from a board and put in a box by the worker on arrival and departure. A latecomer would find only a "late box" to put his disc in. By changing the box at 15- or 30-minute intervals the approximate time of arrival by late-comers could be ascertained and recorded. Overheads would be added to the prime costs of each job usually by adding a flat percentage to labour cost or to prime cost. This percentage would be ascertained from the previous year's financial accounts by expressing the total overhead expenses for the year as a percentage of the year's total direct wages or the total prime costs.

The total of these three amounts—direct wages, direct materials costs and overheads—gave a figure which was accepted as the "actual" cost of the job. But it was not long before the concept of "actual" cost became clouded by doubts. There were differences of opinion as to whether items such as interest on capital, plant obsolescence, and development expenditure ought to be included in costs. Again, how should materials bought at different prices be charged into costs? Should overtime pay be averaged over all jobs or charged only to those done during overtime hours? How should overheads be allocated, and, especially, how should the burden of unused plant capacity be dealt with? These and other difficulties obscured the apparently clear-cut nature of "actual" costs.[47] They certainly made their value somewhat doubtful, whether for purposes of price-fixing or for controlling efficiency. It was, however, only slowly that this came to be generally realized.

In escaping from some at least of the limitations of crudely ascertained "actual costs" there can be distinguished three main lines of advance:

1. Refinements in the apportionment of overheads were introduced, in an endeavour to make the cost records more accurately reflect the facts of the situation.

2. Methods were devised to isolate the effect on costs of changes in the scale of output, so that the effect of changes in other factors could be detected, while at the same time breaking the vicious circle of contracting demand and increasing unit costs.

3. Finally, a technique was developed to separate out and quantify the effect of *all* significant changes in the factors which determine costs.

Any further major advance along the first of these lines seems unlikely but the movement away from "actual cost" to "standard cost" which is what the second and third of the above developments amount to is still

[47]For a fuller discussion of this point see Professor Theodore Lang's paper on "Concepts of Cost, Past and Present," reprinted below, pp. 93–104.

going on. It may be useful, therefore, to consider the way in which these developments have come about.

METHODS OF ATTACHING OVERHEAD COST TO PRIME COST

The treatment of overhead expenses was, in the 1880's, still often incredibly crude. Henry Roland, writing in 1898, describes the method of estimating used by the drop-forging firm of Strieby and Foote, of Newark, N.J., in 1883.[48] The firm used the "Beecher rule," devised by one of the early American drop-forgers, Beecher of Meriden, Connecticut. This rule was to take the cost of materials (the weight of raw material being taken as one-third more than the weight of the finished work), the flat labour cost, and double the total of these two items for other costs. The firm claimed that for average work the rule gave "a wonderfully close approximation to accuracy," though as it had no clearly formulated system of cost-keeping, it is difficult to see how anyone could know what "accuracy" was.

A considerable variety of estimating methods is listed by Thomas Battersby, a Manchester public accountant, who published a small book on the subject in 1878.[49] They included such methods as:

(a) Charging actual materials and wages, 100 per cent. on wages to cover overheads, and 25 per cent. on the total for profit.

(b) Charging a flat daily rate for the use of each machine or tool: to the sum of this charge and the actual wages is added a percentage for indirect expenses and profit: materials are included at cost plus the same percentage addition.

(c) Charging a percentage of wages for the use of tools and to cover all expenses.

(d) Machines and tools were rated according to their purchase price, power costs and operative's wages, and to this charge plus actual wages and materials a percentage addition was made for other indirect expenses. (But these tool rates, says Battersby, were not based on actual costs, being to a great extent "assumed.")

(e) Machines and tools were rated according to their purchase price only. This gave a selling price for the work done, though some deduction might be made to secure a particular order.

(f) A percentage was added to prime cost (*i.e.*, materials and wages)

[48] "An effective system of finding and keeping shop costs." *Engineering Magazine*, Vol. 15, May, 1898, p. 241.

[49] *The Perfect Double Entry Book-keeper (abridged) and the Perfect Prime Cost and Profit Demonstrator (on the Departmental System), for Iron and Brass Founders, Machinists, Engineers, Shipbuilders, Manufacturers, etc.;* Manchester, 1878. In some notes written by Sir John Mann for me, about his early work on costing, he mentioned Battersby's book with Garcke & Fells' *Factory Accounts* and Capt. H. Metcalfe's *Cost of Manufacture* as the only books on costing he could find when he began to study the subject around 1890.

for overheads, and a further percentage added to the total for profit.

(g) A single percentage was added to prime cost to cover overheads and profit. "The *amount* of percentage varies very considerably in different establishments, according to the opinions of the principals."

This last method, said Battersby, was "the general method in use."[50] That it was still a standard practice 20 years after Battersby's book appeared is certainly implied by Roland in 1898.[51] On the other hand, Hamilton Church in 1901 refers to the "percentage on wages" method as the most usual one, "at any rate in Great Britain,"[52] and so does John Mann.[53]

The "percentage on prime cost" method regarded all jobs with equal prime costs as being responsible for an equal amount of overheads. This, of course, was open to criticism on the ground that the cost of materials used on a job (an important part of its prime cost) might be no indication at all of the load which the job imposed on supervision, equipment and factory space.

This was not the only criticism levelled against this basis of allocating overhead but it was the one peculiar to it. In an attempt to meet it, allocation of overhead on the basis of direct labour cost was often practised. It was argued that labour cost would reflect the time spent by a job in the works and that this in turn reflected the call it made on production facilities. But this method also attracted criticism. Products using a relatively high proportion of low paid labour would, even though they occupied as much time in the factory as products using more highly paid labour, be allocated less overhead because the rate per hour paid to the labour was lower. In fact, so the argument ran, such low paid labour might be the cause of proportionately more rather than proportionately less overhead. For example, it might need more supervision, it might waste more material and damage more equipment than high grade and more expensive labour.

In an attempt to defend the use of wages as a basis for allocating production overheads, and to counter the criticism that this was inequitable to work done by expensive skilled labour, the refinement of departmental overhead rates was introduced.[54] This, of course, only met the criticism to the extent that the labour employed in each department was more or less homogeneous. But so long as this was broadly true, much of the sting was taken out of this particular criticism.

[50] Battersby, *op. cit.*, p. 34.

[51] "Cost Keeping Methods in Machine-shop and Foundry," in *Engineering Magazine* Vol. 14, January, 1898, pp. 626–7.

[52] A. Hamilton Church, "The Proper Distribution of Establishment Charges" in *Engineering Magazine*, July, 1901, p. 725.

[53] *Encyclopaedia of Accounting*, Vol. 5, p. 208.

[54] Departmental rates were certainly in use as early as 1870. See, *e.g.*, *The Engineer*, December 23, 1870, p. 428.

In so far as the labour *within* a department was of varying degrees of skill (and consequently of expensiveness) even the use of a different overhead rate (*i.e.*, overheads expressed as a percentage of total direct labour) for each department was still apt to charge a disproportionate amount of overhead to certain jobs. The adoption of labour *time* instead of labour cost as the basis for charging overheads was intended to circumvent this difficulty. By relating a department's overhead to the total direct labour hours worked in it, a departmental overhead rate per labour hour was calculated. This would bear with equal weight on any two jobs which occupied a department for the same time, even though one job demanded expensive skilled labour and the other did not.

The direct-labour-hour basis for charging overheads got round one difficulty only to draw attention to another. It made no allowance for differences in the kind of equipment which different jobs employed. One hour of an operative's time on a light inexpensive machine would attract the same charge for overheads as an hour on a costly piece of equipment. While for purely manual operations the direct labour hour rate might serve well enough, for mechanized operations it clearly left much to be desired.

Early Attempts at a Machine Hour Rate

It was quite obvious to a number of writers by the last decade of the century that no single basis of overhead allocation could be satisfactory. In 1891, for instance, Sir John Mann[55] was arguing for a division of overhead cost into (a) buying costs which vary with the cost of goods bought, (b) selling costs which vary with the sales, and (c) production expenses. So far as the last were concerned he dismissed quantity or value of material as a suitable basis of allocation and pointed out the danger of using wages as a basis where some workers are paid more than others. He emphasized time as the significant factor and put forward some proposals for machine hour rates.

The use of machine hour rates had been noted years earlier by Battersby in his list of estimating methods, but only as a means of allocating those expenses which were directly associated with the machine, such as depreciation, machine maintenance and power. His main criticism of the practice of his day had been that the engineering firms concerned had inadequate data on which to calculate the rates. They were based on opinion and assumption rather than facts. He, therefore, had elaborated a procedure for working out rates to be charged for work done in each separate production department. They included rates per ton of casting in the iron foundry, a rate per indicated horse-power per year for allocating the cost of the steam power

[55] *The Accountant*, August 29, and September 5, 1891.

department and rates per day to be charged for the different machine tools. In the last case the total cost of machine upkeep was divided between individual machines on the basis of capital value, and power cost was allocated on the basis of horse-power. The addition of wages gave the "prime cost rate per day to be charged upon work."

One of his *pro forma* statements for working out the machine rates is worth reproducing as an example.

POWER DEPARTMENT—LATHES AND TOOLS[56]

Total value of Tools .... £	
To .... % for yearly depreciation................................	£
Direct expenses, *viz.*, tools and steel for upholding and repairs, belting, grindstones, oil, waste, etc., as per direct expenses and upholding account in the Direct and Indirect Expenses Book...	
Total cost of tools per year...........	
Equals .... % per £ value of tools	
Then No. 1 Tool, valued at £......... at .... % per £, equals its yearly cost	£
.... horsepower required to work it, at per horse	
Total cost per year of No. 1 Tool...........	£

Which divided by the number of working days, gives its prime cost per day; which added to the workman's wages, gives the prime cost rate per day to be charged upon work.

A register of the numbers and cost rates of the tools was kept for reference.

ALEXANDER HAMILTON CHURCH AND THE IDEA OF PRODUCTION CENTRES

In the last decade of the century, other advocates of machine hour rates were to be heard. But they were quite overshadowed by one, of whom a former President of the Institute of Cost and Works Accountants[57] has said that he "probably did more than anyone, both directly and indirectly, to promote costing as it is now known, chiefly because he promoted thought." This was Alexander Hamilton Church,[58] whose six

[56]Battersby, *op. cit.*, p. 38.

[57]Roland Dunkerley, in a paper entitled "A Historical Review of the Institute and the Profession" read to the eighteenth National Cost Conference of the I.C.W.A. on May 10, 1946.

[58]Church was an English electrical engineer. At one time he had worked for the National Telephone Company in Britain. He settled in the United States around the turn of the century.

articles in the *Engineering Magazine* on "The Proper Distribution of Establishment Charges" in 1901,[59] "at once took rank as a standard reference work on one of the most difficult questions of cost-finding."[60]

His analysis starts with a clear division of overheads between what he calls shop charges and general establishment charges.[61] He relates the different categories of costs and profits in this way:—

Material Wages	Prime Cost			
Shop Charges		Works Cost		
General Establishment Charges			Inclusive Cost	
Profit				Selling Price

Church precedes his own contribution to the problem of allocating overheads by a searching criticism of the methods most common in his own day. Very little of importance has been added to his criticism by subsequent discussion. The "percentage on wages" method he declared to be "not alarmingly incorrect" if "machines are all of a size and kind performing practically identical operations by means of a fairly average wages rate."[62] But in general it was "really quite arbitrary and without any real relation to the actual problem."[63] He turns next to the "Hourly Burden Plan," by which shop expenses are allocated to jobs in proportion to the labour-time spent on them. This method has two virtues which the first lacks. It shows up the expensiveness of cheap labour prolonging and bungling a job: and it brings into full prominence the essential fact that to have work hanging about is a costly business. But it is too simple. It does not discriminate between jobs using large and costly machines and those using cheap and light machines. It works well enough where all the machines used and all the jobs done are fairly

[59]Vol. 21, July–September, 1901, pp. 508–517, 725–734, 904–912, and Vol. 22, October–December, 1901, pp. 31–40, 231–240 and 367–376.

[60]From the Editor's preface to the articles, reprinted in book form in 1916.

[61]In his earlier article on "The Meaning of Commercial Organization" (*The Engineering Magazine*, Vol. 20, No. 3, December 1900, p. 394) he describes this distinction as "a principle the fundamental importance of which had only dimly been realized by the book-keeping mind, and was first given the prominence due to its importance in the Slater Lewis system." J. Slater Lewis, with whom Church had worked in Manchester, was the general manager of P. R. Jackson & Co., Ltd., Salford, and was the author of *The Commercial Organization of Factories* (1896), of which a reviewer in *Engineering* (January 15, 1897, p. 67) wrote: "We know of no other work which treats of commercial organization in the same scientific spirit." It is clear that Hamilton Church learnt much from Lewis.

[62]*Loc. cit.*, p. 726.

[63]*Loc. cit.*, p. 727.

uniform. In similar circumstances, the "percentage on wages" method also works well enough. In such simple conditions almost any method will serve. What is wrong with both the "labour-cost" and the "labour-time" bases is that they produce an averaged result, for which there is as little justification in all but exceptional circumstances as there would be for using average instead of actual wage rates to give the labour cost of a particular operation.

He turns to the machine-hour rate of earlier days only to dismiss it as hopelessly crude. But it does have one advantage over other methods: it does take into account the variation in the cost of work done on different types of machine. It is this idea which Church takes and develops. "What does the expression 'shop' really signify?" he asks. We get no nearer to disentangling costs so long as we look at the shop as an organic whole. But if we regard it as a collection of "little shops" or production centres, the problem suddenly becomes clear. Each "little shop," consisting of a machine, or a bench at which a handcraftsman works, must be charged with its own depreciation, rent, and other running expenses. The cost of each production centre is then loaded on to the work passing through it, at an hourly rate, which he calls the "scientific machine rate." There will still be certain general shop overheads, such as supervision, which cannot be charged other than by an average rate applicable to all work in the shop. But, to a great extent, costs which were formerly averaged over all jobs will now be made to bear on different jobs with differing weight as the facts demand.

The Problem of Idle Capacity and the Supplementary Rate

The development of the idea of the "production centre" made possible the refinement of the machine-hour rate into something very like its modern form. But Hamilton Church did not stop there. He was much concerned with the problem of idle capacity. He saw clearly the absurdity of showing the cost of a particular operation as varying greatly in successive months simply because the shop was fully employed one month and only half-employed the next, the monthly level of overheads remaining steady. The remedy he proposed for this situation was the *supplementary rate.* All shop expenses for the month, both those allocable to specific production centres and those of a general nature, like supervision, were in the first instance to be charged to a shop charges account. "Scientific" machine-hour rates would be calculated for each production centre on the basis that each would operate full time throughout the month. Actual work passing through each centre would be charged at the "scientific" hourly rate, these charges going to the credit of the shop charges account. If at the end of the month all the centres proved to have been fully occupied throughout the period there would be left to the debit of the account a sum representing the *general* shop overheads (*i.e.*, those not allocated to production centres). If all the production centres had *not* been fully occupied, the debit left on the shop charges account would be swollen by the proportion of the allocable expenses not taken up by the "scientific" machine-hour rates. It was this debit balance which was disposed of by means of the supplementary rate. The charges made to jobs by the application of the "scientific" rates had now to be supplemented by further charges, which bore the same proportion to the normal charges as the total unabsorbed expenses bore to the total already absorbed.

This system, Church claimed, had two great virtues. It enabled the producer to compare the cost of jobs worked on at different periods, because the normal overhead rate would be constant and would not distort the results. And the ratio of the supplementary rate to the normal rate would serve as an accurate barometer of the use made of capacity during the period. "*The supplementary rate is the undistributed balance of shop charges due to idleness of productive centres.*" It is this which is "the invaluable complement to the machine rate and which makes the great distinction between the new method and the old machine-rate method."[64]

It is, of course, easy to criticize Church's "supplementary rate." In the first place, the net effect on job costs was to bring them back to the "actual costs" which they would have shown, had the "scientific" machine rate and the supplementary rate not been kept separate in the first place. Second, the fact that the supplementary rate was made up not only of unabsorbed machine expenses but also of the unallocable general shop expenses made nonsense of Church's claims that the supplementary rate was a barometer of shop efficiency: for a rise in the general expenses would raise the supplementary rate even if all machines were being fully utilized. Even a rise in allocable machine expenses caused by a sharp rise in the price-level would raise the supplementary rate irrespective of the degree of capacity usage. And, finally, Church's use of the word "efficiency" is highly confusing. If the production centres of his system were run for the maximum number of hours, the supplementary rate would fall to a minimum. This for him was the sign of "efficiency." But, of course, the volume of production *per machine hour* might fall away very seriously without the slightest effect on the supplementary rate. He seems to regard the full use of plant capacity as synonymous with full efficiency. The distinction in the records between the two, which, at least, is attempted by modern standard costing, belongs to a later period.

Sir Charles Renold has given a graphic account of the working of Hamilton Church's system in the Manchester works of Hans Renold,

[64]*Loc. cit.*, p. 908 (Church's italics).

Ltd., where his father, Hans Renold, had introduced it shortly after the turn of the century. "When I entered the business,"[65] writes Sir Charles, "this system was in its first full flush of enthusiasm. It was developed and refined over the next few years until it became quite unmanageable in its ramifications, elaborations and adjustments. It could never be kept up-to-date and even if it were up-to-date the costs which it turned out, though possibly factually sound, were in a form that gave no convenient guide to action. In producing a cost, bits and pieces of every conceivable kind of expense had gone into the pan and, though each had contributed its flavour, the resulting omelet could not be unscrambled for examination."[66]

It is hardly surprising that, after gaining some support, Church's supplementary rate faded out. But it was not on that account a wholly abortive innovation; for it drew attention to the distinction between "normal" costs and abnormal losses. In his book, published almost 30 years later, he writes about his original proposals that "no element of the new method was more criticized than the 'supplementary rate.' It was (somewhat to the author's surprise) generally recognized that it was no part of true cost and that, therefore, wasted capacity should be charged off to profit and loss."[67] Church's original solution of this problem was clearly not the right one; but it stimulated others to do better. One such other was John Whitmore, to whom further reference will be made below. He is of particular interest to us in connection with the development of standard costing: but another aspect of his work is relevant here. Church's "scientific" machine hour rate was worked out on the basis that machines were worked at their maximum capacity. Whitmore saw that this went too far, and excluded too much from what he called "proper costs." He saw the danger of "assuming an impossibly perfect standard of working." This is well on the way to substituting normal machine usage for maximum usage as a basis for spreading overheads.

Other Methods of Dealing with Overheads

Before leaving the problem of how overheads ought to be apportioned between products in a multi-product firm, we should note that the machine hour rate was not left unchallenged as the best method of apportioning works expenses in all circumstances. In 1907 we find a

[65]In 1906.

[66]*The Cost Accountant*, September, 1950, p. 113.

[67]"Overhead Expense," 1930, p. 384. For an example of this kind of criticism see Whitmore, "Factory Accountancy as applied to Machine Shops," *Journal of Accountancy*, August, 1906–January, 1907, especially at pp. 254–8 (August, 1906). These articles were reprinted in *The Accountant*, Vol. 35 (1906), pp. 605–610, 646–651, 675–680, 746–751, and Vol. 36 (1907) pp. 160–163 and 220–223.

writer on the motor industry advocating the use of not one but a combination of methods.[68] The shops in a motor works are to be divided into two groups, the machine departments (drilling, milling, etc.), and the special departments (foundries, plating, lacquering, etc.), each department being again sub-divided into production centres. Overheads in the production centres of the machine departments are apportioned by a machine hour rate, those in the special departments are dealt with by rates per man hour, per cent. on labour costs, per poundweight of output and so on, according to the nature of the operation carried on in each production centre. These suggestions are, of course, only a refinement of proposals by Battersby and others many years earlier.

A still more elegant combination of methods was proposed by Dr. William Kent in 1916.[69] Recognizing that no one basis could conceivably be right for apportioning all the expenses incurred in a works, he suggested that overheads could be classified under four heads, according as their incidence was related to

(1) man-hours,
(2) machine-hours,
(3) the job,
(4) materials used.

As an example of the way in which expenses might be allocated to each of these categories, he suggested the following:—

Expenses Apportioned on the Basis of:

Man-hours	*Machine-hours*	*Jobs*	*Materials*
Shop supervision.	Tool makers.	Cost clerks.	Storekeeper.
Bookkeeper's wages	Oil, waste and other supplies.	Planners.	Stationery, postage.
Blacksmith's „	Foremen.		Truckmen, cranemen.
Millwright's „	Interest and Depreciation on equipment.		Interest and Depreciation on stores.
Labourer's „	Power.		

The rate per man-hour would be the same for each job: the machine-hour rate would be calculated separately for each class of machine—in effect, there would be a separate rate for each production centre; the job rate would be a flat charge per job; while the materials rate would be differentiated for different classes of materials, and loaded directly on to the cost of the materials.

With this development we can say that the process of attaching over-

[68]"Motor Manufacturing Costs," by D. C. Eggleston, in the *Business Man's Magazine*, October, 1907.

[69]"New Methods of Determining Factory Costs," by Dr. William Kent, *Iron Age*, August 24, 1916, Vol. 98, pp. 392–4.

head expenses to units of product had been brought more or less to completion. From the application of a simple percentage to prime costs we have seen the treatment of overhead expenses become more and more complex, first by the replacement of the simple idea of a homogeneous works by the more realistic concept of a congeries of production centres; then by a distinction first between works overheads and general overheads, and later between different classes of works overheads. Again, from the more or less accidental short-period relationship of actual overheads and actual output, we have seen emerge the calculation of overhead rates first on maximum output and then on normal output. The idea of "normal" cost replaces that of "actual" cost. We shall see later on how that idea in turn is replaced by the concept of a "standard" cost.

Critics of Overhead Allocation

But first let us pick up another thread which can be detected running through the discussions and disputations over the treatment of overhead expenses. The writers which we have considered so far differed, as we have seen, about how overheads should be attached to units of product: but they entertained few doubts as to the desirability of making such an attachment somehow. For if selling prices were to be based on costs, and if the revenue from sales was to be sufficient to cover both prime costs and overheads, what was more natural than that goods should be sold only at prices which showed some margin over and above the cost accountant's computation of average cost, *i.e.*, prime cost plus allotted overheads? It was the very necessity of fixed selling prices that caused such importance to be attached to the choice of the "correct" method of spreading overheads. Cost accountants have, on the whole, continued to attach importance to it for the same reason right down to our own day.

Nevertheless, there have not been wanting heretics to attack the conventional treatment of overheads. Several different grounds for such criticism can be distinguished.

First, there have been those who have argued that overhead expense allocation was not necessary for price-fixing purposes, and that so long as each product made *some* contribution to overheads and profit, while all products together covered the total overheads and desired profit, it was neither possible nor necessary to say how much over and above prime costs each product should earn. On this view, of course, prices are regarded as determined by market conditions; the entrepreneur can only respond to them, he cannot dictate them. This view is supported by Harrington Emerson in an article on foundry costs[70] in 1904. After

[70]Harrington Emerson: "Percentage Methods of Determining Production Costs," *The Foundry*, October, 1904, pp. 80–81.

discussing the application of a uniform percentage of overheads to prime cost for different kinds of foundry work, which in the case he is discussing works out at 82 per cent., he goes on:

> "Selling prices are, however, not made at the whim of the foundry owner, but by competition. It may, therefore, happen that 82 per cent. will carry certain classes of work above competition prices, and carry other classes unnecessarily below competition prices. The foundry owner may therefore . . . assign a different percentage to each (class) provided the totals of all classes, with percentages added, equal his bookkeeper's totals. . . . *The overcharges are distributed, not by some fancy accounting method, but according to the exigencies of competition.*"[71]

The second group of critics of overhead allocation have been those who dismissed it as arbitrary and therefore useless. We may represent the views of this group by quoting from a paper by W. R. Hamilton, writing in 1910:—

> "It is easy to carry this division [of overheads between departments] to a point at which it ceases to correspond to any useful fact. What, for instance, is the use of splitting up a manager's salary between departments? If a department be shut up, can a portion of the manager be dispensed with? If such divisions have any value it is a relative one only, as between one year and another. They have no absolute value for they do not answer to facts which confirm past action, or give rise to new—the only facts worth having in business."[72]

That Hamilton is referring here to the allocation of overheads between departments rather than between units of product does not, of course, diminish the force of his criticism.

Both the views which have just been quoted tended to be rather negative. Those who held them were right to point out the shortcomings of overhead allocation. But they did little to put anything in its place. There was, however, a third line of thought, more constructive in nature, which it is interesting to watch developing into what we now know as "marginal costing."

Variation of Cost with Output

The way in which the cost of producing an article would vary with the amount of it which was produced engaged the attention of a number of

[71]*Op. cit.*, p. 31. My italics.

[72]W. R. Hamilton: "Some Economic Considerations bearing on Costing," *The Accountant*, February 5, 1910. The words of an earlier Hamilton might also be aptly quoted at this point: "When we import a cargo of different kinds of goods which could not well be separated, such as iron and deals, of which the one is necessary for ballast, and the other to complete the lading, it is proper to join them in one accompt, and complete the profit or loss on the whole together. . . . Perhaps there might be gain on the one and loss on the other; but as we were obliged to import both together, it is the success of the whole that we should inquire into." Robert Hamilton, *Introduction to Merchandise*, 1788, p. 408.

economists in the nineteenth century and even earlier, but they were usually more concerned with the output of an industry rather than of a firm. The notion of "diminishing returns" in agriculture was first stated by Turgot in France as early as 1768, and was taken up by Malthus in England in 1814.[73] Yet, "in the original laws of returns the general idea of a functional connection between cost and quantity produced was not given a conspicuous place."[74] It was in the sphere of railway economics, young as the transportation industry was in 1850, when the Irishman, Dionysius Lardner, wrote about it, that the nature of the problem which faced the individual producer was most clearly seen. In his *Railway Economy* Lardner[75] clearly perceived that, in fixing railway tariffs, it was necessary to have regard to the way in which costs reacted to changes in traffic, for an alteration in railway rates would result in a change in the amount of traffic carried and in the total receipts. Only by comparing the change in receipts with the change in total costs could the effect on profits of any tariff change be judged.[76] To do this it was necessary to distinguish between fixed and variable costs, which he does in the following passage:—

> "... the cost of production of the objects of industry, at present, may always be regarded as consisting of two parts, one of which is quite independent of the number of articles produced, and being, therefore, equally divided among them, will render one element of their price precisely in the inverse ratio of their number; but still there will be another component which, depending on the direct application of manual or other labour, and on the immediate consumption of raw materials, will be in the direct ratio of the number of articles produced."[77]

Far from opposing the practice of allocating overheads, Lardner worked out a most elaborate system of allocation, classifying railway overheads into a number of categories according to the way they behaved when the volume of traffic changed. But in emphasizing what we should now call the "marginal approach," as in other matters, Lardner was in advance of his time. His views have become the commonplace of twentieth century economics; and they are still well ahead of much that is written about cost accounting.

In France in 1865, the distinction between fixed and variable costs was appreciated by C. Adolphe Guilbault,[78] though he does no more than mention it. Alfred Marshall, in England, gave prominence to the

[73]In his *Observations on the Effects of the Corn Laws.*

[74]P. Sraffa: "The Laws of Returns under Competitive Conditions," *Economic Journal,* December, 1926, p. 537.

[75]Born in Dublin 1793, died 1859. He was for some years Professor of Mathematics in University College, London.

[76]*Railway Economy*, pp. 249–253.

[77]*Op. cit.*, p. 216.

[78]In his *Traité de Comptabilité et d'Administration Industrielles;* Paris, 1865; p. 120.

distinction between what he called "prime" and "supplementary" costs in developing his theory of business behaviour in 1890.[79] Eugen Schmalenbach, in Germany, drew attention to the importance of variations of cost with output in 1899,[80] and developed the idea 20 years later in a book[81] which had much influence in Germany and went into six editions by 1934. At the end of the last century there was a more general understanding among economists of the significance of marginal variations in cost than there was among accountants. But the idea did gradually gain ground, though by no means universal acceptance, that it was these variations which were important rather than arbitrary allocations of fixed overheads, made in an attempt to perform the "miracle of converting fixed cost into variable cost."[82]

Alfred Marshall obviously learnt something from *Factory Accounts*, by Garcke[83] and Fells,[84] first published in 1887, for he refers to it in approving footnotes in both his *Principles*[85] and in *Industry and Trade*.[86] *Factory Accounts* was by far the best known English work on costing to be published during the last quarter of the nineteenth century, the period which I have described as the costing renaissance, and it reached seven editions by 1922. Its main interest lies in the fact that it integrated the cost accounts into the double-entry system, and it really does

[79]*Principles of Economics*, pp. 359–362, 394–402.

[80]In his paper on "Buchführung und Kalkulation im Fabrikgeschäft" in *Deutsche Metallindustriezeitung*, 1899.

[81]*Grundlagen der Selbstkostenrechnung und Preispolitik*, Leipzig, 1919.

[82]R. A. Gordon; *Short-period Price Determination in Theory and Practice. American Economic Review*, Vol. XXXVIII, No. 3, June 1948, p. 276.

[83]Emile Garcke (1856–1930) was an electrical engineer, becoming a member of the Institution of Electrical Engineers in 1889. He was associated with Brush Electrical Engineering Co. from 1883 to 1893, becoming its Chairman and Managing Director; founded the British Electric Traction Co. in 1895, continuing as its Chairman until 1929; and for about 25 years was Chairman of the North Metropolitan Electric Supply Co. He was a pioneer of electric traction, and is said to have been associated, at one time, with some 80 companies in the industry. He started *Garcke's Manual of Electrical Undertakings* in 1896, founded an electrical journal in 1901, and also founded the Tramways and Light Railways Association and the Electrical Section of the London Chamber of Commerce. His other interests, apart from costing, included industrial co-partnership and philosophical studies.

[84]John Manger Fells (1858–1925), was an accountant. He was Accountant and Assistant Secretary of Brush Electrical Engineering Co. from 1884 to 1889, when he joined the Salt Union, Ltd., becoming its General Manager. He went into practice as an accountant in London in 1899, and became an authority on railway rates, being frequently consulted in connection with cases brought before the Railway and Canal Commission. During the 1914–18 War he acted as Private Secretary to the Surveyor-General of Supply, War Office, and was a member of the Cost Accounting Committee of the War Office. He was a member of the Council of the Society of Incorporated Accountants and Auditors and a Fellow of the Institute of Cost and Works Accountants.

[85]*Op. cit.*, p. 360n.

[86]*Op. cit.*, p. 369n.

represent, as its authors claimed, "the first attempt to place before English readers a systematized statement of the principles regulating Factory Accounts."[87] It has, however, this further subsidiary interest for us, that its authors clearly assert the futility of allocating "fixed" overheads, and must be counted among the founders of the "marginal cost" school of thought. The passage which follows sets forth their view on this point with admirable clarity:—

> "The establishment expense [salaries of clerks, office rent, stationery] and interest on capital should not, however, in any case form part of the cost of production. There is no advantage in distributing these items over the various transactions or articles produced. They do not vary proportionately with the volume of business. A large increase in the value of orders received would not necessitate a like augmentation of the office staff, nor would a sudden and serious falling off in trade enable a firm to effect an immediate or proportionate reduction of general expenditure. The establishment charges are, in the aggregate, more or less constant, while the manufacturing costs fluctuate with the cost of labour and the price of material. To distribute the charges over the articles manufactured would, therefore, have the effect of disproportionately reducing the cost of production with every increase, and the reverse with every diminution of business. Such a result is greatly to be deprecated, as tending neither to economy of management nor to accuracy in estimating for contracts. *The principals of a business can always judge what percentage of gross profits upon cost is necessary to cover fixed establishment charges and interest on capital.*"[88]

Of course there is a good deal of over-simplification in this passage. The distinction between fixed and variable costs (itself an over-simplification) is identified with that between establishment expenses and manufacturing costs. In fact, of course, factory rent is hardly less fixed than office rent. Nevertheless, Garcke and Fells were pretty much on the right lines here. Taken to task by Professor W. J. Ashley for seeming "specifically to exclude establishment expenses and interest as items in the cost of production"[89] the authors agreed that these charges must be elements in the cost of production in the wider sense, but that from the "commercial standpoint of a manufacturer desirous under

[87] *Factory Accounts*, 1st ed., p. v. It is of some slight interest to note that Garcke and Fells may have derived something from a paper by F. R. Goddard, a public accountant in Newcastle, read before the Cleveland Institution of Engineers, Middlesbrough, on January 16, 1873, on "The Balance Sheets of Manufacturing Firms: Their Principles and Theories viewed Analytically," and printed with discussion in the Society's *Proceedings* for the session 1872–73, pp. 79–113. Fells referred to Goddard's paper, in a lecture of his own in 1919, as "so far as I know, the first paper dealing with the subject on broad lines of principle." (*The Accountant*, June 28, 1919, p. 548.) Goddard had discussed job accounts, and the allocation or overheads thereto, in considering the valuation of work-in-progress for balance sheet purposes.

[88] Garcke & Fells: *Factory Accounts*, 1st ed., 1887, p. 74. My italics.

[89] Garcke & Fells: *Factory Accounts*, 7th ed., 1922, p. 119 (footnote).

competitive conditions of obtaining business data on which he could act as to the price of the product, establishment charges, and in some measure interest, would not be regarded as items in the cost of production of particular commodities in so far as it regulates price."[90]

A favourite method nowadays of representing the relationship between total costs and output in a department, works or firm is by the use of a break-even chart. There is nothing very modern about this device. Sir John Mann knew about it in 1904.[91] We find a much fuller account of it in 1903 in a remarkable article by Henry Hess.[92] In this article, Hess takes a set of imaginary figures and divides them into fixed and variable costs. He then plots these costs for various levels of output (measured in terms of men employed and tons produced), together with the total net receipts for each output, and gets a break-even point at which total costs equal total revenue. Because of the incidence of fixed costs, at zero output costs exceed revenue. But as output increases total revenue increases faster than total costs, and eventually overtakes them. This gives the break-even point. As output increases beyond this point, profits appear and increase proportionately with the growth in output. The effect of output changes on profits, assuming that the underlying assumptions as to the behaviour of costs and prices are not falsified, is clearly shown.

Hess's article has another interest for us, for it contains the germ of what we now call a flexible budget. I shall return to this aspect of his work later.

It was only subsequently that the excessive simplication of dividing costs into fixed and variable categories was recognized, and that the need for at least a third category of semi-fixed expenses was seen. John H. Williams, in America, wrote on this in 1922,[93] and suggested that the amount of any semi-fixed expense which could be expected to be associated with any particular scale of output could be found by interpolating between the amounts of expense appropriate to the maximum and minimum outputs. By doing this for each expense, and aggregating, the total expense for any chosen output level could be predicted. The economist, J. M. Clark, represents another point of view.[94] He recommends an empirical approach to the problem of relating costs to output:

[90]*Loc. cit.*

[91]*Encyclopaedia of Accounting*, Vol. V, pp. 217–8.

[92]"Manufacturing: Capital, Costs, Profits and Dividends," *Engineering Magazine*, Dec., 1903, p. 367. Henry Hess was born in Darmstädt, Germany, in 1864, and went to the United States as a small boy. He became a member of the American Society of Mechanical Engineers, 1906, and was its Vice-President, 1914–16. He was associated with the Hess-Bright Manufacturing Co., 1902–12. and the Hess Steel Corporation of Baltimore from 1912 until his death in 1922.

[93]"A Technique for the Chief Executive," *Bulletin of the Taylor Society*, Vol. VII, 1922, pp. 47–68.

[94]*The Economics of Overhead Cost*, 1923, p. 180.

for various scales of output, the amount of each category of expense would be estimated, and the total cost for each level of output arrived at by aggregation. Incremental cost could then be ascertained by taking the differences between the cost totals for each level of output.

The subsequent literature is full of references to the necessity of distinguishing between fixed and variable costs in order to assess the effect of production policy on profits, and a number of empirical studies of cost behaviour were made.[95] But most of these studies were somewhat crude, and it was not until the late 1930's that refined techniques for relating cost to size of output in the short run were developed.

Standard Costs

We must now return from our digression on the development of the distinction between fixed and variable costs to follow up the movement away from "actual" product costs. We have seen that the concept of the "actual" cost of a particular product or unit of product had to be replaced by the idea of normal cost. We now have to trace the further movement from normal cost to standard cost.

The possibility of setting up norms of cost, with which "actual" product and process costs might be compared, is implied by one or two of the nineteenth-century writers on costing. For instance, Garcke and Fells suggest that: "Before any order to manufacture is given it is advisable, as tending to produce greater economy in cost of production, that the person best acquainted with its processes and details should estimate the probable cost to be measured in wages and materials, in the production of the articles in question. This estimate should be a minimum rather than a maximum one, and the storekeeper having been furnished with particulars of it, should not issue more material for the order than is estimated without special authority."[96]

Another early work which deserves mention in this connection is *Textile Manufacturers' Book-keeping*, published in 1889 by G. P. Norton.[97] This book had a great success, running into four editions by 1900. The cost records, which were kept quite separate from the commercial accounts, were designed to allocate costs to departments and processes in such a way that the costs could be compared with the prices that would have been charged by outside specialists, *i.e.*, the trade or "country" prices, as they were called. The results of the undertaking are summarized in a Manufacturing Account, the first part of which

[95]For a survey of such studies between 1920 and 1936, see Joel Dean: "Statistical Determination of Costs, with special reference to Marginal Costs," University of Chicago *Studies in Business Administration*, Vol. VII, No. 1, pp. 13–23.

[96]Garcke & Fells, *op. cit.*, 1st ed., pp. 52–3.

[97]George Pepler Norton (1858–1939) practised for many years as a chartered accountant in Huddersfield. He was chairman or director of a number of companies.

compares the actual sales with the work done valued at the trade prices, the difference after stock adjustments being the amount of profit that would have been made if the work had been carried out at the trade rates. In the second section of the account the "actual" costs (*i.e.*, the costs arrived at after allocations of overhead) of each of the processes, spinning, weaving, dyeing and finishing, are compared with the work valued at trade prices, the difference showing the "profit" or "loss" on each department. The sum of these profits and losses plus the profit from the first section of the Manufacturing Account shows the net profit of the business subject to deduction of certain expenses not allocated between the processes. This comparison of the firm's costs with "outside" values seems to be the nearest that the nineteenth century came to standard costing as we know it. Later, as the practice of putting work out on commission fell out of use, "country" prices ceased to be available, and in his *Cost Accounting and Cost Control*, published in 1931, Norton replaced them by full-blooded standard costs. The evolution in Norton's own mind from "country" prices to standard costs is thus quite clear.

It is impossible to take any discussion of the origins of standard costing far without acknowledging its close connection with the "scientific management" movement in America generally, for standard costs mean little without standard processes and standard operating times, such as F. W. Taylor and his followers developed. No one can read Taylor's famous paper on "Shop Management"[98] of 1903 without seeing that many of the essential elements of standard costing are there, including what is perhaps the first reference to "management by exception."[99]

Credit for the earliest detailed description of a system of standard costing has been given to the American, John Whitmore, who, in a lecture delivered before the New York University School of Commerce in February, 1908, gave a clear account of the use of standards in a shoe factory.[1] In some earlier lectures given by him in the winter of 1905–6, he makes no reference to standard costing.[2] It looks, therefore,

[98] *Transactions of the American Society of Mechanical Engineers*, Paper 1003, Vol. XXIV (1903), pp. 1337–1456.

[99] "What may be called the 'Exception Principle' in management is coming more and more into use; although like many of the other elements of this art, it is used in isolated cases, and in most instances without recognizing it as a principle which should extend throughout the entire field." (*Loc. cit.*, p. 1408.)

[1] "Shoe Factory Cost Accounts," by John Whitmore, *Journal of Accountancy*, May, 1908. This article has been described by Dr. W. B. Macfarland, of N.A.C.A., as "the first of its kind to appear in accounting literature"—see "A Quarter-century of Cost-Accounting Progress" by J. Hugh Jackson, *N.A.C.A. Bulletin*, Vol. 28, No. 19, June 1, 1947.

[2] "Factory Accountancy as applied to Machine Shops," by John Whitmore, *Journal of Accountancy*, August, 1906–January, 1907, reprinted in *The Accountant*, 1906, pp. 605, 646, 675, 746, and 1907, pp. 160 and 220.

as if either his ideas on the subject developed between these two dates or, what is more likely, that during this period he saw a standard costing sytem in operation and decided to write it up.[3]

Before turning to Whitmore's contribution, however, there are two earlier ones which deserve attention. The first is an article on foundry costs by an American engineer, Percy Longmuir, which appeared in 1902.[4] Longmuir asserts quite clearly the value of controlling the cost of *functions* (as distinct from products) by comparison with certain standards of what these functions ought to cost. He proposes that the labour costs of each class of work undertaken in the foundry should be ascertained, each type of labour, *e.g.*, moulders, labourers, etc., being kept separate. These labour costs are then related to the weight per cwt. "Experience," he says, "will readily give standard factors for each class of work and these standards may be plotted on a chart as a fair curve (straight line), the departure from which of the actual weekly cost line will instantly show the degrees of good or bad working." We need not stop to examine this claim. It is sufficient to acknowledge that Longmuir is expressing an important and, for his time, a novel idea. His strictures on the uselessness of job costs which are often worked out too late to be of service to the foundry manager, and his assertion of the necessity of providing management with cost information on the completion of every payment of wages also strike a surprisingly modern note.

A second precursor of full standard costing, this time an English accountant, was H. S. Garry, who read a paper to the Society of Chemical Industry on "Factory Costs" in 1903.[5] Garry expresses himself so ill that his audience of chemists and technologists must have been hard put to it to follow him. But he obviously has the idea of a comparison between actual and standard costs, and separates out, in the illustration which he presented, an "excess of cost, due to partial output," and an "increase in price of material" (in modern jargon, a volume variance and a price variance). On the first of these he says that where there is excess manufacturing capacity "there will probably be a dead weight charge of depreciation, repairs and possibly working expenses, to take into account in the productive cost, which a system of factory accounting should demonstrate."[6] And on material prices, he

[3]A similar view is expressed by J. Hugh Jackson, *loc. cit.*, p. 1203; "From this writing [*i.e.*, Whitmore's 'Shoe Factory Cost Accounts'] one has the conviction that such methods were in use at an even earlier date." In a much later article on "Some Cost Accounting Terms" (*Journal of Accountancy*, September, 1930, pp. 193–200), in which Whitmore looks back to the period we are discussing, he makes no reference to this aspect of his work.

[4]"Recording and Interpreting Foundry Costs," in *Engineering Magazine*, September, 1902, p. 887.

[5]*The Accountant*, July 25, 1903, pp. 954–961.

[6]*Loc. cit.*, p. 955.

says: "In dealing with raw material . . . necessarily the first consideration is to be given to the point of conversion and manipulation; and the second to dealing with the fluctuation caused by increase or decrease in material cost. The first point, therefore, in this is the provision of a normal standard by which we can measure the effectiveness of the factory output, which measure would be needlessly complicated by the introduction of the fluctuation of market prices."[7]

Garry's paper has a secondary interest in that it is one of the very few discussions of costing, at this time, in relation to an industry other than engineering. It is abundantly clear that the engineering industry had outstripped all others in its willingness to study management problems systematically. As Garry put it, in England "the literature of engineering management and costing gives ample evidence of the interest which this subject has for that industry, but up to the present I have not come across any literature dealing with the difficulties attending this subject in respect to the industries which claim the special interest of this society (*i.e.*, the chemical industries)."[8]

Turning back to Whitmore, it would seem that some of his more developed ideas stem direct from Hamilton Church, to whom, therefore, some of the credit for the development of the idea of standard costs must go. In his earlier lectures, as we have already said, Whitmore does not mention standard costs in the accepted sense. But he does there discuss Church's supplementary rate. He disapproved of Church's treatment of idle capacity costs, and proposed instead that they should be charged to an idle capacity account and written off.

In his 1908 lecture he returns to the same theme. But now he takes it and develops it into something of much wider application. If the cost of idle capacity is not a part of the "true cost" of a product, may there not be other costs which ought to be similarly excluded? In the following passage we have the crux of his arguments:—

> "I would say that true or correct cost does not necessarily include every expense incurred in the course of producing an article. Accidents or blunders occur and the cost, as in some instances the cost of unused factory capacity, may be so great that it would be absurd to state it as part of the cost of the product. If this is established, it establishes the principle that improper costs may be separated and stated under a heading which will distinguish between these and manufacturing expenses properly and necessarily incurred. This principle is rather far-reaching; its application may be of the greatest practical value; and it is susceptible of abuse. The danger is of assuming an impossibly perfect standard of working and of failing to allow for an inescapable average of accident and failure. Or again of applying in complex work the standards that are fair where work is simple, or in special work where new means of working to a new end have to be developed, the standards that are fair where processes are throughly established.

[7] *Loc. cit.*, p. 956.
[8] *Loc. cit.*, p. 955.

"It is possible to carry the application of distinguishing between proper and improper cost so far as to use calculations of proper cost, and then to direct the cost accounting to showing the variations of actual from calculated costs. This involves the setting up of complete standards for quality in materials and efficiency in working, and is not be confused with estimates of probable cost which are arrived at by any superficial method or except with the idea of continuously testing actual and calculated costs by each other."

It would be difficult to find a passage written in our own time, of comparable length, which expresses more clearly the basic ideas of standard costing.

Harrington Emerson and Standard Costs

When we turn to Harrington Emerson, the American efficiency engineer,[9] we move on only 12 months in time but we come closer still to the outlook and terminology of our own day. His series of articles entitled "Efficiency as a Basis for Operation and Wages,"[10] revised and published as a book in 1909, are said to have taken place "at once as one of the classics of the literature of industrial engineering."[11] They can certainly still be read with profit, and they deserve some little attention from us in this review of costing development.

The first thing that strikes one about Emerson's work is the very clear-cut way in which he distinguishes between standard costing and all that has gone before:

"There are two radically different methods of ascertaining costs, the first method to ascertain them after the work is completed, the isecond method to ascertain them before the work is undertaken. The first method is the old one, still used in most manufacturing and maintenance undertakings, the second method is the new one, beginning to be used in some very large plants, where its feasibility and practical value have already been demonstrated."[12] The old methods are wrong because the information they provide is hopelessly delayed: and it is "wholly and absolutely incorrect, mixing up with costs incidents that do not have the remotest connection with them, so that analysis of cost statements . . . does not lead to elimination of wastes."[13] "The acceptance of the haphazard is the main characteristic of the old method, still in full and orthodox standing in cost accounting."[14] ". . . Because costs are not standardized, the variations due to inefficiency under identical conditions are in the records either increased or lessened by the much larger variations due to change of conditions."[15]

[9]Born at Trenton, New Jersey, 1853. I do not know when he died.
[10]*Engineering Magazine*, July, 1908–March, 1909.
[11]Editor's note to the book, p. iv.
[12]*Engineering Magazine*, Vol. XXXVI, p. 336.
[13]*Loc. cit.*, p. 336.
[14]*Loc. cit.*, p. 337.
[15]*Loc. cit.*, p. 339.

Two other points are notable. One is his advocacy of the use of the standard hour as "the real standard unit of cost." "The cost of repairing a particular locomotive for a particular mile run," he says, in the course of describing the application of standard costing to a locomotive repair shop, "never has been, never can be ascertained, but the rate of pay for a man for a given hour and his speed of work can be as definitely determined as the length of a race track and the time required by a horse to go round it. . . . Costs of locomotives or of locomotive miles, or of track maintenance, or of anything else will take care of themselves when the unit hours of each man and machine are operating at highest efficiency for standard cost. . . ."[16] A further noteworthy point about Emerson's approach is his reluctant acceptance of the necessity to tie in standard costs with actual current expenditure. He described efficiency engineers as having found this "to their sorrow" and that without tying-in they could not "convince those on whose support they must rely that the methods used are really producing the results promised."[17]

As with Whitmore, so with Emerson. It is impossible to say how much originality is embodied in his articles. In an earlier article, published in 1904,[18] there is no sign of the advanced ideas which he is found advocating in 1908. In his later articles he is describing a system he has seen in operation. We do not know how much he contributed to its devising.

There are two great weaknesses in Emerson's system, or at least in his account of it. First, his idea of what constitutes a standard is confusing and confused. In one place he talks of it as being "always elusively ahead of the actual"[19] and again, "The worker is limited by conditions as they are, but standard time presupposes standard power and maintenance conditions—ideal, not actual, conditions for the worker."[20] Yet later he says that "predetermined standard costs can be attained through the direct and indirect assistance given to the line by the staff."[21] Thus he seems to vacillate between an ideal and an attainable standard. A second weakness in his work is that he makes no attempt to arrive at anything more detailed than an overall variance between actual and standard costs. There is no suggestion of the possibility of analyzing the total variance into its component parts. Thus his repeated claim that his system enables waste to be "located" is hardly justified. That it would come near to enabling the total dollar wastage during any period to be *measured* is probably true enough. But for the *location* of waste in any

[16]*Loc. cit.*, p. 683.
[17]*Loc. cit.*, p. 678.
[18]"Percentage Method of Determining Production Costs," in *The Foundry*, October, 1904.
[19]*Engineering Magazine*, Vol. XXXVI, p. 174.
[20]*Loc. cit.*, p. 178.
[21]*Loc. cit.*, p. 178.

sense of the word which is at all significant we must look not to Harrington Emerson but to others whose work lies a little nearer to our own time.[22]

The Change of Emphasis from Cost Ascertainment to Cost Control

It will be seen by comparing the summarized account of Longmuir's ideas with that of Whitmore's that they approach the idea of standard costing from somewhat different angles. Longmuir wants standards as a check on the economy with which various functions in the business are being performed. Whitmore is more concerned with the elimination from "actual" costs of adventitious or wasteful expenditure in order to arrive at a "true" cost, and this brings him also to standards. It will be seen from this that the extension of the use of standard costs was not immediately accompanied by a change of emphasis away from the use of costing as a technique for the ascertainment of product costs towards the control of expenditure and the location of wastes. The introduction of standards seemed more satisfactorily to serve both these functions. The suggestion that the two functions may be incompatible and that there should be a change of emphasis from cost ascertainment to cost control was to be heard only somewhat later.

Budgetary Control

Budgeting, in the sense of forecasting and acting on forecast, is a very old practice. Joseph, in Egypt, made a budget of corn supplies and planned Pharaoh's investment and consumption policy in the light of it. In less remote times, in Great Britain the practice of drawing up a government budget each year is about 200 years old. In the United States it dates back only to 1921.

Even in the humbler sphere of business, budgeting is of respectable antiquity. De Cazaux, whose work on agricultural accounting was referred to earlier, is the first writer I have found to show an interest in accounting for the future as well as for the past, and in the 1825 edition of his book, he devotes a chapter to budgeting.[23] "Future conduct," he says, "is to be traced from an account of successes and failures of the past. Thus one can determine one's needs in the coming year and can compare them with the resources one will have. This statement of resources and needs is called a budget." And he goes on to explain that it is desirable to foresee not only what demands on one's resources will

[22]H. S. Garry, as I pointed out above, separated out price and volume variances. But these were not, as we should now say, "controllable" variances, *i.e.*, they did not reflect avoidable inefficiency.

[23]*Élements d'Économie Privée et Publique*, Book II, Chap. III, pp. 105–108.

be encountered but also exactly when these demands will arise. "Hence the necessity to establish *monthly budgets*, elements of the *general* or *annual budget*."[24]

BUDGET DE (1)

INDICATION DES RESSOURCES ET BESOINS.	RESSOURCES.		BESOINS.		EN PLUS.		EN MOINS.	
	Quantité.	Valeur	Quantité.	Valeur	Quantité.	Valeur	Quantité.	Valeur
ART.								
1.er Froment, à 12^{f} l'hectolitre	200 h.	2400^{f}	100 h.	1200^{f}	100 h.	1200^{f}		
2. Vin, à 15^{f} l'hectolitre	300 h.	4500	70 h.	1050	230 h.	3450		
3. Fourrages secs, à 3^{f} le quintal métrique	1800 q.	5400	1500 q.	4500	300 q.	900		
4. Paille, à 2^{f} *id.*	500 q.	1000	700 q.	1400	....	....	200 q.	400^{f}
etc.								
...Journées d'ouvriers, à 1^{f}	1500 j.	1500	2600 j.	2600	....	....	1100 j.	1100
etc.								
...Besoins de la famille autres que ceux mentionnés	....	....	....	2000	....	....	....	2000
...Pour cas imprévus	....	....	....	1000	....	....	....	1000
...En caisse, aujourd'hui 1.er janvier	....	1500	....	....	....	1500		
TOTAUX	....	16300^{f} *a*	....	13750^{f} *b*	....	7050^{f} *c*	....	4500^{f} *d*

(1) Indiquer le mois, si c'est un budget mensuel; et l'année, si c'est un budget annuel récapitulatif des 12 budgets mensuels. (*On a rempli, en partie,* hypothétiquement *les colonnes du tableau, supposant que ce fût un budget annuel*).

Nota. b soustrait de *a* doit donner le même résultat que *d* soustrait de *c*, sans quoi, il y aurait erreur. (Ce serait *a* qu'il faudrait soustraire de *b*, et *c* de *d*, si les besoins excédaient les ressources.)

[24] *Op. cit.*, p. 105.

The form of farm budget which de Cazaux recommended is reproduced above. As "resources" he shows the quantity and value of produce which he expects to get from the farm, and the amount of labour to be provided by (presumably) the farmer's family. As "needs" he shows the expected consumption of produce by the family, and the *total* amount of labour needed during the period, the family's purchases from outside and a provision for contingencies. The net result will be an addition to the farmer's capital of 2,550 frs. for the period. De Cazaux's budget is a combined business and family budget. As such, while it is of great interest, it is of course not quite typical of business budgets as we now know them.

Budgeting, today, serves several different purposes. It may function, as in government, primarily as part of the machinery of financial procurement. It may serve, in business, as a device to aid systematic planning. Or it may aid the delegation of authority, by fixing limits up to which subordinates may be allowed to spend. It is, however, in the incorporation of budgets into the cost records for the purpose of controlling expenditure that we are specially interested here. This practice seems to have developed early in the present century.

S. H. Bunnell described such a system in 1911.[25] He explained that each item of overheads was to be budgeted and charged into costs at this budgeted figure. Subsequently actual expenditure under each head would be compared with the budget and the differences examined. He claimed two advantages for the system. First, costs did not fluctuate as a result of the purely arbitrary incidence of actual expenses. Second, the differences between budgeted and actual expenses gave a control over efficiency.

We have here an early example of standard costing coupled with budgetary control. The budget, however, is a fixed budget. Like all fixed budgets, it does not take account of fluctuations in output, so that differences between actual and budget expenditure which might at first glance look like excess spending might in fact have been justified by an expansion of output. On the other hand, the complete agreement of budget and actual expense would be quite compatible with the existence of wasteful expenditure.

Bunnell's claims for his system of budgetary control—for that is what it is, though he does not use the term—cannot therefore really be substantiated. His budget lacked flexibility in that the figures were not adjusted in the light of changes of circumstance which supervened during the period for which the budget was drawn up. The basic idea of what we now call a flexible budget had, as a matter of fact, already been expressed by Henry Hess in his remarkable article of 1903 to which

[25]"Standardizing Factory Expense and Cost," *Iron Age*, November 16, 1911.

reference has already been made.[26] Discussing the use of expense forecasts, Hess says:—

> "Forecasting is quite useful but far more important is to make sure that results agree materially with such forecasts and to find the causes for whatever divergencies there may be. . . . There is nothing new in the idea of following up costs in detail and by groups and comparing these with some ideal; rarely do the results agree with that, and very often are discrepancies attributed to the influence of a fluctuating output; there is generally just enough truth in that excuse to prevent the responsibility for a falling off being definitely located, owing to the haziness of knowledge of the actual influence of such fluctuation."[27]

Hess then proceeds to expound a simple graphical method of comparing actual and budgeted expenditure. For each main group of expenses he plots a straight line representing the relationship of the expenses to output. The horizontal axis measures both output (say, in tons) and time. At the end of each month (or other appropriate period) actual expenditure is plotted on the diagram.

DIRECT PRODUCTION LABOUR COSTS

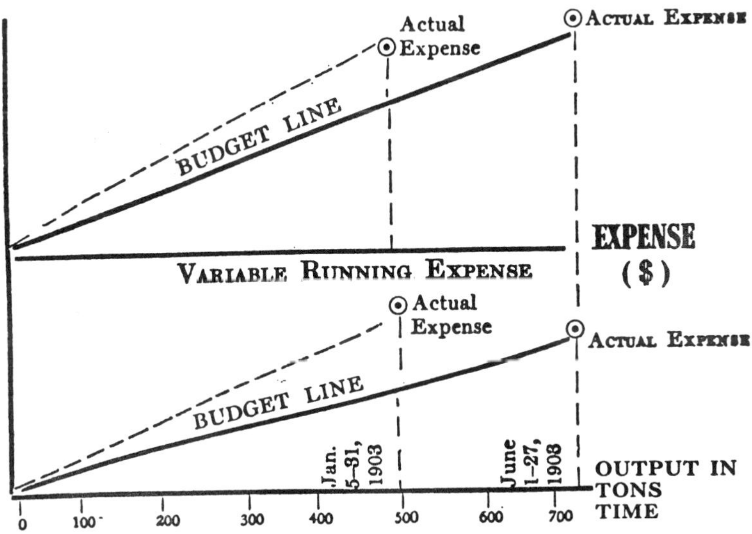

By arranging the charts for the various expense groups under each other, and by having a common date line, Hess claimed that the record for each period could be followed up very quickly and the serious departures from budget investigated. By having a line instead of a point

[26]"Manufacturing: Capital, Costs, Profits and Dividends," *Engineering Magazine*, December, 1903.

[27]*Loc. cit.*, pp. 376–7.

for his budgeted expense, he expresses clearly the variability of certain expenses as output varies. His lines are straight lines and represent, therefore, an over-simple relationship between output and expense. But the harnessing for control purposes of the distinction between fixed and variable expenses which he had earlier discussed in relation to questions of output policy shows Hess to have been well in advance of most of his contemporaries.

The Later Development of Standard Costing

From about 1912 onwards, the literature of standard costing becomes richer, and it becomes increasingly difficult to trace the genealogy of new ideas. We find a growing volume of criticism of retrospective costing; and the change of emphasis, to which I have referred, from the ascertainment of what it costs to make something to the control of what it costs to carry out an industrial process or function can be seen developing. The newer view is put thus by W. E. McHenry, writing in 1914 " 'What it costs to *do* things' and 'What it costs per HOUR' may some day supplant much present detail, laboriously worked out 'per ton'."[28] And the same writer, two years later, gives us an admirably clear illustration of the application of standard costing techniques to the operation of a blast furnace.[29] In this illustration he separates out what we would now call volume, efficiency, and expense variances, and shows how a straight calculation of cost per ton would give an unfavourable (and misleading) impression of the efficiency of a works in a month in which the blast is off for seven days out of 30, without a corresponding fall in the monthly expense of operation. McHenry makes no claim to originality. "The general method of distributing indirect expense by means of 'standard' rates, so that the product is only charged with its *proportion of the services actually used*, has been before the public for several years," he says. But it is "little understood."[30]

One more pioneer of standard costing must be mentioned. This is G. Charter Harrison.[31] Becoming associated with Harrington Emerson in 1909, he took up his ideas and developed them in 1911 into the first *complete* standard costing system known to exist.[32] A series of articles[33]

[28]"Cost per ton": *Engineering Magazine*, February, 1914, p. 791.

[29]"Is your cost system scientific?" *Engineering Magazine*, August, 1916, pp. 681–3.

[30]*Loc. cit.*, p. 686.

[31]Born in London, 1881, became an Associate of the Institute of Chartered Accountants in England and Wales in 1905, and forthwith settled in America. From 1911–16 he was head of the Systems Department of Price, Waterhouse & Co. From 1918 he practised independently as a management consultant for over thirty years in Madison, Wisconsin. He kindly prepared some notes for me about his early work.

[32]This was for the Boss Manufacturing Co., of Kewanee, Illinois, makers of work gloves.

[33]"Cost Accounting to Aid Production," *Industrial Management*, October, 1918–June, 1919.

which he wrote in 1918 have a sureness of touch and a comprehensiveness in their treatment which shows standard costing to have left the experimental stage and to have attained the status of established practice. In these articles he produced the first set of formulae for the analysis of cost variances.[34]

Any detailed account of Charter Harrison's ideas would encroach too far into the field of modern costing, for his articles and his book are not only milestones in the development of the subject—they are still part of its current literature. Harrison viewed the growth of standard costing, not as a new departure but rather as a return to the principle of predetermining costs which in earlier times had found general acceptance but had become obscured by the complexity of modern business. And for justification of his view he quotes from St. Luke's Gospel: "for which of you intending to build a tower sitteth not down first and counteth the cost."

Uniform Costing

The development by trade associations of uniform costing definitions and methods for adoption by all member firms and others in the industry is the last costing evolution which I shall try to describe.[35] It is by no means a recent development. We first encounter it in America, where the National Association of Stove Manufacturers, formed in 1872, had by 1889 developed a uniform "formula" for costing the industry's products. Similar activities in the printing industry were afoot before 1887 but only resulted in the formal adoption of the Standard Uniform Cost Finding System for Printers by the United Typothetæ of America in 1910.[36]

Since the 1914–18 War, uniform systems have had a chequered career in the United States. In 1925, adverse decisions by the Supreme Court in the Hardwood Lumber and Maple Flooring Cases brought under the Sherman Anti-Trust Law made trade associations wary about developing this side of their activities. On the other hand, the National Recovery Administration under the New Deal, during the period 1933–36, had power to prohibit sales below cost—and uniform costing was greatly encouraged as a result. In 1950 there were probably about 150 *effective* schemes in the United States though a vastly greater number certainly existed on paper.

[34]In an article entitled "Scientific Basis for Cost Accounting," *Industrial Management*, December, 1918, p. 459 *et seq*.

[35]For a fuller study of this subject, see my "Uniform Cost Accounting—a Survey," *Economica*, August and November, 1950.

[36]On this, see "Typothetæ Experiments with Price Maintenance and Cost Work," by Leona M. Powell in *Journal of Political Economy*, February, 1926, pp. 78–99.

3

In Great Britain, it was in the Birmingham iron bedstead trade that uniform costing seems to have been first tried out, in the last decade of the last century. The prime mover in this development was E. J. Smith, himself a bedstead manufacturer, and having organized his own trade, he set out to spread the light elsewhere by starting the New Trades Combination Movement. This was to ensure a quiet life for industrialists by fostering price agreements based on cost within each industry, and uniform costing was to play its part. "It is part of my scheme," he wrote, "to establish in every trade a system of cost taking which, while it may not be all that could be desired when tested by the special circumstances of any individual business, is still all that is needed for the purpose of fixing throughout an entire trade a selling price for each manufactured article which will bring a legitimate and reasonable profit to each maker without unduly taxing the purchaser."[37] Smith was active in a number of trades, but virtually nothing is left of his work for uniform costing for, so far as I know, none of the still extant schemes owes anything to him.

The oldest existing British scheme is that of the British Federation of Master Printers. The Federation was founded in 1900, and almost from the start costing occupied much of its executives' time. A form of printers' cost system was issued in 1909 and in 1911 a representative of the Federation went to America to learn what he could from experience there. Two years later, after further discussions, the first edition of the present scheme was issued as a cost manual after formal adoption by a Cost Congress held in London.[38]

Since 1913, the printers have been followed by many other trade associations. Not all the schemes launched have survived. There were in 1950 probably not more than 25 in effective operation.

Conclusion

This survey of costing history makes no pretensions to completeness. A full history would have to concern itself with many aspects of the subject which have been altogether omitted here, such as the development of mechanized means of keeping cost records, the growing integration of costing and production control, the application of costing to selling and distribution functions, and its application to governmental activities.

If there is one conclusion to be drawn from the foregoing study, it is that there is remarkably little in modern costing which our fathers did not know about. What can be fairly claimed for the period 1910–1950,

[37]E. J. Smith: *The New Trades Combination Movement*, p. 30.

[38]For a detailed account of these developments, see *The British Federation of Master Printers, 1900–1950* by Ellic Howe.

however, is that great strides were made in converting ideas into widely adopted practices. In that process, two world wars played no inconsiderable part. But that there is room for further advance both in the theory and practice of industrial accounting hardly needs to be said. I should like to think that this book, by making the studies which follow more widely known, may play some small part in helping that advance forward.

The Maner and Fourme how to kepe a Perfecte Reconyng

By Professor David Solomons

BERNARD Shaw made one of his characters say of book-keeping that it was the most "damnable waste of human life that ever was invented." We do not know how he would have answered the question, "Why, then, was it invented ?" After all, waste of human life is no small matter. The question, therefore, is not one to be treated lightly. Besides, if Shaw is right, a number of other people, not less distinguished in their way, have been wrong. Goethe's Wilhelm Meister called double-entry book-keeping "one of the fairest inventions of the human mind", and Sombart described it as "born of the same spirit as the systems of Galileo and Newton, . . . the first cosmos constructed on the basis of mechanistic thought". When men of such eminence differ, the difference is surely worth investigating.

Moreover, we stand on the threshold of a new era in the art of accounting, an era dominated by the electronic valve. If the past can illumine the future, is this not a good time to look back over the way we have come to check our bearings ? The recent appearance of a volume of twenty-four essays[1] on the history of accounting makes this a pleasurable as well as a profitable thing to do, for those who use accounts (and which of us does not ?) as well as for those who prepare them.

Yet whatever the debt which accountants owe to historians for their researches into the origins and development of the accounting art, it is small by comparison with the debt owed by historians to the accountants of antiquity. A substantial part of the epigraphic and documentary evidence from which our knowledge of the ancient world and the early Middle Ages has been obtained consists of accounting records. Indeed, the first written records known to us—the clay tablets left

---

Mr. Solomons is Professor of Accounting in the University of Bristol.

[1] *Studies in the History of Accounting*, ed. A. C. Littleton and B. S. Yamey (Sweet & Maxwell, 1956. xi + 392 pp. and 8 plates, 50/-).

by the Sumerians of the fourth millenium B.C.—are priestly records of temple incomes, and it has been suggested that the very art of writing was invented because of the need to keep accounts. Since that time, accounts have been kept in every conceivable form—by inscription on stone, wood, metal and on wax tablets, on potsherds, on papyrus, parchment and paper, as notches cut in tallies, as holes punched in card or paper, and as impulses on magnetic tape.

ACCOUNTING IN GREECE AND ROME

The central theme in any history of accounting must be the origin and development of double-entry. Yet double-entry did not make its appearance until after some five millenia of accounting by simpler methods. This is one of the principal conclusions reached by Mr. G. de Ste. Croix in a fascinating essay in this collection on Greek and Roman accounting.[1] It had long been thought, on the evidence of a single passage in the Elder Pliny's *Natural History*, that Greek and Roman accounts were kept in the bilateral form used in our own day—receipts on one side, payments on the other. Mr. de Ste. Croix shows with a wealth of evidence that such was not the case, and that the Greeks and Romans did not as a rule have the idea of an orderly arrangement of debits and credits, much less a complete system of double-entry. There are a few accounts, both on stone and on papyrus, in which the figures are arranged in an orderly manner in columns. But these are the exceptions. The typical account is in the form of a continuous narrative, without tabulation of the figures and without any regular segregation of receipts or payments.

From the second century A.D., Roman book-keeping, such as it was, went into decline and by the fifth century the practice of keeping private accounts (except by bankers) is said virtually to have ceased. The reason is not without its moral for us. Taxation of the property-owning classes had become penal, and accounting evidence of the ownership of intangible property (e.g. book debts) which might be made the basis of yet further tax burdens, was best avoided. Apparently the more sophisticated expedient—the keeping of two sets of books—was not resorted to in the ancient world, or at least there is no evidence of it.

The reason for the backwardness of Greek and Roman

---

[1] *Op. cit.*, pp. 14-74.

accounting was, Mr. de Ste. Croix argues, the clumsy numerical notation which they used. Like us, of course, they used the decimal system "simply because all men have ten fingers and find it useful to count on them." But their system of writing numbers was greatly inferior, since they could not express the value of a number by its mere position in relation to other numbers or to zeros. This meant that in the Roman script and the Greek acrophonetic script, a long string of oft-repeated symbols was required to express what we can express with four or five; or in the Greek alphabetic script, twenty-seven different symbols were used to do what we do with ten. As place-value did not exist, to tabulate figures made it easier to check them, and in inscriptions had aesthetic value, but it was not essential for computation. This had to be done mentally or on the digital computer with which Nature has equipped us, or, when this was inadequate, on an abacus. Hence, it is argued, there was little stimulus to the orderly arrangement of figures, much less to the segregation of debits and credits.

Now this question of numerical notation may well be basic to the origins of double-entry. In Mr. de Ste. Croix's view, the introduction of double-entry is bound up with the spread of Hindu-Arabic numerals in Europe and the gradual supersession of the much clumsier Roman system from the tenth century onwards. This view has hitherto failed to find much favour because, although double-entry accounts are found from the early fourteenth century onwards, most of those which have come down to us, for the next 200 years, were kept in Roman numerals. Even where Arabic numerals were used for dates and folio numbers, Roman figures were used in the accounts proper, as these were thought to be more difficult to alter.[1] Yet it is clear, as Mr. de Ste. Croix points out, that in fact Arabic numerals were being used, though not widely, for account-keeping in Tuscany by the end of the 13th century, and right at the beginning of the century Leonardo Pisano, the foremost mathematician of his time, had demonstrated in his *Liber Abbaci* (1202) the superiority of the Arabic notation for accounting as for other purposes.

Mr. de Ste. Croix's thesis is that it was men like Leonardo who "were responsible for the introduction into Europe of the practice of arranging figures—Arabic figures—in accounts in

[1] It is interesting to see excessive caution putting a brake on accounting progress here, just as the suspicion of loose-leaf records did during the first quarter of this century.

regular columns . . . " and that, stimulated by the expanding economy of the later Middle Ages,

> Once figures began to be disposed in a *single* column, instead of being scattered all over the page and reduced to order only outside the account-book, on the abacus or in the mind, the advantages of having *two* clearly separated columns, simply to facilitate computation, would very quickly become apparent; and this would of itself result in the emergence of the bilateral form of account, with debits and credits visibly distinguished. The final step, the further advance to double entry, could then equally well be made by those (no doubt still the large majority) who continued to employ Roman numerals.

This may be so. We shall probably never reach the final truth on this matter. I would only point out that the speed with which a clerk could add on an abacus would be considerably increased if, instead of having to search in a narrative account for the figures he wanted, these were systematically set down in columns. This would be just as true for one numerical notation as another. The growth in the volume of transactions as medieval trade expanded would, therefore, have provided a stimulus to the tabulation of figures, for the sake of those using an abacus, even if Roman numerals had not been superseded.

THE FORMATIVE YEARS OF ACCOUNTING

From what we know of English manorial and household accounts of the early Middle Ages, accounting in this country at that time seems still to have been in much the same state as the Romans had left it in, despite the fact that by the end of the thirteenth century manorial accounting was being taught at Oxford. But in Northern Italy, the golden age of accounting was about to dawn. In a masterly survey of the medieval period down to 1500, by which time Pacioli had published the first treatise on double-entry book-keeping in Venice, Raymond de Roover, drawing on what is probably an unrivalled knowledge of the sources in not one but half-a-dozen European countries, gives us a detailed picture of the beginnings of modern accounting.[1]

The view, once held, that Pacioli was the first and sole inventor of double-entry—a claim he never made himself—has long been discredited. His treatise, published in 1494, may not even have been the first written on the subject. Moreover, we

[1] "The Development of Accounting Prior to Luca Pacioli according to the Account-Books of Medieval Merchants ": *Studies in the History of Accounting*, pp. 114-174.

now know of many sets of books kept by double-entry from early in the fourteenth century onwards. There are even fragmentary records from before 1300 which may have been parts of a double-entry system, though opinions differ as to whether they were or not.[1]

The accounts of the stewards (*massari*) of the Commune of Genoa for the year 1340 have for many years been accepted as being the oldest genuinely double-entry accounts known to us. Though we do not have any earlier records of the *massari*, it seems likely that the same system was in use from 1327, when the Commune's book-keeping arrangements were overhauled as a result of several frauds. The ledger sets out debits and credits in tabular two-sided accounts, a form already much more common in Genoa and Northern Italy than in Florence and the rest of Tuscany, and every transaction is entered twice. The Genoa accounts reveal, incidentally, an ingenious method of raising public loans without contravening the Church's ban on usury. The Commune purchased merchandise—pepper, silk, sugar, wax—on credit and sold it for cash at a loss. This method of raising funds by buying on credit was, it seems, not uncommon in the Middle Ages. The device is still used in some of the under-developed countries.

Recent research has brought to light new records of earlier date in a number of Tuscan cities, but especially Florence, which have some at least of the distinguishing features of double-entry, though the ledger accounts, where we have them, are usually still in the narrative or paragraph form of the pre-double-entry era. It would not be worth while, here, to follow Professor de Roover in his discussion whether they do or do not pass the double-entry test. What is important is that we now have a picture which shows double-entry developing simultaneously in a number of centres in Italy between 1250 and 1350, and being fully developed in principle though not, of course, in detail, by the end of that period.

---

[1] A complete double-entry system is one which recognizes that every transaction can be analysed in two different ways, i.e. according to answers to the questions (1) " *What kind* of benefit was gained or given up? " and (2) " *What was the source or destination* of the benefit gained or given up? " As there are for any business many transactions to be analysed, the quantitative answers to these two questions are, so to speak, filed away in the ledger accounts. There will, in a complete system, be accounts for incomes, expenditures, assets, liabilities and for the proprietor's equity. It is the last which makes a double-entry system balance, and which essentially distinguishes double-entry from single-entry, for single-entry does not have proprietorship accounts. Unless a substantial part of the records relating to a particular business have survived, it may be difficult to say whether its system was a " balanced " one or not.

Professor de Roover attaches considerable importance to partnership as a factor in the development of accounting. Clearly, it introduces two important new elements. The firm becomes an accounting entity distinct and separate from its proprietors; and the striking of an accurate profit figure becomes altogether more important, for the rights of the partners relative to each other depend on it.

The considerable complexity which Italian business organization had attained during the fifteenth century, and the way in which accounting methods had already developed to meet the new demands made on it, are well illustrated by the history of the Medici Bank, which was founded in Florence in 1397 and which flourished throughout most of the ensuing century.[1] At one time, the bank had five branches in Italy, in addition to its head office in Florence, and four abroad—in Avignon, Bruges, Geneva (later moved to Lyons) and London. In addition to their banking activities, the Medici controlled three textile manufacturing shops in Florence. Each branch and the manufacturing enterprise was organized as a separate partnership with its own books. The Medici held a controlling interest in each partnership, the businesses being managed by active resident partners.

An examination of the bank's records shows that the best accounting practice of the early fifteenth century was in several respects in advance of the earliest treatises on the subject written much later. Each branch, for instance, had several ledgers rather than a single ledger and a balanced set of final accounts could be prepared from the combination of ledgers. The books were closed and balanced at least once a year, and a copy of the balance sheet was sent to Florence, sometimes with a report from the manager. Some of the specimens which are still extant bear witness to the fact that they were carefully scrutinized, especially for bad debts. In one of the branch balance sheets, a debt due from a deceased cleric is noted as being doubtful of recovery because his surety, a layman, is indifferent to the threat of excommunication which, as papal bankers, the Medici could bring down on his head for failing to pay over Church revenues. Provisions for bad debts were commonly made, and so were provisions for accrued

[1] Professor de Roover has written more fully on the Bank in his *The Medici Bank; Its Organisation, Management, Operations, and Decline* (New York, 1948): but much of the accounting material on which he writes in his present study has come to light since his book was written.

wages and reserves for contingencies. Not all the modern touches are equally praiseworthy, however. In the balance sheet of the Bruges branch for 1464, it is noted that as profits are small, the bank's depositors have not been credited with the interest due to them. As de Roover puts it, " 'window-dressing' does not seem to be anything new, either."

Outside Italy, the standard of accounting by 1500 was in no way comparable, to judge from the rather fragmentary evidence. This is somewhat curious, because although treatises on book-keeping " after the Italian manner ", as double-entry was still called as late as the eighteenth century, did not become available until 1494 in Italy and later still in other countries, the foreign branches of some Italian merchants and banks were using the system and one might have expected the expatriate Italians to influence the merchants among whom they lived. The Borromeo Bank, of Milan, opened a branch in London in 1436 for example, and its ledgers for the years 1436-39, which are still extant, reveal a high level of accounting. Yet English merchants did not approach this level till a century later. It is usual to explain this backwardness outside Italy by saying (as de Roover does) that, not having such elaborate business organizations as the Italians, other countries did not feel the need for such refined accounting methods. No doubt this is true. Whether the argument can then be turned round, so as to make the lack of refined accounting methods a contributory factor of economic backwardness—a pirouette which de Roover skilfully executes—is much more doubtful.

BOOK-KEEPING AND THE RISE OF CAPITALISM

This brings us to one of the most interesting questions raised by a study of the history of accounting. Did the emergence of double-entry in the fourteenth and fifteenth centuries, and its subsequent spread, play a vital part in the rise of modern capitalism, by facilitating the measurement of profit and hence making possible the rational direction of investment and enterprise? Many authorities both on capitalism and on the history of accounting—Max Weber, Sombart, Nussbaum, Schumpeter, de Roover and Littleton among them—have leaned to this view.

The argument is not merely that systematic book-keeping made for better control of business. What is in issue concerns business planning rather than control. Those who think that the rise of double-entry was synonymous with the development of a rational approach to profit-seeking have generally based their view on broad grounds of probability, rather than a detailed examination of cases. " One can scarcely conceive of capitalism without double-entry book-keeping: they are related as are form and content ".[1] Only recently has research into book-keeping records in medieval Italy, especially Tuscany, begun to give substance to the view that it was as an improved method of profit measurement that double-entry was valued.

The case " against " double-entry, so to speak, has perhaps been put best by one of the editors of this collection, Mr. B. S. Yamey, both in his introduction and more fully in an earlier paper published elsewhere.[2] Basing his view on a careful study of the early book-keeping treatises, he concludes that profit measurement was not considered an important advantage of double-entry, as is evidenced by the infrequency with which books were balanced and profit figures and a balance sheet drawn up. Balancing, when it is done at all, serves predominantly to provide a check on the arithmetical accuracy of the books. " Throughout the period the process of balancing . . . appears to have served limited objectives of a technical ' book-keeping ' nature ".[3]

On neither side of the argument is the evidence conclusive. As de Roover has pointed out, because Pacioli's treatise is based on Venetian practice and so many of the later treatises derived so much from Pacioli, neither his book nor its successors can be relied on to give an adequate description of the procedures outside Venice. It so happens that Venetian accounting was marked by infrequent balancing.[4] And since it was concerned so much with maritime trade, it leant heavily towards " venture " accounting: that is, towards keeping separate accounts for each voyage or venture on which the trader embarked. In this kind of accounting, so long as separate profits and losses on each venture are being calculated, a general balancing of the books does not have much significance from the point of view of business direction.

---

[1] W. Sombart, *Der Moderne Kapitalismus* (6th Ed. 1924) Vol. II, part 1, p. 118.

[2] " Scientific Book-keeping and the Rise of Capitalism " in *Studies in Accounting* (ed. W. T. Baxter, 1950), pp. 13-30.

[3] Yamey, *loc. cit.*, p. 26.

[4] Too much should not be made of Venetian slackness in this respect. Pacioli's advice on this matter is sound enough. " It is always good to close them [i.e. the ledger accounts] each year ", he writes, " especially he who is in partnership as the proverb says—frequent accounting tends to lasting friendship ".

ACCOUNTING IN TUDOR ENGLAND

Reference was made earlier to the relatively backward state of accounting outside Italy, at a time when so much progress was being made inside that country. In England, by 1550 we had reached a stage which the Italians had reached a hundred years earlier. Mr. Peter Ramsey's examination of some Tudor merchants' accounts throws light both on the state of accounting in England at that time and on the contribution of double-entry to rational profit seeking.[1] One of the ledgers he writes about is the earliest known example of a ledger kept by double-entry in England. It belonged to Thomas Howell, a member of the Drapers' Company engaged mainly in the Spanish trade, and it contains entries for the years 1522-26. It is kept in Roman numerals still and has the debit entries on the left-hand page, the credit on the right.

Of these Tudor records, it is perhaps the journal of Sir Thomas Gresham for 1546-47 which is of greatest interest to us, in part because of Gresham's eminence as a merchant. Like so many account books of its kind, it opens with a resounding dedication:

> In the name of God, Amen. This present boke shalbe the Jornall called & apperteyning to me Thomas Gresham of London mercer for therin to wryte with my owne hande or els with the hand of my prentys Thomas Bradshawe alle my hoole trayne and doynges and out of the said Jornall to wryte it into the greate booke called the Leger which shalbe holden by poundes shillinges and pence of money of Englande. Pleaseth God to give me profytt and prosperitye to defend me from evill fortune losse and damage. Amen.

Then follow two hundred folios which show in detail how Gresham's business was conducted. Amounts were written in the narrative of the journal in Arabic figures but were extended into a single money column in Roman numerals.

The entries in the journal were roughly in chronological order. No attempt was made to group purchases or sales or to segregate cash or bill transactions into specialized books. One important feature is that a separate trading account was kept for each commodity dealt in, so that the profitability of different commodities could be determined. Trading profits on one or other of these accounts were struck from time to time, unsold goods being valued for this purpose at cost price: but the accounts were never all balanced together, so

---

[1] "Some Tudor Merchants' Accounts": *Studies in the History of Accounting*, pp. 185-201.

that the total profit for a period was never arrived at, at least so far as can be discerned from the books. A single-entry type of profit calculation was most probably resorted to. This and other features of the accounts of Gresham and of the other Tudor merchants he considers leads Mr. Ramsey to share Mr. Yamey's scepticism as to the importance which early users of double-entry attached to its use as a profit-measuring technique.

PACIOLI AND HIS INFLUENCE

By Gresham's time, the earliest treatises on double-entry book-keeping had made their appearance—six in Italy (of which four were Venetian), two in Germany, one in the Low Countries, one in Spain and one in England. Of these, Pacioli's, the first of them all, and Hugh Oldcastle's, the first in England, have a special interest for us.

Luca Pacioli was born at Borgo San Sepolcro (between Florence and Perugia) between 1445 and 1450.[1] As a young man he was a pupil of Piero della Francesca, and afterwards went as a tutor to the family of a Venetian merchant. During the six years that he spent in Venice, he no doubt learnt much about commerce, and this may have given him an interest in book-keeping. After joining the Order of the Franciscans Minor at about the age of 25, he spent most of his life in teaching mathematics at universities and courts up and down Italy and his work on book-keeping consists of one section of a treatise on mathematics which he published in 1494.[2] He also published other mathematical works. Nothing is heard of him after 1514, when he received a papal summons to teach at the Academy in Rome, and the date of his death is not known. In spite of his authorship of a book on chess, he emerges as a somewhat sombre personality, and this impression is reinforced by the portrait of him attributed to Jacopo de Barbari which now hangs in the Naples museum.

It is not now thought that much, if any, of Pacioli's work on book-keeping was original, even as an account of " the method employed in Venice ", as he described it. But original or not, it (or the unacknowledged manuscript on which his book was based) became the model for countless later works.

---

1 " Luca Pacioli ", by Professor R. Emmett Taylor: *Studies in the History of Accounting*, pp. 175-184. Professor Taylor has published a full-length biographical study of Pacioli, entitled *No Royal Road. Luca Pacioli and his Times* (University of North Carolina Press, 1942).

2 *Summa de Arithmetica, Geometria, Proportioni et Proportionalità*. The section on book-keeping is called *De Computis et Scripturis*.

Some of them are little more than translations. It is hardly too much to say that Pacioli's grip on the subsequent development of book-keeping is comparable only to Aristotle's hold on natural philosophy, though it did not last so long; or rather, since Pacioli did not originate anything, through him the methods used in Venice at the end of the fifteenth century took on a canonical authority in matters of detail which led, in the seventeenth and eighteenth centuries, to what de Roover has called " a period of stagnation ". Indeed, it took the advent of mechanization in our own day to sweep away such useless relics as " to " and " by ", and a whole lot of clutter with which practitioners of the art have been wont to turn a useful technique into a mystery.

In England, the first to follow where Pacioli led was Hugh Oldcastle, teacher of arithmetic and book-keeping in the parish of St. Olave's in the City of London. Of his book, *A profitable treatyce called the instrument or boke to learne to know the good order of the kepyng of the famous reconyng, called in latin Dare et Habere, and in Englyshe Debitor and Creditor*, published in 1543, no copy has come down to us, and it is known only through a reprint issued by John Mellis in 1588. It is sufficiently different from Pacioli's work to pass as more than a translation, but it nevertheless follows its Italian model closely.

It is closely followed, in its turn, by the second English book on book-keeping, *The Maner and fourme how to kepe a perfecte reconyng, after the order of the moste worthie and notable accompte, of Debitor and Creditor*, by James Peele, 1553, although, as we know Oldcastle's book only through Mellis's 1588 reprint, we do not know whether and to what extent Peele borrowed from Oldcastle or Mellis borrowed from Peele. By the middle of the century, English merchants had no excuse for continuing ignorance of double-entry, for after 1547 they had also an English translation (via the French) of Ympyn's *Nieuwe Instructie*, which was itself a Dutch translation of an Italian manuscript which had come into Ympyn's hands. Mr. R. R. Coomber, who contributes an essay on Oldcastle to the present collection,[1] suggests that both he and Pacioli may have used the same manuscript as Ympyn, which the latter acknowledged as being by one Juan Paolo di Bianchi.

Who can say where authorship ends and plagiarism

---

[1] *Op. cit.*, pp. 206-214.

begins? Nearly all these old writers on book-keeping added something to the clarification of the subject, if not always to its development. Their books, and the many which followed them during the next 200 years, are not less distinctive, one from the other, than our modern text-books; and their titles—*The pathewaye to perfectness in the accomptes of Debitour and Creditour; The Merchant's Mirrour; The Apprentices Time-Entertainer accomptantly; Amphithalami, or, The Accomptants Closet*—have an alluring quality which we, with our eternal Principles, Elements, Introductions and the rest, have long since lost.

THE FUTURE OF DOUBLE-ENTRY

We cannot here follow the subsequent history of accounting down to the present day. Much of the story can be found in these *Studies*. Probably it could have been said of the vast majority of small businesses during the last 600 years, as in fact it was said of the Japanese in 1640, that " they have not the Italian Manner of Keeping Books, and yet fail not in their Calculations ". But it is unlikely that the growth in the size of businesses which took place during the nineteenth century, made possible as it was by the spread of limited liability and joint stock, could have been so fruitful if a system of orderly account-keeping had not been readily to hand; and although orderly account-keeping and the " Italian manner " are not necessarily synonymous, they have usually gone together.

This fact seems to have been recognized exactly a century ago in the Joint Stock Companies Act of 1856, for the model set of articles contained in Table B of the Act (which became Table A of all later Acts) required that " The Directors shall cause true accounts to be kept . . . Such Accounts shall be kept, upon the Principle of Double Entry, in a Cash Book, Journal and Ledger ".[1] This specification that the accounts should be kept by double-entry, which of course a company could avoid by modifying or not adopting Table B, has not survived to the present day, but the more stringent accounting regulations enacted in later statutes have really made such a requirement superfluous.

It is possible that we may already have seen double-entry pass its zenith. At least before long it may come in for rough handling. Its great virtue—perhaps the only one it does not

[1] Quoted by H. C. Edey and P. Panitpakdi in their essay on " British Company Accounting and the Law 1844-1900 ", *op. cit.*, p. 362.

share with less elegant methods—is that, as every transaction is recorded twice, the balancing of the books provides a *prima facie* proof of their accuracy. The more we reduce the scope for human fallibility, the more we play down double-entry's strength. This is exactly what the mechanization of accounting has been doing, and what its " electronification " will do even more. We no longer have to look to double-entry to ensure that " it is impossible for an error of the most trifling amount to be passed unnoticed ".[1]

There is another reason why double-entry as it has hitherto been practised may now call for radical modification. Traditionally, accounting has been based on the so-called " cost principle ". When a business acquires assets, it enters them, and continues to carry them, on the books at cost, except in so far as it is necessary to recognize any *loss* in market value of current assets or the diminution in value of fixed assets through their loss of expectation of life. The records remain anchored to historic cost. Changes in the value of money are ignored. A monetary unit which bears the same name at two dates is taken to be the same thing. It goes without saying that this belief has been shaken by recent monetary upheavals but it has survived nevertheless. It may have survived because the " cost principle " seemed to be implicit in double-entry. If accountants are ever driven to recognize that £'s at different dates are different things, index number techniques are ready to hand to put this recognition into effect. These techniques will not abrogate double-entry; but they will transform it, as perhaps nothing else since 1494 has done, into something which Pacioli would be hard put to it to recognize.

DAVID SOLOMONS.

Bristol.
September, 1956.

[1] These words form part of the title of Edward Jones's *English System of Book-keeping* . . . (1796). Jones and his contemporaries are the subject of an essay by Mr. B. S. Yamey, *op. cit.*, pp. 313-324.

MANAGEMENT ACCOUNTING FOR TODAY'S BUSINESS

A review of the development of management accounting from its earliest days to the present time.

SESSION CHAIRMAN

J. D. Cormie, MA, FCA
Finance Director
Reed International Ltd.
(Member of Council)

From Early Times to 1950 D. Solomons

If you look in the index of almost any book on the economic development of Britain, America or any other developed country, do not expect to find a reference there to management accounting. Specialised books by scholars do sometimes make a passing reference to the contribution that accounting made to economic growth in the nineteenth century and subsequently; but compared with the space devoted to developments in technology, one has to be grateful if accounting gets as much as a mention.

Yet it is obvious that without accounting, a complex economic system based on private property and free enterprise could not have developed. So long as transactions remain simple, and are for the most part promptly settled for cash, business can be conducted with only rudimentary records or with none at all. But as soon as the use of credit becomes at all extensive, and when enterprises have to look outside for capital, the need for accounting becomes pressing. It is above all the separation of ownership and management that makes accounting an essential ingredient of our economic system.

Most of this conference will be concerned with the future; but I shall unashamedly be looking to the past, to see where management accounting has come from. My colleagues in this session will carry the story forward from 1950. There is no way to compress the history of almost 500 years into a twenty minute presentation and all one can hope to do is to pick on a few highlights. I shall mention a few names of those who contributed to the development of our subject; but to do so is inevitably to do an injustice to the multitude of others who cannot be mentioned and who played, perhaps, no less a part.

I believe that by 1950 the foundations of everything important that has happened to date in the management accounting field had already been laid. That thought, if it is true, should make us humble. What passes for innovation more often than not turns out to be imitation. Which is not to say that we should stop trying to be innovative.

The Beginning

Let us go back to the beginning. Whether capitalism could have emerged in the thirteenth and fourteenth centuries without double-entry bookkeeping is still an unsettled question, and perhaps it always will be. Though the first written work on double-entry, Luca Pacioli's "Summa", appeared in 1494, we know that bookkeeping systems like the one he described were in use long before that. The beginnings of double-entry have now been pushed back to about 1300, for records that old have been found and deciphered.

I make no apology for taking you back 500 years. I was glad to see, as I entered the exhibition at this Centenary Conference, the portrait of Pacioli. It would certainly not be fitting to ignore the man who, at least so far as the literature of our subject is concerned, really "started it all".

The Industrial Revolution

There is no other single date that has as much significance in accounting as 1494. If we jump over the next 300 years, we find ourselves - in Britain - in the middle of the Industrial Revolution. I have read several attempts by historians to explain why that phenomenon came when it did and why it came first in Britain, and I have found none of them convincing. As one writer put it: "The question about the origin of the Industrial Revolution which concerns us... is not... how the material for the economic explosion was accumulated but how it was ignited; and, we may add, what stopped the first explosion from fizzling out after an impressive initial bang. But was a special mechanism necessary at all? Was it not inevitable that a sufficiently long period of accumulating explosive material would, sooner or later, somehow, somewhere, produce spontaneous combustion? Perhaps so. Nevertheless, it is the "somehow" and "somewhere" which must be explained; all the more so as the way in which an economy of private enterprise brings about industrial revolution raises a number of puzzles. We know that in fact it did so in some parts of the world, but we also know that it failed to do so in other parts, and took a rather long time doing so even in Western Europe." 1

Britain in 1880

The year of the Institute's Charter, 1880, just about divides in half the interval that separates us from the explosion that we call the Industrial Revolution. During the century before the charter, the population of Britain grew from about 10 million to about 30 million. The proportion of the population engaged in agriculture fell from about 40% to about 12%. A railway system of about 16,000 miles had been built, and British capital had helped to build far greater mileages in Europe and the United States. It is interesting to note that this year is the 150th anniversary of the opening of the first passenger railway line in Great Britain. The stimulus resulting from the investment in railways changed the face of the economy, increasing the importance of heavy industry (especially coal, iron, and engineering), and swept three-quarters of the population into the cities. When the Institute received its charter, Britain was producing nearly 50% of the world's coal, 40% of its steel, and almost 50% of its cotton cloth, while in shipbuilding it was far ahead of the rest of the world. Naturally this economic transformation called for financial and management information more sophisticated than had ever been needed before.

1 *E.J. Hobsbawm, Industry and Europe (1969, The Pelican Economic History of Britain, Vol. 3).*

Management Accounting in 1880

In 1880, management accounting was more the preserve of the engineer than of the accountant. The accountant was still, at that time, though with some notable exceptions, largely preoccupied with such matters as bankruptcy and deceased estates. Industrial engineers saw that, with increasing mechanisation, overhead costs had become much more important than they had formerly been. The extreme case was seen in the cost structure of the railways themselves, where heavy fixed costs overshadowed variable costs in importance. This growth in fixed costs posed two different but related questions, one concerned with cost-finding or cost determination, the other with cost behaviour.

Management accounting meant cost accounting in 1880, and one of its main concerns was the allocation of costs to the products that flowed from the factories in ever increasing variety. This is the era that developed the systematic recording and allocation of materials and of time worked, and above all overhead rates that enabled costs to be traced to products. In an age of keen competition, a business that did not have cost data to help it set selling prices was less likely to survive than one that did.

Most of the last quarter of the nineteenth century was a period of depression in Britain and even more so in Western Europe and America, and there was plenty of incentive to improve cost-finding techniques. During this period, several novel methods of applying overhead to products were developed, some of which later contributed to the development of standard costing. But it would be a mistake to think that advanced methods of cost accounting were yet in widespread use. Alexander Hamilton Church, an English electrical engineer who emigrated to America at about that time and whose work powerfully influenced the development of cost accounting, wrote in 1900 that "the majority of firms of any size have some sort of cost method, however rough and home-made, which enables them to tell how much labour and what value of material have been expended on any particular job. Between this elementary stage and the next there is a very wide gap which is bridged by comparatively few firms even in the go-ahead United States."[2] Other sources could be cited to support the view that in general the level of cost accounting to be found in practice was not high at that time.

Harking back to the "Great Depression" that settled on most of the developed world in the last part of the nineteenth century, in our own inflationary times it is hard to believe that the index of wholesale prices actually fell from 152 (1900=100) in 1873 to 88 in 1896. When Britain emerged from that long depression, she had lost her position of supremacy as the "workshop of the world," and she never recovered it.

Some Accounting Pioneers

Although, as I have said, it was engineers rather than accountants who were developing cost accounting before 1900, there were important exceptions. John Manger Fells (1858-1925), an incorporated accountant, joined forces with Emile Garcke (1856-1930), an electrical engineer, and their book, "Factory Accounts", first published in 1887, ran through seven editions by 1922 and was still in use many years later. It was the first book successfully to show how cost and financial records could be integrated, a matter no doubt of more appeal to accountants than to engineers. Another noteworthy name among the accountants who were developing cost accounting at that time was George Pepler Norton (1858-1939), a chartered accountant, whose book, "Textile Manufacturers' Bookkeeping", published in 1889, showed how the costs of the successive processes in the textile industries could be compared in the books with standards derived from the prices charged by outside specialists. His work can thus also be seen as contributing to the later development of standard costing after the turn of the century.

Cost Variability

A second concern of cost accountants in the nineteenth century was cost behaviour. The way in which costs varied with the quantity of a product produced became more important as production became more capital-intensive and, as I have already mentioned, it was the

[2] *Engineering Magazine, Vol. 20, No. 3, December 1900: "The Meaning of Commercial Organisation," p. 394.*

railways that drew attention to the increased importance of fixed costs. Dionysius Lardner, writing in 1850 on railway economics, discussed the significance of the distinction between fixed and variable costs for the purpose of setting railway rates. Economists, engineers and accountants have since then all expanded our knowledge of cost behaviour. Henry Hess gave us the breakeven chart in 1903, and in the same article he graphically represented a simple form of flexible budget. We had to wait some time for the application of the statistical technique of regression analysis to the study of cost behaviour. The main advance here was Joel Dean's work in America in the early 1930s, culminating in the publication of his book, "Statistical Determination of Cost, with Special Reference to Marginal Cost", in 1930. However, for multiple regression to be a widely available technique, it was necessary for the computer to be invented. That too had been accomplished before 1950.

Standard Costing

The third development in cost accounting that, together with budgeting, can be said to have transformed cost accounting into management accounting, was standard costing. I regard this as the most impressive technical development in accounting since double-entry itself. Though no one date stands out in this connection as 1494 does in the other case, and no one name stands out as Pacioli's does, standard costing as we know it took its rise in the first decade of this century (and even earlier if Norton's use of "country prices" as standards in the textile industry is accepted as an example of standard costing). The technique of standard costing, complete with formulae for the analysis of variances, had been fully worked out by 1918, though its widespread adoption took much longer.

Standard costing represents a synthesis of several different forces - the introduction of work standards by F. W. Taylor and others as part of the "scientific management" movement, the recognition that for control purposes processes were more significant than products (and also easier to account for because they were less numerous), and the need to distinguish between cost variations that represented managerial shortcomings and those that represented uncontrollable fluctuations in prices, wages and the level of activity. It also provided the building blocks with which to construct improved budgets. It moved management accounting away from the rather rudimentary function of cost determination towards the control of business operations and the integration of planning and control by means of a single accounting system. I believe that standard costing had a profound influence on accounting thought, mainly because it forced accountants to look forward as well as backward and brought the planning function and the control function into focus with each other.

Cost Accounting's Spread Beyond the Factory

Management accounting started in the factory and workshop, but it did not stay there. As markets expanded in the early part of this century, the need to know more about the costs of distribution became more important. Distribution costs had become a significant part of the total cost of supplying products to consumers, and marketing was taking its place beside production as an important factor in business success. Articles dealing with distribution costs can be found in the literature before the First World War. Of course the railways were the first important service industry that raised important questions of cost accounting, as far back as 1850, so that it was not remarkable when costing later moved out of the factory into other spheres.

Divisionalization

One of the most striking features of the modern corporation is the diversity of its activities. Diversification of products and of markets probably could not have proceeded as far as it has, and as successfully as it has, without the divisional form of organization that almost all large companies have now adopted. Divisionalization makes it possible to disperse authority throughout a large business down to subordinate levels of management, and it does so by delegating responsibility for making a profit to subordinate managers. Thus management accounting plays a vital role by providing this essential element, divisional profit measurement, that makes decentralization work.

Divisionalization came to Britain some time after it was already common in America. The pioneers of the multi-divisional form of organization in the United States in the 1920s were Dupont and General Motors. The Dupont family were the dominant stockholders in both companies and in 1921 both companies were headed by a Dupont, so it is perhaps not remarkable that they evolved along similar lines. Their methods of financial control, and especially their emphasis on the rate of return on investment as a measure of performance, exercised a powerful influence on American accounting, and also subsequently in Britain. But in America, these developments came between 1920 and 1950, whereas in Britain they came after 1950, when American companies were penetrating deep into the British market. It has been suggested that family control of many British companies before then slowed the adoption of a form of industrial organization that had already been proved to be successful across the Atlantic.

Other Developments Before 1950

I have time to claim only two more important developments in the management accounting field for the period before 1950. One is the professionalization of the subject. All of the professional bodies with an interest in it were well established long before 1950, both in this country and in America. The Institute of Cost and Management Accountants here and the National Association of Accountants there were both founded in the same year, 1919, incidentally, though with slightly different names from their present ones.

Finally, what about the computer, that last word in modernity? Depending on how you define it, it was around well before 1950. Charles Babbage built his difference engine in 1822. Hollerith's punched card machine dates back to 1890. And even if you insist that nothing short of what we now call a computer will qualify, I can just pass that test. In the entrance to the Moore School of Electrical Engineering in my University in Philadelphia stands a plaque that reads as follows: "In this building the ENIAC, first electronic large-scale general-purpose digital computer was conceived, developed and constructed 1943-46".

D. Solomons, BCom, DSc(Econ), FCA
Professor of Accounting
Wharton School,
University of Pennsylvania

History of Public Accounting in the United States. *James Don Edwards.* The University of Alabama Press, 1978. xiv + 370 pp.

There was no coherent account of the rise of the public accounting profession in the United States before the original publication of Professor Edwards's study by Michigan State University in 1960, and we are now indebted to the Academy of Accounting Historians for bringing it back into print. As Edwards says, 'most of the histories of accounting begin with Assyria and Babylonia, leap to Italy in the days of the well-known Renaissance tutor, Pacioli, then hurry across Europe to devote their remaining space to the origin and growth of public accounting in Great Britain. By the time the histories have covered the period from the South Sea Bubble to the organization of the British Societies during the third quarter of the nineteenth century, the authors have exhausted their space, and give but little thought to the United States.' Edwards was a pioneer in helping to remedy this imbalance. His book developed out of his doctoral dissertation, which was written at the University of Texas and completed several years before this fuller version was published.

The first edition of Edwards's book carried a foreword by John L. Carey, then executive director of the American Institute of Certified Public Accountants, commending the book as 'a readable, reasonably concise history of the accounting profession from its beginnings to the present day.' Carey may well already have been working on, or at least have been contemplating, his own much fuller account of the same events, published in two volumes in 1969 with the title *The Rise of the Accounting Profession.* Carey spent his whole working life in the service of the AICPA, and so was intimately involved in or was close to many of the developments about which he wrote. He had joined the Institute as its assistant secretary in 1925, at the age of 21, and had become its secretary in 1930. He retired, full of honours, in 1969. Inevitably his book overshadows Edwards's work. It is richer in detail, it is better organised and its sources of information are vastly more numerous. As Carey says in an appendix listing his source materials at the end of his first volume, 'much of what appears in this book is based on unpublished sources—minutes and transcripts of meetings, memorandums and correspondence in the files of the American Institute of Certified Public Accountants, in addition to the personal observations and recollections of the author, who was on the scene from 1925 onward.' In evaluating Edwards's book, it is impossible to avoid comparison with Carey's. Carey would have had to be a much less skilful author than he was for his advantages not to make his book the preferred source for anyone who wants to learn about the development of public accounting in the United States, at least from 1896 onwards.

The history of a profession can be written chronologically or it can be written topically, that is by identifying the main facets of the unfolding story. Edwards says that he chose to follow a chronological sequence because it 'seemed to present less difficulty to the reader.' That is a matter of opinion. If it is less difficult for the reader, it is undoubtedly also less illuminating; and in the limit, as in parts of his chapter dealing with the 1950s, one is confronted by what is little more than a miscellany of unrelated events—international congresses, an Institute committee on long-range objectives, AICPA films, an anniversary meeting of CPA examiners, a change in the Institute's name and ARB No. 44, all within the compass of five pages.

The chronological scheme chosen by Edwards divides the history of public accounting in the USA into five periods. His first period runs from 1748 to 1895. He takes 1748 as his starting point because in that year Benjamin Franklin sold his interest in a printing company and asked one of his partners, James Parker, to prepare an account of the settlement on the sale. Edwards asserts that this may have been the first public accounting engagement in the American colonies, though there is no evidence that Parker practised as an accountant.

The second period runs from 1896 to 1913. The start of this period is marked by the passage of the first state law giving recognition to the designation 'certified public accountant.' This was in the state of New York. Pennsylvania followed in 1899, and, by 1913, 31 states had such laws. The end of this period is marked by the passage of the 16th Amendment to the US Constitution, which gave Congress the right to enact a federal income tax law.

Edwards's choice of the terminal dates for his third and fourth periods are somewhat more arbitrary. The third period ends in 1928, just before the onset of the Great Depression, and the fourth period ends in 1949. There seems no better reason for the choice of 1949 than that it left Edwards free to devote his last chapter (except for a summary chapter) to the 1950s, at the end of which decade his book was published.

Once a chronology of events has been established, it is much easier for later writers to see how a logical structure might be imposed on those events, and John Carey must have benefited from the trail that Edwards had left. Carey devoted less space than Edwards to the period before 1896 but, since he published later, he was able to carry the story down to 1969. He chose 1936 as the dividing line between his two volumes, that being the year in which the two competing organisations that then made up the American public accounting profession were reunited. Carey did not ignore chronology—obviously no historian can—but his chapters are more than mere intervals of time, for each one represents a recognisable component of the evolving structure.

Carey pointed the way towards a structure for a history of our profession (as distinct from a history of accounting) and no doubt future historians will improve on it. There seem to be five broad themes that mark the development of an accounting profession, whether in the United States, Britain or any other advanced economy. There is the growth of professional organisations, their schisms and mergers and their struggle for public recognition. This recognition has been generally achieved by rising standards of professional education and rigorous examinations; that is the second theme. A third theme, which distinguishes accounting from most other professions, is the growth of a small number of large firms that have come to occupy a dominant position within the profession. The remaining two themes are the development of accounting and reporting standards and the development of auditing standards. Most of the legal battles in which members of the profession have been engaged over the years have involved alleged infractions of accounting or auditing standards or have arisen because of the absence of explicit standards. Litigation can therefore be considered in relation to those standards, and so can the impact of legislation such as the Companies Acts in Britain or of government agencies such as the Securities and Exchange Commission in the USA.

There are far more people interested in and working on accounting history now than there were when Edwards's book was first published. The very formation of the Academy of Accounting Historians, which came into existence in 1973, attests to that fact. If all this effort is justified, it must be because 'the past is a guide to the future,' as Carey wrote in introducing Edwards's book.[1] Unfortunately, it is at least as easy to misread the past as to read it correctly. A splendid example is given by Edwards (probably unintentionally, since he could not have foreseen, in 1959, how much litigation would confront the US profession in the next two decades) in a quotation from *The Accountant* of 1940 on the McKesson and Robbins case: 'McKesson and Robbins was not one case in a hundred, or even one case in a million; it was the grand exception unlikely ever to be repeated and unworthy of being the occasion for the laying of burdens and expense on a community in which, after all, honesty is the prevailing rule.' If that prediction had proved to be true, there would now be fewer practitioners licking their wounds on both sides of the Atlantic.

The Wharton School David Solomons
University of Pennsylvania

[1]Did Carey show uncanny foresight in predicting the Academy's motto, *Praeterita illuminant postera*, or did the Academy borrow from Carey?

Accounting Education

THE INTEGRATION OF ACCOUNTING AND ECONOMIC STUDIES*

By DAVID SOLOMONS

While it would be too much to say that no economist before Irving Fisher had taken any interest in accounting, it is, I think, true that he was the first to use systematically the ideas and techniques of a branch of knowledge which was well established more than 400 years before he wrote his *Nature of Capital and Income*. In his preface to that book, he describes it as forming "a sort of philosophy of economic accounting," which, he hopes, "may supply a link long missing between the ideas and usages underlying practical business transactions and the theories of abstract economics."

Fisher's book was published in 1906. This was an era which saw a considerable growth in the academic study of accounting in America, and it also saw the introduction of the subject into university curricula in this country. That these developments brought the two disciplines closer together cannot be doubted. Yet, by 1929, when John B. Canning, a disciple of Fisher, published his *Economics of Accountancy*, the process of cross-fertilisation had not gone very far; and in 1936, George O. May could still say, without much fear of contradiction, that "there is little to suggest that the course of accounting has been consciously influenced to any considerable extent by economic thought."[1]

While May's judgment is still substantially true so far as concerns the influence of economics on what is commonly called financial accounting, the last twenty years have seen a good many developments which have helped the practitioner of each subject to become more aware of the work of the other. For instance, some economists have felt the need to include in their books some description of elementary accounting. One of them, P. W. S. Andrews, justifies this use of his space by saying that "Business accounts have an important place in the minds of business men, who are used to thinking of their activities in terms of the ways in which their accounting position will be affected, and look to their accounts for a summary of the results of those activities. . . . Further, significant differences in the economic characteristics of businesses often show themselves in the accounts."[2] And Samuelson introduces his appendix on "The Elements of Accounts" by saying that "It is necessary for every student of economics to have some understanding of the

* A paper read on January 6th, 1955, in London, at the annual meeting of the Association of University Teachers of Economics.

[1] *Twenty-five Years of Accounting Responsibility*, Vol. II, page 305.

[2] P. W. S. Andrews, *Manufacturing Business*, page 31.

two fundamental accounting statements: the balance sheet and the statement of profit and loss. . . .[3] Again, economists have recently shown a growing interest in the asset-structure of enterprises, and therefore in their balance sheets. The work of Boulding and the Lutzes obviously comes to mind in this connection.

On the other side, it has been the pressure of economic events rather than of new ideas which has brought accountants to a growing recognition of the relevance of economics (or at least of some parts of it) to their work. I refer, of course, primarily to the steady fall in the value of money, which has now continued for twenty years and which has forced accountants to call in question the significance of historical cost as a basis for income-measurement, and also, though less strikingly, its significance as a basis for price-determination.

Perhaps I might refer to just two further pieces of evidence of the drawing together of the two professions, one from either side of the Atlantic. In this country there was set up, in 1945, a Joint Exploratory Committee of the Institute of Chartered Accountants on the one hand and the National Institute of Economic and Social Research on the other, to enter into discussions "with a view to a closer understanding between accountants and economists regarding the principles applied in their respective fields of work."[4] The Committee decided that its first task must be "an examination of the major accounting concepts and of the more important terms commonly used by both accountants and economists." This task was largely delegated to a sub-committee, and the main Committee's report, entitled *Some Accounting Terms and Concepts*, appeared in 1951. Although this disposed only of what they referred to as their "first" task, the Committee seems to have dissolved itself on, if not before, the publication of the report, and nothing has been heard of it since. I wish I could say that its one and only report had brought the two professions noticeably closer together, but this, alas, is not the case. The Committee split wide open on the rock of "changing price levels," but more seriously, in my view, it threw away an opportunity of doing much useful work for the reason that the economists on the Committee and Sub-committee, so far as one can judge from the report, seem to have confined their attention almost exclusively to aspects of the subject bearing on national income accounting. This is not, as I shall explain, the aspect to which I should give primacy. Perhaps the Committee, had it continued its work, might have recovered from its disappointing start.

The development on the other side of the Atlantic took the form of an inquiry into the nature and measurement of business income, which was sponsored by the American Institute of Accountants and financed jointly by the Institute and the Rockefeller Foundation. This inquiry was narrower in scope than that of the Joint Exploratory Committee in this country, but it was more ambitious in that it attempted a four-pronged attack on the subject,

---

[3] P. A. Samuelson, *Economics: An Introductory Analysis*, Appendix to Chapter 6, page 134.

[4] *Some Accounting Terms and Concepts*, page 7.

by bringing together not only economists and accountants but lawyers and business men as well. The Committee on Business Income, as it was called, produced its report in 1952, under the title, *Changing Concepts of Business Income.* The discussion engendered by this quadripartite inquiry has certainly stimulated interest, especially in the United States, in work in the borderland between economics, accounting and law.

I hope I have said enough to establish the point that we have made *some* progress in the last half-century towards closing the gap between economists and accountants. This, of course, is very far from amounting to an *integration* of economics and accounting. Yet even here, real progress has been made. It is only necessary to examine the contents of the five volumes of *Accounting Research* which have appeared to date to see how difficult it is to classify many of the contributions as lying clearly in the field of either economics or accounting, rather than in a vaguely defined common ground between the two. Social accounting has, of course, been a powerful integrating force, using as it does, for the economist's purposes, both the data provided by the accountant and his double-entry technique. Again, the development of cost accounting has set accountants thinking along lines parallel with those of the economist, though I doubt whether they are to any considerable extent in his debt in this connection. The cost accountant has been interested in the distinction between fixed and variable costs for as long as the economist; and the widespread use of formal budgets by industrial accountants, a practice which has been established for well over 50 years, shows how wide of the mark is the economist's gibe at accountants for being backward-looking. The distinction between an *ex ante* and an *ex post* approach was certainly known to British and American accountants long before these terms were imported by economists via Sweden. Indeed, over much of the field, accountants and economists are only prevented from realising that they are talking about the same things by their persistence in the use of different terms. At the same time, one has to admit that they are often prevented from realising that they are talking about different things by the use of the same terms.

I do not want to appear to exaggerate the extent of this area of common ground. There are, and must continue to be, substantial parts of each of our two disciplines which have little relation to any part of the other. It is capital theory, the theory of the firm, industrial organisation and, to a lesser extent, public finance to which accounting obviously has the greatest relevance, and it is here that the greatest scope for the integration of our two branches of study lies.

Let me now turn to the educational aspect of all this, which is properly the subject of this paper. I do not propose to spend time arguing that the fusion of accounting and economic studies is a good thing, for I take this for granted. What in fact I want to urge is not merely that the study of accounting and economics should be fused, but that a case can be made out for making the study of accounting the basis for micro-economic studies, in much the same way as *The Social Framework* type of approach has been made the basis of further work in macro-economics.

The first thing a student of elementary accounting learns to do is to analyse the effect of simple business transactions on the enterprises which are parties to them. He soon learns to see a complex business situation as made up of relatively simple elements—purchases, sales, receipts and payments of cash, the incurring and settlement of indebtedness, and so on. Transaction analysis is really the key to accounting, and once the student has mastered it, he should be able to see quite readily how out of any particular complex of transactions there emerges an enterprise income of determinable, if arguable, amount, a determinate enterprise asset structure and a capital structure. In learning how the accountant deals with the depreciation of long-lived equipment, the student gets an introduction to some of the problems of inter-temporal relationships. By working on simple problems involving compound interest calculations, he will equip himself with some very useful tools for later work in the theory of interest and capital, business finance, problems of engineering economy and the like. Towards the end of such a course, discussion of the accountant's valuation conventions would prepare the ground for a consideration of their effects on national income figures, on tax revenues and on dividend policy: but there could hardly be time, at the elementary level, for these matters to be more than touched on.

Such an introductory course as I have been describing would provide a realistic basis for the micro-economic side of economic studies which is, at present, very often lacking. It would complement and be complemented by a social accounting approach to macro-economics. The student of economics would then be equipped to start his theoretical studies, for he would have some knowledge of what he was theorising about. When he talked about "maximising profit" he would know how a business man thinks of profit and how he measures it. When he talked about factors of production he would think, one hopes, of the multifarious services a business buys, the expenditure on which appears in the profit and loss account, rather than homogeneous land, labour or capital. Having become familiar with some of the financial problems of corporate enterprise, he would think of the entrepreneur more realistically, perhaps, than he might otherwise do. Again, much of the mystery would have been stripped from banking, for it is surely not too much to say that banking is, to a considerable extent, account-keeping. And, if we may include statistics with economics in this survey, the student would, from his practical work in constructing accounts from the data provided, have gained some added insight into the processes of analysis and aggregation of which so much elementary statistical work consists.

I do not propose to dwell on the subject of accounting and changing price levels, for the simple reason that so many writers have given the impression that this was the *only* ground on which accountants and economists could meet, even if only to air their differences. It should be clear from what I have said that I do not share this view. It would be most unfortunate if the impression were given that, in an era of stable prices, accountants and economists had nothing to say to each other. Nevertheless, it would be equally foolish to ignore the opportunities for useful discussion which are presented by the accounting problems of fluctuating prices. The serious limitations of the conventions used by the accountant in measuring profit, the different meanings to be attached to the notion of maintaining capital intact, the effects of taxing "accounting" profits when money values are changing—all these matters, and many others, provide excellent discussion material which can illuminate the student's later work in economics. It is not likely that much time can be found for them in an introductory course, but it would be a mistake to pass them by altogether.

From a first-year course which did no more than I have just described, the student who was going to do no further work in accounting would have gained a good deal. If time can be found, side by side with his early work in economic theory, for an introduction to cost accounting, much more will be gained; for some realistic content will be given to the economist's concept of cost, which is much closer to the accountant's than most economists seem to suppose. Moreover, the scene will be set for work on a whole range of problems in decision-making, in which a choice has to be made between alternatives. This is material which surely goes to the heart of economics. I have in mind problems of a kind calling for decisions on whether to make or buy, on the substitution of one process for another, on machine replacement, on industrial location, on pricing and the like. Ideally, the data for these problems would be drawn from actual business situations, but not too much is lost if we have to fall back, as we usually do, on invented situations and imaginary data. Such problems, if carefully presented, make the student bring to bear on them his knowledge of accounting, of economics, and perhaps of statistics, too. They therefore promote an integration of knowledge in the best sense of the word.

Let me anticipate and answer at once one possible objection to my proposal. Students often complain that they find the "book-keeping" stage of a beginning accounting course unduly difficult, and it may be thought that there is a great risk that they might be put off economic studies altogether if they were introduced to them, in part, *via* accounting. There is, I believe, force in this argument only if beginning courses in accounting continue to be presented, as they so often are now, as if all the students taking them were going on to become professional accountants. On this view, since the difficulties have to be encountered sooner or later, it does not matter how soon they are met. The same view also has the unfortunate result that the beginning course—the only one, probably, which economics specialists will take—gets cluttered up with technical matter of little importance to any except accounting specialists, and often even to them.

Fortunately, this objection is easily met, for many of the difficulties can be pushed back into second- and third-year courses, to be taken only by accounting specialists, and some of them can be eliminated as not being relevant to a university course in accounting at all. Another solution would be to have separate beginning courses in accounting for students preparing for work in advanced economics on the one hand and advanced accounting on the other, but this is a luxury which, so far as I know, no university in this country permits itself, and I am not at all certain that it would not have greater disadvantages than virtues. In America, one place in which such an arrangement can be found is at Stanford, where the Economics Department conducts its own accounting courses quite separately from those in the Graduate School of Business. No doubt similar arrangements could be found elsewhere. Yale, Princeton and Johns Hopkins, which do not have business schools and therefore do not turn out accounting majors, nevertheless offer accounting courses for students of economics.

I have devoted most of my attention to the integration of accounting and economic studies at the elementary level, but of course plenty of opportunities for more advanced work exist. One group of problems which offers such opportunities is concerned with a more advanced consideration of the nature and measurement of income, on which accountants and economists must surely one day come to terms with each other. Another group of problems exists in the field of cost theory, and includes such topics as the statistical and accounting determination of marginal cost, full-cost pricing, the use of cost data for governmental price-control, inter-firm cost comparisons and the like. Again, in the field of business finance, there are considerable areas in which it is difficult to say whether the problems encountered are problems of accounting or of economics. If our two subjects are taught in an unintegrated fashion, it is certainly not for lack of suitable material. To a much greater extent I suspect it is due to a lack of suitable text-books and to our own shortcomings as teachers. But both these deficiencies are slowly being remedied.

Let me close on a challenging note. I think that the combining of courses in accounting and economics into an integrated structure must benefit both disciplines, and I am not at all sure that it is not economics which stands to benefit more, for accounting can give to economic studies a realism and a quantitative tool which they can dispense with only at their peril. Among the many wise things which G. O. May has said in the course of his long career, I do not think that any is more penetrating than that contained in the quotation with which I should like to end this paper:

> The fact is . . . that accounting is a tool of business, and that the development of accounting, like the development of business law, has been determined by the practices of business men. Where accounting and economic thought are found to run along parallel lines, it is probable that both will be found to be running parallel to good business practice. Where accounting treatment diverges from economic theory, a similar divergence is likely to be found between economic theory and business practice.[5]

London

[5] G. O. May: "The Nature of Accounting," in *Twenty-five Years of Accounting Responsibility*, Vol. II, page 305.

ACCOUNTING EDUCATION FOR NEW RESPONSIBILITIES – I

by DAVID SOLOMONS, B.COM., A.C.A.
Professor of Accounting in the University of Bristol

IN creating this chair of accounting, with the help of the three industrial companies whose names are associated with it, the University of Bristol joins its sisters in Birmingham, Cambridge and London and its Scottish half-sisters in Edinburgh and Glasgow in giving to the study of accounting a recognition which is still a cause of surprise to some people, both in university circles and outside. Those who feel this surprise would no doubt find themselves in sympathy with the Cambridge don who was recently asked by a friend of mine why Cambridge was so slow to introduce management studies into the curriculum there. After all, my friend pointed out, Cambridge had taught agriculture for many years, why not industrial management? 'Ah', said the don, 'but agriculture as a subject of study was introduced when people *lost* money on farming!' This rather unenthusiastic attitude is one to which I shall return in a minute.

Professor David Solomons

There could be few places more fitting than Bristol to become a centre of accounting studies. When double-entry book-keeping was still in its infancy so far as this country was concerned, Bristol's merchants were helping to extend its use. Again, Bristol is the home of the oldest existing firm of accountants in England, a firm which claims a continuous history since 1780.[1] It was Bristol, too, that was the home of the greatest hoax in the history of book-keeping, which yet, because it attracted so much attention, stimulated new thought and so left a permanent mark on the development of the subject. I refer, of course, to the publication by Edward Thomas Jones, accomptant of this city, of a work which bore the resounding title of

'Jones' ***English System of Book-keeping by Single and Double Entry***, in which it is impossible for an error of the most trifling amount to be passed unnoticed. Calculated effectually to prevent the evils attendant on the methods so long established and adapted to every species of trade. Secured to the Inventor by the King's Royal Letters Patent, Bristol, 1796.'

Launched after extensive advertising, in which the most extravagant claims were made for the book, it ran into sixteen English editions, several American editions, was translated into German, French, Italian and Russian, and is reputed to have brought its author a fortune of £25,000. Yet the advantages which Jones claimed for his system over the so-called Italian method of book-keeping were wholly illusory. It was enormously complicated without giving any greater assurance of accuracy, and the only really astonishing thing about it is that Jones was able to take in men of such eminence as the father of Sir Robert Peel and the Governor of the Bank of England to the extent of obtaining from them testimonials which he included in his prospectus. Jones has been described by one writer on the history of book-keeping as occupying

> 'In Book-keeping the place which Macpherson with his "Ossian" fills in literature. Both prove that success can be achieved by unblushing impudence.'[2]

Bristol can perhaps take pride in Jones' enterprise, if not in his integrity.

If Bristol was the birthplace of the greatest accounting hoax in history, it was also the scene of one of the greatest insults ever offered to the accountancy profession. It was at the Summer Assize in Bristol in 1875 that Mr Justice Quain, in the case of *The Queen v. James Winge*, a prosecution for fraudulent bankruptcy, saw fit to use these words:

'That the whole affairs in bankruptcy should be

An inaugural lecture delivered in the University of Bristol, on December 8th, 1955.

[1] The firm, founded by Josiah Wade, now practises as Tribe, Clarke & Co, in Bristol and elsewhere. See *The Accountant*, March 14th, 1953, page 311, for a letter from the firm's senior partner giving the evidence in support of this claim.

[2] 'History of book-keeping', by J. Row Fogo, in *A History of Accounting and Accountants*, ed. Brown (1905), page 167. See also 'Edward Jones' "English system of book-keeping" ', by B. S. Yamey, *Accounting Review*, October 1944, pages 407–416.

> taken out of the hands of solicitors – a respectable body, subject to the control of the Court – and handed over to an ignorant set of men called accountants, was one of the grossest abuses, in my opinion, ever introduced into the law.'

These were hard words, even in 1875, and produced indignant letters to *The Times*. In creating this chair, the university may, perhaps, be regarded as in some small measure making amends.

The Universities and Professional Education

I referred just now to the surprise still felt by some that accounting should be accepted as an academic subject at all. I hope it is not necessary, at this time and in this place, to spend many minutes in defending the position already won for it, or in refuting the view that, as a 'purely professional subject' it has no place in an academic curriculum. The division of knowledge into the cultural and the vocational, into the academic and the professional, has long ago been discredited, and a striking change of opinion as to the role of the universities in our society has taken place since John Stuart Mill, in an inaugural address at St Andrews, in 1868, declared that:

> 'The proper function of a university in national education is tolerably well understood. At least there is a tolerably general agreement about what a university is not. It is not a place of professional education.'

Indeed, it is now widely recognized that, in the words of Sir Alexander Carr-Saunders,

> 'it was as schools of professional training that the medieval universities came into existence; it was their undisputed task to train for the professions of divinity, law and physic. Since the great officers of state were clerics, the profession of divinity included what we now call public service.'

And he goes on to assert that

> 'the view that there is an antithesis between a liberal and a vocational education [has] worked and still perpetuate[s] great mischief in modern society'.[1]

Strong support for the same view is now widespread. The philosopher, Samuel Alexander, expressed himself clearly on this point. A university, he wrote,

> 'does not only pursue the sciences for their own sake, but, so far as the larger part of its members are concerned, pursues them in preparation for the professions. I had almost said', he goes on, 'that the purpose of a university was to prepare for the professions, and I should be ready to defend this, provided that the qualifying words, "in a liberal spirit" are not merely not omitted but emphasized. . . . It is impossible to divorce the work of a university from its practical issues in life. A university is not and never has been a society of persons cultivating the sciences for their own sake, in the sense that that is its purpose. That is rather its method than its purpose.'[2]

To the support which I have drawn from a social scientist and a philosopher for the view that the universities are the rightful home of professional studies, let me add that of a natural scientist, Bertrand Russell.

> 'The conception of the "education of a gentleman" ', he writes, 'has had a bad effect upon universities. . . . It is possible to spend the university years in the acquisition of knowledge which has some professional utility, but conservative academic types view this with horror. I think they are mistaken. I think many clever young men become vapid and cynical through the consciousness that their work has no real importance while they are at the university. This does not happen to those who are studying medicine or engineering or agriculture or any subject of which the utility is obvious'. And he goes on: 'Pure learning as an ideal has its place in the life of the community, but only for those few who are going to devote their energies to research. For those who are going to be engaged in some other profession, it would be better to spend the last few years of education in acquiring such knowledge as would enable them to pursue their profession with intelligence and breadth of outlook.'[3]

I shall not labour this point further, for in this university, in so far as I am addressing my own colleagues, I am in large part preaching to the converted. But perhaps the university teacher of accounting may be forgiven if he is sometimes oversensitive to the danger of being attacked on two fronts. His professional critics outside the university are apt to think that his hair is too long, while some few at least of his colleagues inside the university think that it is too short. In this respect, he is worse off than those of his colleagues who teach engineering, law, medicine, agriculture, education, and other professional studies which make up such a large part of the university curriculum today, for their subjects either have a long academic tradition, or demand for their development resources which cannot easily be found outside the universities.

The Need for a Review of Accounting Education

In 1944, conversations were begun between the Committee of Vice-Chancellors and Principals and representatives of the accountancy profession, and there was worked out, by the McNair committee, a scheme to enable prospective accountants to take a university degree based on the related disciplines of economics, accounting and law, and then to proceed to take a professional qualification. It is now just a decade since teaching under this scheme began. It therefore seems to me that, with the experience of this decade behind us, this is an appropriate time to

[1] A. M. Carr-Saunders: 'The functions of universities in the modern world'. *The Sociological Review*, Vol. XXXII, Nos. 3–4 (July–October 1940), page 141.

[2] Samuel Alexander: 'The purpose of a university'. *The Political Quarterly*, Vol. II, No. 3 (July–September 1931), page 337.

[3] Bertrand Russell: *Education and the Social Order* (1932), pages 156–8.

look at the whole problem of accounting education, especially with a view to seeing what further part, if any, the universities have to play in it.

If I had to find any other excuse for my choice of subject, I should say that, because academic posts in the field of accounting in this country are relatively few in number, there are not many men outside the technical colleges who combine a professional interest in education with an educational interest in the profession. As one of the few, I feel that I have a duty and, in this lecture, the occasion to survey the educational scene and to report back. As a result, I might at least succeed in provoking a useful discussion.

I am not alone in thinking the subject of education for the profession worthy of consideration. It was a sense of the importance of the problem which led the Institute of Chartered Accountants of Scotland to set up a special committee in 1953 to consider the examination and training of apprentices. The committee's report is expected early in 1956. It was a sense of the importance of the problem, too, which led the American Institute of Accountants, in 1952, to set up a commission on standards of education and experience for C.P.A.s. The Commission's work is still far from finished.

The Structure of the Accountancy Profession

In order to get the nature and size of the problem in this country into perspective, let me give a few elementary facts and figures, which will be familiar to many of my audience but will be new to some. The accountancy profession resembles that of engineering rather than law and medicine in that there is no statutory restriction on the right to call oneself an accountant. There is a statutory restriction imposed by the Companies Act, on the right to audit the accounts of companies other than exempt private companies, but that covers only a limited if important part of the work which accountants do. Such protection as the public gets from inexpert advice in the accounting field must come from the quality of the professional qualifications held by those accountants whom they seek to employ.

Of these qualifications there is no end, but the great bulk of professional accountancy work in Great Britain is in the hands of the members of four bodies which are, in order of seniority, the Institute of Chartered Accountants of Scotland, the Institute of Chartered Accountants in England and Wales, the Society of Incorporated Accountants and the Association of Certified and Corporate Accountants. It will be convenient hereafter to refer to these four bodies as the Scottish Institute, the Institute, the Society and the Association. The four bodies are by no means of equal size and importance. As regards size, the Institute is by far the largest, and by the end of this year will have about 18,800 members. The Society, by the end of the year, will have about 10,700 members, the Association will have about 9,500 members and the Scottish Institute will have about 5,800. The combined numbers of the English and Scottish chartered accountants are, therefore, substantially greater than the combined numbers of the other two bodies, whose membership is spread on both sides of the border. But mere numbers, while they favour the chartered accountants, yet do not adequately reflect the predominant position which they hold in the profession.

When, in 1930, the departmental committee on the registration of accountants looked into the matter, it found that of some 5,500 companies whose shares were dealt in on the London Stock Exchange, 90 per cent had as auditors firms whose partners were all chartered accountants. I doubt whether a similar inquiry today would show a very different result, although since 1930 the relative importance of auditing among all the services provided by accountants to the business community has probably declined. Nevertheless, in the light of the figures I have cited, I feel justified, in what follows, in devoting most of my attention to the arrangements, present and future, for educating chartered accountants, since these arrangements must be of crucial importance for the whole profession. Indeed, limitations of time will force me to concentrate most of my attention on English chartered accountants, as distinct from those in Scotland, though the Scottish educational arrangements are interestingly different from the English, and I shall not entirely ignore them.

The Universities' Present Role in Accounting Education

At the present time the universities in England play a very small part in the education of new recruits to the Institute. I understand that approximately 8 per cent of those entering into articles are graduates. Of these, I estimate that slightly more than one half take degrees in which accounting is a major subject. The percentage recruitment of graduates into articles at the present time is about the same as it was before the war, while the absolute numbers have doubled: for the total number of newly-registered articled clerks each year in recent years has been about double the pre-war number. The total number of first degrees awarded by the universities in England and Wales has also about doubled as compared with before the war. Comparing the pre-war and post-war periods for the Institute then, we can say that there has been no material change either in the proportion of new articled clerks who are graduates or in the proportion of graduates who become articled clerks.

The figures I have just given relate to the numbers of graduates entering into articles, i.e. commencing their professional training. But articled clerks do not by any means all eventually become chartered accountants, for the failure rate in the Institute's examinations is high. From an investigation I made into a small but representative sample of those qualifying as chartered accountants during the period 1950–54, it would seem that about 10 per cent of the new members of the Institute are graduates. The fact that the percentage of graduates among new members is greater than among new articled clerks is not surprising since we would expect that fewer graduates would fail their professional examinations than is the case for articled clerks as a whole.

I do not have similar figures for the Society and the Association, but from such information as I do have, I think it is safe to say that the number of graduates they recruit between them would not exceed one-fifth of the number recruited by the Institute. This would give a graduate recruitment for the profession as a whole in England and Wales of something like 6 per cent.

If we compare the recruitment of graduates by the accountancy profession with the figures given by Professor Gower for the two branches of the legal profession, we find a striking difference. Of the solicitors' articled clerks who passed the final examination of the Law Society in 1949, 36 per cent were graduates, and of these graduates, 73 per cent had law degrees. Of students called to the Bar in 1949, 57 per cent held degrees of English universities, and it is estimated that 70 per cent of these degrees were wholly or partly in law.[1]

(*To be continued.*)

[1] L. C. B. Gower: 'English legal training': *Modern Law Review*, Vol. 13, No. 2 (April 1950), page 151.

ACCOUNTING EDUCATION FOR NEW RESPONSIBILITIES – II

by DAVID SOLOMONS, B.COM., A.C.A.
Professor of Accounting in the University of Bristol

The Position in the U.S.A.

IF the difference in the extent of the part played by the universities in educating entrants into the legal and accountancy professions in this country is a striking one, the difference in the amount of university recruitment by the accountancy professions of this country and the United States is no less striking. Any comparisons between the professions in the two countries are made difficult by the fact that, whereas in this country qualified accountants hold their qualifications by virtue of their membership of voluntary organizations of which, as I have noted, there are several, in the United States there is a single qualification of certified public accountant, granted separately by each of the forty-eight States on the strength of a uniform examination but on terms as to experience and educational requirements which vary a good deal from State to State.

I have not been able to obtain any reliable information about the percentage of newly-qualified C.P.A.s who are graduates. But there is no doubt at all that the amount of graduate recruitment into the profession in the United States is far greater than it is over here. In 1952–53 in America, over 7,000 first degrees in accounting were awarded. The number in this country was probably less than 100. Two of the most populous States, New York and New Jersey, require a degree as a prerequisite to qualification as a C.P.A., and other States are moving in the same direction. A strategically placed informant writes to me from New York in these terms:

> 'I believe it would be quite unusual at the present time for an important C.P.A. firm to hire a man who was not a college graduate.'

All this leaves little room for doubt about the important part which American universities are playing in the education of entrants into the accountancy profession over there, as compared with the diminutive contribution which we are making over here.

The Apprenticeship System, Past and Present

If the typical chartered accountant is not a university graduate, how does he get his professional education and training? The answer is that he is the product of a system of apprenticeship combined with correspondence tuition. The apprenticeship system is quite basic to the present system of training chartered accountants and it is their refusal to countenance any alternative to apprenticeship as a prerequisite to membership which distinguishes the English and Scottish Institutes from the Society and the Association.

Apprenticeship for would-be accountants is much older than the oldest professional body of accountants in Great Britain, which came into existence in Edinburgh in 1854. Indeed, it is as old as the first organization of accountants of which we have any knowledge, the *Collegio dei Raxonati*, which was founded in Venice in 1581. This body attained considerable power in that city by the middle of the seventeenth century, and its membership was closely controlled. Admission was by examination following on an apprenticeship of six years in the office of a professional accountant. A somewhat similar college in Milan, founded in 1739, required a five years' apprenticeship as a prerequisite to membership.

Apprenticeship as the method of training accountants in this country was well established long before our professional organizations came into existence in the middle of the last century. In 1784 we find an advertisement by a Glasgow firm of accountants which runs:

> 'Wanted, an apprentice: none need apply unless they intend to give an apprentice-fee.'[1]

Apprenticeship was the already-established method of training solicitors and the qualifications for entry into The Institute of Chartered Accountants in England and Wales which were written into the original charter, granted in 1880, were modelled on those regulating admission to the roll of solicitors.

In the professional education and training of chartered accountants, apprenticeship still plays a dominant role. There has never been any hint, in any pronouncement by the Institute, that it entertained any doubts about the rightness of this, or that it conceived it possible that a method of training which was the best available in Venice in 1600 or in England in 1880 might possibly be ripe for modification in our day. Indeed, in a rejoinder to the report of the Carr-Saunders Committee on Education for Commerce, which the Institute issued in 1951, it reasserted its belief that:

> 'A person cannot be a chartered accountant unless he knows how to do the work of his profession and this knowledge can be acquired in one way and one way only – by learning as an apprentice under the guidance of others.'[2]

Concurrently with the practical training which he

The first part of this inaugural lecture delivered in the University of Bristol on December 8th, 1955, was published in last week's issue.

[1] *History of Scottish Chartered Accountants* (Edinburgh, 1954), page 12.

[2] *Education and training for membership*: a report by the Council of the Institute. March 1951, page 8.

obtains as an apprentice, the would-be chartered accountant pursues his theoretical studies by means of a correspondence course provided by one of a small number of highly specialized coaching establishments. This is a generalization one can make with great confidence, for the Institute has published figures which show that, among the candidates for its examinations between November 1949 and November 1950, those who did not take a correspondence course represented less than 0·75 per cent of the total entry,[1] and nothing has happened since then to change the picture. Correspondence tuition for the Institute's examinations, in its present highly organized form, is not quite as old as the Institute itself, but the oldest of the existing correspondence colleges serving the profession was founded in 1884, only four years after the granting of the charter.

The Institute appears to entertain no more serious doubts about the means by which its recruits obtain their theoretical instruction than it does about the apprenticeship system of practical training. In a memorandum put in to the Carr-Saunders committee in answer to questions put by the committee, the Council of the Institute declared that it

> 'has no reason to believe that the present facilities for correspondence tuition are inadequate or unsatisfactory',[2]

and it strenuously rejected the recommendation of the committee that a major part of the theoretical instruction for the profession should be transferred to the technical and commercial colleges.

Some Comparisons

The accountancy profession in England and Wales is now almost the only major profession to be content with apprenticeship coupled with correspondence tuition to provide the practical and theoretical instruction considered necessary for its members. Wherever one looks, whether to other professions in this country or to the accountancy profession in other countries, one finds that some element of institutional training has been introduced and in some cases it has ousted other forms of instruction.

It is a hundred years since apprenticeship ceased to play an important part in the training of medical practitioners. Would-be solicitors are required to attend university law classes or the Law Society's own School of Law in London regularly during their 'statutory year'. Aspirants to membership of the engineering institutes, where they are not already university graduates, commonly qualify by taking one of the Higher National Certificates and this usually involves attendance at a technical college. If we turn to look at the principal organizations in the accountancy profession itself in other parts of the world, we find that almost everywhere the English system of training has been discarded. In the United States, as I have already mentioned, the first step towards preparing for entry into the profession is commonly by attendance at a university. In Scotland and in South Africa, part-time attendance by articled clerks at university classes is obligatory. In Australia, the largest body of accountants, the Commonwealth Institute, accepts a university degree in accounting as exempting the holder from the greater part of its own examinations, so that university attendance is a common means of preparing for the profession. The same is true in New Zealand. In the Netherlands, full-time or part-time attendance at the universities forms a normal part of the preparation for the profession, and in Germany the *Wirtschaftsprüfer* is almost always a university graduate. Is it possible that everyone is out of step but ourselves?

The Development of the Profession since 1880

Consider the changes which have transformed the position of accountants since 1880, when the Institute of Chartered Accountants received its charter. Then, one of the professional accountant's main preoccupations was the administration of insolvent estates, for the Bankruptcy Act of 1869 had abolished the Official Receiver and had given creditors the power to appoint their own receivers. Usually the receiver appointed was an accountant, and the Act had brought a great access of work to the profession. One has only to look through the early issues of *The Accountant*, which had commenced publication in 1874, to see the extent to which its pages are almost monopolized by insolvency matters. The other main source of work in those early days was the audit of company accounts, which had become more important with the passing of the Companies Act of 1862.

Taxation, which now demands so large a part of the accountant's attention, was then quite unimportant. Death duties were brought into existence only in 1894 and the maximum rate of duty levied, on estates exceeding £1 million, was then 8 per cent. In 1894, the standard rate of income tax was 8*d* in the £, but rose to 1*s* in 1900. Supertax was introduced only in 1909. Profits tax did not come into existence until much later. The rise of the accountancy profession has obviously been greatly stimulated by the increasing burden of taxation: but there is no reason to think that this played any important part in the thinking of the men who formulated the methods of educating and training accountants which we have inherited.

Nor could their thinking have been much influenced by the needs of what we now call management accounting, for there is little evidence that more than a handful of men were interested in accounting as an aid to management in 1880, and the men who were so interested were as likely to be found in the ranks of engineers as among accountants. You will certainly find just as frequent reference to cost accounting in the columns of journals such as *The Engineer* or

[1] *Education and training for membership*, page 18.

[2] *Loc. cit.*, page 22.

Engineering in that period as you will in the pages of *The Accountant*.

The Institute started its career as an organization of *professional* accountants, i.e. of accountants practising as independent practitioners. It is doubtful if the founders could ever have envisaged that members working in industry and commerce would come to represent such a large and important part of the total membership as they do today. It is not possible from the published information to say just how large a part this is, but a test carried out by the Institute in 1947 showed that at December 31st, 1946, it was just under 50 per cent.[1] Today the proportion would probably be greater. If the system of education and training worked out in 1880 happens to be well adapted to the needs of industry as distinct from the profession, it must be so by accident rather than by design.

Not only has the accountant since 1880 won for himself an important place as a staff officer on the managerial headquarters, he has become an important contender for a share of command itself. In Dr Copeman's study of the directors of public companies in this country, 16 per cent of the 1,243 directors who answered his questionnaire gave their original occupation as accounting, about the same number as gave engineering. When the sample was analysed as between those over 50 years of age and those under 50, the percentage of those starting as accountants went up from 15 per cent of the over 50s to 18 per cent of the under 50s, showing that the young accountant's chance of promotion to board level had increased, whereas the chances of the young engineer and the young lawyer are shown by the same inquiry to have diminished.[2] We shall do well, in considering how we ought to educate those who enter the accounting profession, to remember that we are doing much more than educating future accountants. We are also educating men and women who are destined, in substantial numbers, to be found among the future leaders of British industry.

Changes in Technique since 1880

While these changes in the nature of the demand for the accountant's services have been coming about, other changes have been taking place 'on the supply side', so to speak. There has been nothing less than a revolution in clerical procedures and many routine clerical operations which formerly had to be done by hand have been mechanized and rendered largely foolproof. Much routine checking formerly carried out by the professional auditors of large businesses is now done by internal audit staffs or rendered unnecessary by good control systems. Statistical techniques are being developed and put into use so as to reduce to a minimum the amount of checking which still has to be done. All of these changes have diminished or are diminishing the amount of routine audit and accounting work which has to be done, relative to work calling for higher intellectual qualities and expert knowledge.

I am confident that in the next decade or two we shall see other changes which could work in the same direction. We are moving out of the age in which business decisions were taken by 'hunch' into one in which most problems will be considered to be capable of a more or less precise quantitative solution. The technique of linear programming is already being successfully applied to problems of product maximization and cost minimization which defy solution by more traditional methods except at an exorbitant cost. The advent of the electronic computer, of course, enormously increases the scope and possibilities of these techniques. These developments could greatly and fruitfully add to the field of activity of the accountant, for what is he if he is not the manipulator and interpreter of quantitative business data?

Yet I fear that the profession, by failing in the past to require of its recruits a high standard of mathematics and by failing to equip them with an adequate grasp of statistics and economics, is in danger of having to confess itself unable to grasp these opportunities, and of having to stand aside and see them taken by the statisticians and econometricians.

Educational Implications of Changes in the Profession

The changes which I have outlined as having taken place during the last seventy-five years, and those which we may expect in the near future, have an obvious bearing on the problem of accounting education. With the diminution in the importance of routine skills, a lengthy apprenticeship is surely destined to become a less effective method of training than it formerly was: for it is routine skills rather than expert knowledge which apprenticeship training is particularly well suited to instil. The decline of apprenticeship in industry has been due to much the same phenomenon on the more humble level of the factory floor. As the processes to be learnt demand more cerebration and less dexterity, the more important is skilled institutional instruction likely to become, at the expense of the rather haphazard and inefficient learning which alone apprenticeship makes possible. Even factory apprenticeship now means something very different from what it meant fifty years ago, for a large part of the apprentice's instruction is now obtained from skilled teachers in an apprentices' school, not painfully picked up from a working journeyman.

I am not saying that practical experience is any less important than it formerly was, nor do I dissent for a moment from the statement by the Institute, in its pronouncement on education and training, that

[1] See a paper by Sir Harold Howitt, on 'The future of the accountancy profession': *The Accountant*, January 3rd, 1948, page 7.

[2] G. H. Copeman: *Leaders of British Industry*: (Gee & Co (Publishers) Ltd, 1955).

'a person cannot be a chartered accountant unless he knows how to do the work of his profession. . . .'[1]

What I do say is that, in the changed circumstances of today, much of the educational value of practical experience will be lost if the ground has not adequately been prepared in advance. To take a boy straight from school, turn him loose in an accountant's office and expect him to learn from practical experience at the same time as he is beginning to acquire a rudimentary knowledge of accounting by means of a correspondence course is, if I may quote a remark of Professor Shackle's in another context

'as though one should ask a man to swallow a tablespoonful of coffee-berries and then pour a cupful of hot water down on top of them in the hope that the two ingredients will somehow get appropriately mixed up in his inside'.

Practical experience is what the professional man distils from the impressions which come to him in the course of his daily work. It is not, like a photograph, an impression made on a passive sensitized plate. It is the result of an active process of selection, and a trained mind will make a different and, one hopes, a more valuable selection from that made by one less well prepared. This is the answer to those in the profession who say that practical experience is all that matters. 'Practical experience' is just as much the result of the way we prepare the mind to receive experiences as of the experiences themselves.

Correspondence Tuition and Students' Societies

On the second constituent of education for the accountancy profession as it stands today – correspondence tuition – I shall not waste much time. I find it utterly incomprehensible that any profession should think it other than a third-rate substitute for real education. It is, of course, not without its virtues as a counterpart to the existing system of apprenticeship. It is cheap. It does not interfere with the routine of office work. As a method of imparting technical knowledge in a readily digestible form, it is not less efficient than the methods used in institutions of higher learning. There is the added advantage that each student can proceed at his own pace. I have known of several instances where university students have supplemented their university courses with correspondence courses, because they found it easier to acquire knowledge that way. This does not say very much for our skill as teachers. But whereas correspondence tuition begins and ends with the imparting of knowledge, real education does not. The true aims of professional education have been well put by an American engineer, Professor Teare:

'It is clear that in professional education we must do more than acquaint the student with facts, principles and existing procedures; we must, in so far as possible, teach him to use fundamental principles in dealing with situations that are new to him and also teach him how to continue to learn throughout his life from his professional activity'.[2]

Correspondence tuition hardly begins to do this. There have been men – I know of one – whose imagination was fired by a correspondence course, who were stimulated to question an established procedure or to want to push back the frontiers of knowledge. But such men are rare. Maybe our university students, too, are not often enough so stimulated. But at least their horizons are not wholly bounded by examination results.

Before leaving the system of education for the accounting profession as it stands today, it is necessary to say a word about the place of the students' societies which exist within each of the professional organizations. These societies arrange lectures and industrial and other visits for apprentices and it is now becoming common for them to arrange short residential courses as well. One cannot speak too highly of the work which their officers, who are often themselves busy practitioners, put into these societies, and it is to them that credit must go for such liberalizing elements as are to be found in the present system. But their scope is naturally limited by the fact that they have to operate in the interstices of the apprenticeship system. Within the framework of that system, they achieve, no doubt, as much as can be achieved. But it is not and cannot be enough to transform a scheme of professional training into a system of professional education.

A Proposal for Educational Reform

What then, would constitute a worthy system of professional education and training for the accountancy profession? I do not have any serious doubts as to the main outlines which the long-term answer to this question should take, though there is plenty of room for argument about details. There is room for argument, too, about timing and speed of implementation. But I do not think that anything less than a radical change will do. The system I would propose would require every entrant to the senior professional accountancy body, at least, who was not already of mature years,[3] to spend three years at a university reading for a degree based on economics, accounting and law. Having obtained his degree, the graduate would proceed to three years of practical training in the profession with, however, this vital difference from the present scheme. The three-year period after graduation would be divided into three equal stages of one year, each made up of ten months of office work followed by two months of full-time instruction on practical lines, in a suitable training establishment. At the conclusion of this training period, the trainee would take his final professional

[1] *Loc. cit.*, page 8.

[2] Professor B. Richard Teare, Jr. (Buhl Professor of Electrical Engineering, Carnegie Inst. of Tech.) in *Education for Professional Responsibility*, page 136 (Carnegie Press, 1948).

[3] Special provision would have to be made for the older entrant.

examination before admission to the Institute.

That, in barest outline, is my scheme. Let me now sketch in one or two details, before turning to answer the objections which will certainly be raised against it. At the hub of the proposal is a compulsory university degree. Imperfect as our university education still is, it is the best instrument which has yet been devised for equipping men and women to take their place in society, and for laying the broad foundation on which later experience may be based. The justification for placing the universities at the centre of my scheme has been put so well by Whitehead that I shall content myself with quoting his words:

'. . . . Qualities essential at a later stage of a career are apt to be stamped out in an earlier stage. This is only an instance of the more general fact, that necessary technical excellence can only be acquired by a training which is apt to damage those energies of mind which should direct the technical skill. This is the key fact in education, and the reason for most of its difficulties.

'The way in which a university should function in the preparation for an intellectual career, such as modern business or one of the older professions, is by promoting the imaginative consideration of the various general principles underlying that career. Its students thus pass into their period of technical apprenticeship with their imaginations already practised in connecting detail with general principles. The routine then receives its meaning, and also illuminates the principles which give it that meaning. Hence instead of a drudgery issuing in a blind rule-of-thumb, the properly trained man has some hope of obtaining an imagination disciplined by detailed facts and by necessary habits'.[1]

As for the detailed content of the degree courses, I would not want to make any drastic changes in our existing arrangements. The essential feature of the course taken by those students choosing accounting as their special subject of study both in this and in other universities in England and Wales is that it is a broadly based course, in which accounting is not allowed to get out of perspective by being studied in isolation, but is studied throughout the three years in conjunction with economics, law and other subjects chosen from the field of the social sciences. It is in this respect that the university study of accounting differs fundamentally from its study in the professional curriculum.

Although our present university course was broadly worked out by the McNair committee in 1944 to meet the needs of the accountancy profession, it has proved to give an education admirably suited to much wider purposes. One such purpose is the provision of a way into the field of general industrial management. Sir Charles Renold has pointed out the difficulty which exists.

'The field of general management', he writes, 'really only begins at a comparatively high level and the necessary maturity has to be acquired in one or more of the specialized fields of activity, because the general management field cannot in the nature of things provide its own ladder of experience from the bottom upwards.'[2]

One of the specialized fields from which general management is apt to be recruited is the accounting field, and the arts graduate who has read accounting at the university is equipped, after he has had some training in industry, for a specialist job, much as the engineering or science graduate is. He can thus learn responsibility in a limited field before being given wider responsibilities.

An Alternative to Correspondence Tuition

As for that part of my proposal which relates to post-university training, I have suggested a period of three years, of which only two and a half years would be spent in an office, the remaining six months being spent in three terms, at a professional training school. While, superficially, this may have the appearance of reducing the present period of three years which a graduate spends under apprenticeship in an office, it would in fact, I am confident, result in a much more fruitful use of a slightly shorter period, so that the quality of the training received would be improved, and even the quantity would probably not be less, for working time would no longer be eroded by leave to attend lectures or by pre-examination study leave, since this would be covered in the periods of institutional training. What is even more important is that the period at the university would have prepared the student's mind to get the best out of his practical training, and he would start learning effectively from it right from the outset. If the professional bodies consider, as they at present do, that three years' practical training is adequate for those who graduate in classics, modern languages or history, then two and a half years can hardly be too little for those whose university studies have been more vocationally oriented.[3]

As for the training school, in which the universities would have no part, the essential thing about it is that the instruction it gave would be personal, not by correspondence, it would be practical rather than theoretical, since the theoretical side would have been taken care of at the university, and it would be intensive. The school would be able to start where the university left off. Recommended reading would be done by the students during the periods between attendances at the school.

One very important issue which would have to be settled would be whether the training school should be set up *ad hoc* by the profession or whether the job should be put in the hands of the existing

[1] A. N. Whitehead: *The Aims of Education* (1929), pages 44–5.

[2] *The Advancement of Science*, Vol. 10 (1953/54), p. 302, on 'Training for management'.

[3] I do not exclude the possibility of reducing this period if the improvement in the *quality* of training under my scheme proved to be as great as I think it would.

technical colleges. This is a delicate question which time fortunately does not permit me to explore. The technical colleges have not hitherto had any success in attracting away from the correspondence colleges any material number of students working for the examinations of the major accountancy bodies. But it does not follow from this that they ought not to be entrusted with the rather different task which I have in mind. The alternative course has been taken by the Law Society in setting up its own School of Law in London, but there again the task is different from that I envisage, in that the School of Law is attempting to give a mixture of basic legal education and practical professional instruction, whereas in my scheme the basic accounting education would have been received at the university before practical training commenced. The closest parallel that I can think of to what I am proposing is the combination of pre-clinical study at a university followed by clinical training in a hospital by which many medical students are prepared for *their* profession.

Articles or No Articles?

I do not attach much importance to the question whether the period of practical training is or is not to be carried out under articles of apprenticeship, for I do not think that the formal relationship which exists between principal and clerk is what matters. A young man who joins an industrial firm as a management trainee does not get an inferior training because he has not entered into a contract of apprenticeship, nor is his intention to qualify for a particular type of post any the less

> 'recognized at the outset, so that throughout the term of service his work, experience and studies can be arranged with that object in view'.[1]

a matter which the Institute regards as

> 'a fundamental requirement'.

What does matter, of course, is that the training obtained shall be a good one and this is secured as often in fields where articles of clerkship are unknown as in those where they are the rule. American C.P.A.s do not obtain their practical experience under articles, yet I doubt whether they are generally less well trained than accountants in this country.

Objections to the Proposed Scheme

I cannot do other than devote the few minutes which remain to me to considering the more important objections which will be raised against my proposals. Most of these objections will be summed up in the one word 'impracticable', even by those who agree with me that the changes in accounting education I have envisaged are in themselves desirable. And the first ground for regarding them as impracticable will be that they would impose an impossible burden on the universities.

I myself shared this view for some time. But the present plans for increasing the number of scientists and technologists produced by the universities, involving among other things an increase in the size of Imperial College from 1,650 full-time students to 3,000 in from five to ten years, shows how misconceived this objection is. There is nothing unalterable about the numbers or distribution of students in our universities. An intake of undergraduates sufficient to maintain the present flow of new members into the Institute and allow for a 25 per cent wastage *en route* would, after allowing for the graduates already joining the Institute, require about 900 additional university places each year. This represents an increase in the total number of full-time graduating and first diploma students entering the universities of England and Wales for the first time of about 5 per cent, or 6¾ per cent if we exclude Oxford and Cambridge, which do not at present teach accounting. This is a modest figure compared with the 60 per cent increase in the size of the university population which has taken place since 1939, or the further increase of up to 40 per cent which we may have to accommodate by 1965. On the score of numbers, there is nothing inherently impracticable about my proposal, if there were a strong enough desire to put it into effect. Nor do I think that the universities would have any grounds for fearing a dilution of the quality of students they would be asked to take. It would need a lot to convince me that the intellectual qualities required to obtain a first-rate professional accounting qualification are inferior to those required to obtain a respectable degree. Indeed, complaints that precisely the opposite was true have recently been heard from professional quarters.

In my consideration of the quantitative aspect of my proposals, I have considered only one part of the accounting profession, the Institute. One has, after all, to start somewhere, and it is unlikely that, if the senior body did not give a lead in the direction I have indicated, any other body in England and Wales could do so. In Scotland the lead would have to come from the Scottish Institute, and it is in that enlightened quarter that I, in fact, place my highest hopes. A leader-writer in *The Times* recently told of a

> 'board of directors who, whenever they had anything particularly disagreeable to convey, always chose their Scottish director. They had come to the conclusion that even the most unwelcome things said in a Scottish accent sounded less painful and more acceptable than in any other'.

Let us hope that, failing a move from any other quarter, Edinburgh's persuasive accents will before long lead us towards the light.

Another ground on which I shall be accused of making an impracticable suggestion is that my scheme would put an unwarrantable burden on would-be accountants who do not live in a university city or, as regards the second part of my scheme, who do not live in the centre or centres chosen for the training schools. The simple answer to this is that the requirement that a medical student shall obtain his

[1] *Education and Training for Membership*, page 8.

training at a teaching hospital also puts a burden on those who do not live in a university city, but we do not accept lower standards of medical training on that account. If one were looking round for burdens to describe as unwarrantable in the field of accounting education and training, we might more appropriately start with the apprenticeship system, with its premiums and lengthy period of unpaid or low-paid labour.

There will be some who will regard my proposals as representing a desirable long-run objective, but not a practical proposition in the foreseeable future. For these there will be attractions in some compromise plan of part-time university attendance such as has been adopted for solicitors' articled clerks outside London and by apprentices of the Scottish Institute in Scotland. For me these compromises have little appeal, for they distract the university from its real job and they do not give the articled clerk or apprentice a sense of belonging to the university or the zest for learning which that sense brings with it. According to Professor Gower,

> 'there seems to be fairly general agreement among teachers at law schools that this statutory year's attendance [for solicitors' articled clerks] is of very doubtful value',[1]

and there seems to be no reason for expecting any better results if it were adopted by the accountancy profession.

A Grave Danger ?

I feel bound, at the conclusion of this lecture, to refer briefly to some remarks made in this city, a month ago, by the President of the Institute. His speech contained these words:

> 'Whilst I think that the special degree courses now being provided at certain of the universities have a place in our system of professional education, I can foresee grave dangers unless university lecturers and professors are careful to avoid feeding their students with arguments and propositions which they are not mature enough fully to appreciate or even digest properly. . . . I don't want them to feed the young on champagne and caviare before they are properly weaned.'[2]

I hope that the President will, on some future occasion, enlighten us as to the arguments and propositions which he thinks represent grave dangers. He agrees, it seems, with Mark Twain that

> 'Soap and education are not as sudden as massacre, but they are more deadly in the long run.'

Is it, I wonder, Truth or the Institute's Recommendations on accounting principles which the President thinks are in danger? As regards the latter, I am sure he will agree with me that the critical discussion of accepted ideas is one of the principal purposes for which universities exist. If received doctrine is not to be questioned there, who is to question it? If, on the other hand, it is Truth for whom the President fears, he must look for her enemies elsewhere: for it is not in the universities that he is most likely to find them.

(*Concluded.*)

[1] Gower, *loc. cit.*, page 152.

[2] *The Accountant*, November 19th, 1955, pages 589–590. For a later comment by the President, made after this lecture was delivered, see *The Accountant*, December 17th, 1955, page 688.

This hard-hitting article probably represents the extreme of adverse criticism of the Report of the Committee on Education and Training, the debate on which is still in progress. The article of course commits nobody but its author.

The Report on Education and Training: Failure of a Mission

By Professor David Solomons, B.Com., F.C.A.*

WHEN THE INSTITUTE of Chartered Accountants in England and Wales received its charter in 1880, the educational landscape was very different from what it is today. Compulsory elementary education was barely ten years old, and was not everywhere free. Technical and commercial education did not exist in the modern sense. There were no universities (outside Scotland) except Oxford, Cambridge, Durham and London; the University of Manchester was just coming into existence. The problems confronting the accountancy profession were also very different from what they are now. Insolvency administration was the main preoccupation at that time, and taxation and management accounting were little thought of. It is by no means surprising, therefore, that in 1958 the Council of the Institute should have moved to set up a committee "to consider the education and training appropriate for entrants to the profession, the existing arrangements and facilities therefor, and the changes, if any, which should be made so as to ensure the provision of an adequate supply of trained candidates suitable in all respects for admission to membership of the Institute: and to make recommendations." Now, after nearly three years of hard labour on the part of the Committee, its report is before us. While it will be for the Council of the Institute to decide what action, if any, is to be taken on the Report, every member of the Institute who has any concern for its future has an obligation to form his own judgment on the result of the Committee's work.

The Committee had a choice between two diametrically opposite approaches to its task. It could start by asking itself what kind of system it would recommend if it had not inherited certain arrangements from the past, and it could then see to what extent the existing arrangements could be retained without prejudicing the reforms which its study had shown to be necessary. This approach would have called for a careful comparative study of the educational systems developed by other professions and by the accountancy profession itself in other countries. This would be a natural approach for those who think that a system of education and training which may have been the best available to the accountancy profession in the nineteenth century is conceivably not the best that is possible in the second half of the twentieth. Alternatively, the present system could be regarded as hallowed by tradition, and as only to be changed in detailed ways which would leave traditional practices undisturbed. There is little doubt that it is this latter approach which has produced the Report now before us. And it is for that reason that it represents, as it seems to me, a completely inadequate response to the challenge with which the Committee was faced.

Why the Committee's Recommendations Are Inadequate

For the benefit of those who are as yet unfamiliar with the Committee's findings, I think it is fair to say that they reject all proposals for radical change, but that they propose to modify the present arrangements in a number of ways, the most important of which are:

1. to reduce from five years to four the period under articles required of candidates who have remained at school until the age of 17½ and have passed two subjects in the G.C.E. at advanced level;
2. to amend the examination syllabus by including some elementary economics and statistics, and to increase the attention devoted to management accounting;
3. to arrange for the provision of three courses of full-time oral tuition, each of not more than three weeks' duration, the first to come soon after the beginning of articles, and the second and third at intervals thereafter;
4. to increase the minimum total allowance of study leave to twenty-six weeks;
5. to permit a principal to second an articled clerk, with his concurrence, to other members' firms for periods not exceeding six months in all.

* The author, who is a Fellow of The Institute of Chartered Accountants in England and Wales, is Professor of Accounting in the Wharton School of Finance and Commerce, University of Pennsylvania. From 1955 to 1959 he was Professor of Accounting in the University of Bristol and before that was Reader in Accounting in the University of London.

There are, of course, a good many other recommendations, but I cannot regard any of them as being of major importance. Indeed, it is doubtful whether the last item on the above list is really entitled to be so considered, for it is already possible for an articled clerk to transfer from one firm to another, with the consent of both principals, and secondment is merely a simpler means of attaining one of the purposes of a transfer of articles, namely an extension of the opportunities for gaining experience.

So far as these positive recommendations are concerned, the first, second, fourth, and fifth of those noted above are easy to accept. The third is of much more doubtful value, and I shall return to it later when considering the Committee's views on "classroom tuition." But it is because of its sins of omission, not of commission, that I hold the Committee to have failed in its task.

There is a brief but revealing passage in the Report itself which sums up the cause of my dissatisfaction. The Committee is considering the provision of experience in management accounting for articled clerks, and states: "To what extent a practical insight into the use of accounting by management can be provided by the principal during articles will depend very much on the nature of his practice and on the extent to which this use of accounting has been developed by or for his clients. Significant development has taken place in recent years, and it is continuing. We believe, however, that this development has still a long way to go before worthwhile experience in this field for articled clerks could be found in a sufficient number of undertakings. . . . *Unless there can be a reasonable assurance that all pupils can acquire that particular experience, it cannot be represented as being of the essence of the newly-admitted member's qualifications*" (para. 93—italics supplied). In other words, the training which a prospective chartered accountant needs to have is, by definition, the training which can be obtained through the articled clerk system in approximately its present form. Therefore, the articled clerk system in approximately its present form is a satisfactory means of training prospective accountants. Q.E.D.

Study and Experience—A Misguided View

I believe that if one looks at the present system with an open mind, three conclusions are inescapable.

1. That with the evolution of accounting and management out of the craft stage into at least highly sophisticated arts (I hesitate to use the word science), practical experience is destined to lose some, perhaps much, of its formerly predominant place in the system of education. When wars were fought with bows and arrows, skill and practical experience on the part of the archers was no doubt more important than their educational attainments and their understanding of ballistics. Different criteria are relevant in an age of ICBM's. "Practical experience" too often means learning the rapidly obsolescing methods of one's predecessors, and learning them, moreover, slowly and inefficiently.

2. That continued reliance on correspondence tuition for theoretical instruction is keeping the English accountancy profession in a unique state of educational backwardness vis-à-vis every other major profession in Britain or anywhere else.

3. That, assuming the system of training under articles is to be retained, some means must be found within it of extending the limited opportunities for experience which can be found in all but a small number of large firms. The evidence which the Committee presents to show that "well over half the present students are receiving their practical training in the smaller practices" (para. 7) gives added urgency to this need.

The first and second of these conclusions hang together, for the educational backwardness to which I refer is undoubtedly to be explained by the relative lack of importance attached to theoretical studies by the leaders of the profession, as compared with the exaggerated importance attached to practical experience. There is little if any recognition in the Report that it is the quality of experience, not its quantity, that matters, and that its quality and what is got out of it are largely determined by the quality of the theoretical preparation for it. It is clear that the Committee, when it thinks of theoretical studies, thinks of them always as merely preparation for the examinations. Thus, in rejecting a suggestion by the Association of University Teachers of Accounting that full-time attendance at classes at selected technical colleges for a total (though not a continuous) period of eighteen months should replace correspondence courses, they say, "We do not see how periods of the length suggested could possibly be spared . . . without giving tuition for the examinations a disproportionate place in the system of training as a whole" (para 147). Tuition for the examinations is simply not the point. It is preparation for professional life that matters. It is precisely because the Institute seems to be incapable of thinking about theoretical study without relating it to examinations that it never talks the same language on this point as its educationist critics.

The proposal for "block releases" for full-time study at the major technical colleges and the establishment by the Institute of its own school of accountancy seem to have been the only serious alternatives to correspondence tuition which were put to the Committee. They are probably the only immediately practical alternatives worth serious consideration. The Committee's rejection of the idea of an Institute school of accountancy (except as a last resort), on the grounds that it would be excessively costly and would replace one undesirable educational monopoly by another, is, in my opinion, sound. The rejection of the "block release" idea is quite another matter. The period of eighteen months originally suggested by the Association of University Teachers of Accounting for these courses was based on the assumption that for non-graduates the period of articles would remain at five years. Had it been contemplated that the Committee might recommend a reduction to four years for more mature non-university recruits to the profession, some modification of the proposal might have been offered. The Committee itself considers such a modification and concludes that "from the aspect of time alone, this might be a feasible proposition" (para. 148), but having cleared away one difficulty, it raises another. "We are doubtful," it says, "whether it would meet the requirement, which we rate high, that, as a feature of professional upbringing, the initiative for study should be left largely with the articled clerk." I cannot believe that anything quite as absurd as this has ever before been said about professional education. Either it amounts to a wholesale rejection of formal education beyond the school-leaving age, in which case all our universities, technical colleges and adult education activities must be held to be a vast misdirection of effort; or it implies that the Committee thinks that the value of education is enhanced by making it irksome, drab and haphazard; or it stems from a failure to understand just how much room for initiative a well-devised educational programme based on oral tuition can leave to students of articled clerk age. There is not much doubt that this last explanation is the true one, for the disparaging references later (para. 158) to what the Committee quaintly calls " 'classroom' teaching" make it clear enough that it thinks of formal education as consisting wholly or mainly of lectures or some other form of instruction in which the student plays a completely passive role. No one familiar with modern education could harbour such a misconception. Limitations of space make it impossible here to discuss the numerous ways which exist to transform " 'classroom' teaching" into an exciting experience for both teacher and student—case discussions, role-playing, straight discussions of theoretical issues, problem-solving, game-playing, and others. Though the Committee seems to think otherwise, even private reading has its place in such a programme! Indeed, when the Committee describes the arrangements it favours—"ideally we should like to see a pattern of examination study [here we are again; not study, but examination study] in which the main emphasis is upon private reading and writing under a tutorial guidance which includes appropriate contact with both tutor and fellow students, the whole supported by a programme of lectures designed not primarily to impart knowledge but to embellish it" (para. 158)—it is describing a university scheme of study. Whether an abbreviated technical college programme would achieve this could only be established by careful experimentation. But if such experiments are to be tried, it will apparently have to be without the support or even the blessing of the Committee; which means, of course, that the experiments will not be made.

The Examination Syllabus

The Committee's recommendation that some work in elementary economics and statistics should be included in the syllabus is to be welcomed, for one of the most serious criticisms that can with justice be levelled against the education and training of chartered accountants is that it is extremely narrow and does little to equip the men subjected to it to understand questions of public economic and fiscal policy on which later they are frequently expected to pronounce judgments. The increased attention to be given to management accounting is also to be applauded. Whether the curriculum changes go far enough is a matter for debate; but half a loaf is better than no bread.

On the other hand, the Committee did not react favourably to various suggestions made to it that some element of flexibility should be introduced into the examinations. There is really no good reason why all articled clerks should study precisely the same subjects to precisely the same depth, as the present curriculum requires. It is easy to agree with the Committee that "the qualification of a chartered accountant should continue to be a general qualification and that specialisation should follow admission to membership and not be permitted or encouraged during articles" (para. 113). But while the A.C.A. should properly continue to be a general qualification, this does not mean that there is no scope at all for allowing some small degree of latitude to articled clerks to pursue some subjects in greater depth than others, while requiring a reasonable minimum coverage of all subjects in the curriculum by all candidates for membership. Thus one suggestion was that candidates with a special interest in professional practice might carry their study of auditing to a higher level than their study of management accounting, while candidates with a special interest in industrial accounting would reverse this process. This could hardly be called specialisation. It would merely be providing some slight opportunity for articled clerks with different enthusiasms to indulge them a little, without prejudice to the value of the A.C.A. as ensuring a reasonable degree of competence in all fields. The admitted fact that many men do not have definite career intentions at the time they qualify has little to do with the matter. Anything which stimulates intellectual activity is worth trying, and indulging a student's personal interests to a limited extent is one way of doing this. However, on this point as on so many others, the Committee takes a negative attitude.

The Role of the Universities

It was no surprise to find the Committee saying of the scheme whereby most of the universities in England and Wales (other than Oxford and Cambridge) provide courses leading to a degree based on accountancy, economics, and law that "the only conclusion we can reach is that even after fifteen years there is still not enough evidence to show whether in general the scheme should be encouraged or abandoned or changed or left as it is. We therefore favour leaving it substantially as it is, pending still further experience of its value" (para. 132). Certainly the Report offers little enough evidence to support any conclusion at all, but whether this is because the evidence cannot be obtained or because the Committee did not seek it is not clear. The only statistic adduced, that out of the forty-two "scheme" graduates who entered into articles in 1952 only 60 per cent. passed the final examination at the first attempt, as compared with 81 per cent. of other U.K. graduates, while it certainly reflects no credit on the "scheme," must be regarded as having little evidential value. Such a small number of graduates, picked from a single year, is no basis for an argument (and indeed the Committee does not make it one). For the rest there is only a vague reference to "such slender evidence as we have been able to get from professional firms," again inconclusive. Since the "scheme" is the only attempt to break new ground in education which the profession has seen since 1880, it might have been thought to be worth closer study.

Unfortunately, the Committee's apathetic attitude to the Universities Scheme is very much in line with the Institute's attitude of indifference to university studies in accounting during the last decade. Pious words like the Committee's "We should very much like to see the Institute more closely identified with the Universities" (para. 175) have to be read in the light of the Institute's palpable failure to do anything to show that it shares this sentiment, and of a similar failure on the part of the large firms in the profession. The contrast with the position in the United States is quite striking. There, several of the major firms of C.P.A.'s have established educational foundations to support prizes and fellowships in accounting at the universities. To take one or two examples, the Haskins and Sells Foundation annually makes seventy-five awards of $500 each in colleges all over the country for scholastic excellence in accounting, as well as annual grants of $1,000 each at thirty colleges to assist junior teachers of accounting to pursue higher studies; the Price, Waterhouse Foundation makes a number of grants each year to the accounting departments of university schools of business, ranging in amount from $1,000 to $5,000, to be spent at the discretion of the departments, but most commonly to assist a junior teacher with advanced study or research, in addition to providing a stipend and facilities for extending the practical experience during university vacations of a small number of teachers who can benefit from such arrangements. For many years until recently, the Arthur Lowes Dickinson Fund, established at the Harvard Graduate School of Business Administration by Price, Waterhouse & Company, made possible the Dickinson Lectures in accounting and related fields. Continuing this list of benefactions by American professional firms in support of accounting education, the Arthur Andersen Foundation makes ten awards each year of $5,400 to enable junior teachers to pursue advanced pre-doctoral studies and also pays their tuition fees for the year; Arthur Young & Company make a number of grants of $1,000 each year to graduate students of accounting; Lybrand, Ross Bros. and Montgomery help teachers to gain experience while paying them a stipend; the Institutes of Certified Public Accountants in a number of states award prizes for outstanding performances by university students of accounting. This list has no pretensions to completeness; and many other ways could be cited in which the American accountancy profession shows by deeds, not words, that it considers accounting education to be a good investment. The contrast with the position in Britain is made even more striking when it is recalled that of the three notable British benefactions in this field since 1945, two—the instituting of the Leverhulme Fellowships in management accounting and the founding of the Chair of Accounting at the University of Bristol—were financed by industry, not by the profession, while the third, the P. D. Leake bequest — the only one with which the Institute was associated—was used primarily to promote the study of economics.

A comparison of the position of university teachers of accounting in Britain and the United States is also revealing. In the United States, teachers sit with their professional and industrial fellows on the governing bodies of the various state Institutes of Certified Public Accountants, while in the American Institute of Certified Public Accountants itself they are well represented on the governing body, on the research staff and on the education and examinations staff. By contrast, in Britain teachers are entirely without a voice on the Council or Committees of the Institute, and they do not even play more than a subordinate role in the conduct of the examinations. The very composition of the Committee on Education and Training, which included not a single member of the Institute whose daily work is primarily concerned with education, is in significant contrast with the composition of the Commission on Standards of Education and Experience for Certified Public Accountants, which reported in 1956, and whose twenty-four members were made up of twelve practitioners, six professors of accounting, four deans of university schools of business, and two others, one a former dean and the other a university vice-president.

These are the facts against which we must judge such statements as the Committee's "We should very much like to see the Institute more closely identified with the universities." Deeds, or the lack of them, speak louder than words. Well may Mr. Bertram Nelson say, in his Statement of Reservations, that "any chartered accountant might hesitate to take up work for which so little support was available from his profession" (page 84).

The Proposal for Short Courses

Even this Committee cannot declare itself wholly satisfied with the present arrangements for tuition. "The general pattern of study," it says, "has settled into a comparatively narrow groove. . . . Looking to the future . . . we cannot believe that this situation is beneficial" (para. 156). And what does the Committee offer us as a cure for this deep-seated malaise? A three-weeks introductory course in book-keeping! This is as sensible as giving an aspirin to a person suffering from malnutrition.

But let us examine the Committee's proposals for short courses with the seriousness which the problem deserves. The introductory course in book-keeping for recently articled clerks is the only one which it is proposed to make compulsory. One does not have to take sides for or against such a proposal, for it really has very little to do with education in any important sense. If there is one thing that can be adequately handled by correspondence tuition, it is probably the inculcation of double entry. That an early knowledge of book-keeping is necessary for a clerk to benefit quickly from his office experience is obvious enough; but it does not follow that for such a pedestrian purpose oral tuition has much advantage over correspondence. I have already argued that the Committee misunderstands the purpose and nature of theoretical studies. In this proposal the same misunderstanding is apparent.

When we come to the later optional courses of oral tuition, lasting at the most for three weeks in each case, which the Committee recommends in connection with preparation for the proposed Parts I and II of the Final examination, it is obvious that the Committee has a much less clear conception of their purpose than in the case of the introductory course. They are apparently "designed to set the stage for study, to indicate the points of difficulty which are likely to be encountered, and to a limited extent to dispose, in advance, of certain matters on which for one reason or another many students spend time unprofitably" (para. 166). I confess that here, to my astonishment, I find myself in agreement with Mr. Coulson when he remarks in his Statement of Reservations that "It may be that the Committee has in mind . . . an attempt to clear misconceptions before misconceptions have arisen in the minds of students, but such a proposition—the clearance of errors before they have arisen—will, it is submitted, hardly stand up to consideration" (page 91).

The fact is that short courses have their uses, when it is desired to achieve some quite limited objective—to teach computer programming, or to give foremen some knowledge of work study, say, or to give a "shot in the arm" to mature men whose formal studies lie far behind them. But articled clerks do not need a shot in the arm. They need a nourishing intellectual diet for the long pull. They need to acquire the habit of asking questions and not accepting easy answers. To superimpose short courses on to a curriculum which continues to be based on correspondence tuition is merely to tinker with the problem. However, it probably cannot do much harm. At the best, it might foment even more discontent on the part of articled clerks with their otherwise drab diet, and in this thought at least there is hope.

Practical Experience and the Articled Clerk System

"The system of articles," says the Committee, "has been described to us in a memorandum by one group of Institute members as being 'encrusted with sentiment, like the Maypole or Beefeaters or the Horse Guards' " (para. 26). That this assessment of it is no less than just is amply borne out by the Committee's own approach to the system. "For our own part," they say, "we are convinced that the prime requirement for prospective members of the Institute is a good professional upbringing. This is not at all the same thing as tuition for written examinations. . . . Nor is it the same thing as the mere provision of practical experience. We believe that it goes much deeper, to the roots of professional ethics and outlook. . . . Upbringing implies the existence of a 'parent' and of a relationship with him which in character is essentially different from that between employee and employer or between pupil and school-teacher. We know of no better means whereby this relationship can be created than by the system of articles" (para. 27). I believe this appraisal of the system to be pure mysticism and not a rational judgment at all. It implies that the medical profession, which somehow manages to get along without this mysterious "relationship," has a lower standard of professional ethics or a poorer professional outlook than does the accountancy profession; that barristers (who are content to call their protégés "pupils"), officers of the armed forces, ministers of religion, university dons and stockbrokers, none of whom confuse the force of example with "parenthood," are inferior to chartered accountants because they obtained their professional upbringing by means other than those which we inherited from our solicitor forebears. High professional standards, of which chartered accountants are rightly proud, are not the monopoly of any one profession, nor are they the product of any one system of training, and it is nonsense to pretend otherwise. Only when this point is acknowledged can the system of articles be seen in perspective and its shortcomings prescribed for.

Basically, there are two weaknesses in the system of articles. The first is that there is no reason why a man who is a capable practitioner should also be a good teacher, or even why he should have any particular interest in the education and training of articled clerks. That so many members of the Institute do in fact have enthusiasm for instructing their successors, and the skill to do so, alone makes the system as effective as it is. One day, perhaps, accountants and lawyers will discover what most other people have known for a long time, that training is a job for experts and, though something does rub off from principal to clerk in the rough and tumble of professional life, this is a slow and inefficient way of imparting skills. I doubt whether, within the limitations of the system of articles, much can be done to remedy this weakness.

The second basic weakness is that, in any but the largest practices, it is impossible to provide all-round experience, and there may be serious gaps both in the type of work to be done and in the type of clients to be served. It has always been possible to mitigate this weakness in the system by arranging for articles to be transferred from one firm to another when they were part-way through. The provision whereby articled clerks could be seconded for up to six months to an industrial concern opened up a further possibility of strengthening the training offered. Not much use has been made of either of these remedies. Transfers of articles are probably not welcomed by practitioners, and a maximum of six months in industry is not long enough to be really useful.

The Committee's recommendation that it should be made possible to second an articled clerk from his own firm to others without a formal transfer of articles is a step in the right direction, but its value is greatly reduced by the limitation of the periods of secondment to six months in all. The Committee considers that transfers of articles, while they should continue to be permitted, should not be advocated: it declines to recommend that the six months' limitation on service in industry should be raised, in spite of the fact that it was "very strongly pressed" to do so (para. 87); and it rejects what was probably the most effective proposal put to it for extending the range of experience obtainable within the articles system, namely, that it should be possible for a clerk to be articled to a group of firms organised for this purpose so that he could move from firm to firm within the group, learning what he could from each, on the lines of the group apprenticeship schemes which make it possible for small firms in industry to provide effective training for apprentices. The scope of this arrangement could be usefully extended by including members in industry and members in the public service in such groups.

This generally negative reaction on the part of the Committee to all attempts to increase the effectiveness of the system of articles stems from the "mystical" theory of articles to which I have already referred. To quote the Committee, "Our attitude to all these suggestions is governed by our conviction, already expressed, that the prime requirement for an articled clerk is a good professional upbringing and by a belief that this upbringing can best be secured in the circumstances of a special relationship between the principal and his articled clerk which is essentially not casual or transient but carries mutual obligations and responsibilities for the whole period of the articled service. To encourage changes of principal is to undermine the continuity of this relationship" (para 84). It is a pity that the Committee was unable to see that, if there is something valuable in a continuing relationship between principal and clerk, it is a continuing sense of mutual responsibility, but that this does not imply that the clerk's experience has to be limited by the facilities which can be offered by a single firm, any more than the continuing mutual responsibilities between a student and his tutor at a university means that he may not be taught by other teachers or take work outside his tutor's department. Within a group apprenticeship scheme, the *primary* responsibility can still be between the clerk and a single principal, if this is thought to be important.

Conclusion

Perhaps once in a generation, an opportunity for educational advance presents itself which, if taken, becomes a historical landmark. The Education Acts of 1870, 1918, and 1944 were such occasions. For the British accountancy profession, the 1961 Report of the Committee on Education and Training might have been such another. Instead, it is notable only for its timidity. Whenever it can find specious reasons for opposing change it does so. A good example of this reluctance to innovate is seen in the Committee's rejection of the proposal that the Institute ought to appoint a Director of Studies. Its objections to this proposal are almost unbelievable. "It would concentrate more responsibility on a single individual at the centre than we should think desirable," and there would be a "tendency to restrict competition in new ideas and new methods" (para. 177). In fact, of course, the Director would not only be anxious to stimulate and collect new ideas, from whatever source they came, but he could also do much to remedy the weakness of the present situation, where "what is everybody's business is nobody's business." Perhaps the real objection to having a Director of Studies is that he would presumably have to be someone with a professional interest in and knowledge of education, or at least he would soon acquire a professional attitude. For some reason, the Institute has always preferred to take advice on its educational policy from amateurs.

Another example of specious reasoning is to be seen in the Committee's rejection of the idea that the Institute should prescribe a minimum scale of remuneration for articled clerks. Whatever the merits of this proposal (on which I have no strong views myself), I can make no sense whatever of the Committee's argument that "this would have a 'levelling down' as well as a 'levelling up' effect" and that it "would be a measure which might restrain the scale of reward for the best candidates" (para. 209). Why should a *minimum* scale restrain the reward of the best candidates? But the full absurdity of the Committee's argument is seen only when one reaches the next paragraph, and finds that it has turned a nimble somersault and expresses its "anxiety lest, for lack of adequate information, some principal may be led by the competition from industry and elsewhere to offer articled clerks scales of remuneration which are *excessive*" (para. 210, italics supplied). What is one to make of such logic?

Many thousands of articled clerks will be subjected to the profession's archaic training methods before the system is again the subject of review. This is a sobering thought; for a great opportunity has been lost, and the price will be paid not by those who are already members of the Institute but by those whose professional education might have been but now will not be worthy of a great profession.

Professional Certification

David Solomons
Arthur Young Professor of Accounting
The Wharton School, University of Pennsylvania

There may be some participants at this Roundtable who are skeptical about the appropriateness of including a session on professional certification in a conference devoted to accounting education. It is true that accounting educators find among their students many who have no intention of entering the accounting profession, however widely we define it, and who have no interest in obtaining a professional qualification. Nevertheless, we cannot close our eyes to the fact that a large proportion of accounting students are destined to become professionally qualified accountants, and even those who are not are going to find themselves, during their working lives, working with (or sometimes against) those who are.

There is a creative tension between educators, on the one hand, and those responsible for controlling entry into the professions on the other, in that the quality of professional recruits is to a considerable extent dependent on the efforts of the educators, while some part at least of our university and college curricula are determined for the educators by the professional regulators. Thus any failure on the part of these two groups to work together to a common end cannot fail to be damaging to both of them.

I shall not here go into the question of whether the public interest really requires the regulation of the professions, and in particular of the accounting profession, although there are some persons, such as Milton Friedman, who have serious doubts about the necessity for regulation. Friedman, in his provocative essay on "Occupational Licensure," distinguishes between three levels of control: registration, certification, and licensing.

> By regulation I mean an arrangement under which individuals are required to list their names in some official register if they engage in certain kinds of activities. . . . The second level is certification. The governmental agency may certify that an individual has certain skills but may not prevent, in any way, the practice of any occupation using these skills by people who do not have such a certificate. . . . The third stage is licensing proper. This is an arrangement under which one must obtain a license from a recognized authority in order to engage in the occupation.[1]

It is licensing against which Friedman delivers his broadside, seeing it as an unwarranted interference with the free market. Certification is also objectionable to him, though much less so. But he notes that in the case of CPAs, "certification is frequently only an intermediate stage. In many states, there has been a tendency to restrict an increasing range of activities to certified public accountants. With respect to such activities there is licensure, not certification."[2]

The American Institute of Certified Public Accountants, it need hardly be said, does not agree with Milton Friedman. In the preamble to their Model Accountancy Bill, they assert: "The public interest warrants the licensing and regulation of persons professing expertise in accounting who perform professional accounting services, including the expression of opinions on financial statements and other information upon which the public necessarily relies." They then go on to quote in support the dictum of the Court of Appeals of the State of Tennessee (1957): "The state, under its police power, may pass laws to protect the public against fraud, deception or the consequences of ignorance and incapacity, and may exact the requisite degree of skill and learning of persons in professions and pursuits which affect the public health or welfare, such as accountancy."[3]

Whatever significance the certification of accountants may have for the public, there is no question that it has great significance for accounting educators. The requirements which have to be satisfied by a candidate for certification help to define the end product of much of our educational activity. The profession's requirements for certification are one way, perhaps the most direct way, in which the profession tells educators what it thinks to be important in the professional preparation of its future members. These requirements also have an important effect on the motivation of our students. Though we may deplore this situation, we cannot ignore it. We cannot be blind to the fact that the amount of interest shown by some students in the various parts of the accounting curriculum is directly related to their coverage in the CPA examination or in some other professional examination of a similar kind.

The Problem of Diversity

Discussion of the professional certification of accountants has to confront a number of special difficulties. The first, and I believe the most important, stems from the very diverse work that accountants do. It is not simply that they are found in public practice, in industry, in government, and in other parts of the not-for-profit sector. Many of the most successful accountants go into general management and engage in entirely nonaccounting activities, while continuing to hold an accounting qualification. It is unfortunate that a single qualification, the CPA certificate, is so widely used as a qualification in fields for which it was not designed. In evaluating the CPA certificate, one has to bear in mind that it is primarily concerned with *public* accountants and the demands of *public* practice, even though more than half of the 150,000 holders of the certificate now work outside that field.

The other kind of difficulty which complicates an evaluation of the CPA qualification results from the multiplicity of jurisdictions which share responsibility for it. Though all fifty-four of the state and other territorial boards now use a uniform examination, their educational and experience requirements, and now their continuing education requirements, exhibit considerable diversity. This diversity of regulations is not confined to the accountancy profession. Of course it also affects medicine, law, and the other professions. What makes it particularly troublesome for accountants is that their practice, unlike that of many other professionals, is not generally confined within state boundaries, so that problems of reciprocity are much more serious. The joint AICPA-NASBA Committee on Professional Recognition and Regulation, which was appointed in August 1970 and reported in July 1973, took a gloomy view of the prospects of an improvement in this situation. "Uniformity," they say, "is not attainable under the present structure;"[4] looking back, they expressed the belief "that the profession has not made any significant advances in the past decade in achieving uniformity in statutory provisions for regulation, education and experience, ethics and interstate practice."[5] A subcommittee on professional recognition noted:

> comments were received that states are gradually moving closer to uniform requirements in the more important provisions. Undoubtedly this is true for some requirements. It is also true that new laws are being enacted which introduce additional and unique variations so that progress, if any, toward uniformity moves at a snail's pace. The subcommittee concluded that substantial uniformity among the fifty-four jurisdictions is all but impossible under present procedures.[6]

The solution the committee recommended was the joint establishment by the AICPA and NASBA of a national qualification service to enroll individuals who had fulfilled prescribed requirements for education, experience, completion of the uniform CPA examination, and continuing education. This would virtually amount to the institution of a super-CPA certificate.

Even the one part of the certification procedure which is uniform across the country, the CPA examination, is affected by the diversity of educational requirements. In New York, a candidate may not sit for the auditing paper until he has satisfied the experience requirement—two years with a baccalaureate degree, one year with a master's. Presumably it is thought that the auditing paper should test what has been learned from the period of work experience as well as what has been learned from formal education. Yet in Illinois there is no experience requirement at all for the CPA certificate, and in Florida there is no experience requirement for candidates who hold a master's degree. All of these candidates take the same auditing examination. Either the examination is unfair to candidates from Illinois, Florida, and the other states which do not demand prior work experience, or it fails to test what the New York State Board appears to think that it tests.

In other parts of the English-speaking world, different situations bring different problems. There professional certification is in the hands of private organizations, not of public boards. But even in Britain, a relatively small country with a unitary form of government—at present, though perhaps not for much longer—there is more than enough disuniformity. In Great Britain and Ireland together, there are four accountancy bodies whose members in public practice are officially recognized for the purposes of the Companies Acts, and two others which occupy important positions in management accounting and the public sector respectively, to say nothing of numerous lesser bodies. Each of the six major organizations conducts its own examinations and has its own other requirements for membership. In Canada, the chartered accountants' qualification is awarded by the ten provincial Institutes of Chartered Accountants, all of which use the Uniform Final Examination conducted for them by the Canadian Institute of Chartered Accountants. (This examination is also taken by candidates from Bermuda.) Other conditions for qualification as a chartered accountant in Canada do differ somewhat from province to province, but the differences are not as important as they are among the states of this country. In Australia, the responsibility for certification is for the most part divided between the Australian Institute of Chartered Accountants and the Australian Society of Accountants. As another session of this conference is devoted to what we can learn from other countries, I shall not pursue these international differences any further.

Having noted earlier that the CPA qualification is not really designed to test all the skills which are relevant to accounting work outside the field of public practice, we should recognize a potentially important newcomer to the list of professional qualifications, the

Certificate in Management Accounting, which has been offered since 1972 by the Institute of Management Accounting. I shall have something to say about this qualification later. However, most of my remarks will be concerned with the CPA certificate, if only because of its numerical preponderance and the degree of official recognition accorded it.

The Nature of Professional Qualifications

What has until now been a process of "becoming qualified" is in our day turning into a process of "staying qualified." Qualification is seen as a state, not as a one-time achievement. Continuing education, peer review (though so far we have seen it applied only to firms, not individuals), and periodic examination (as in Florida) are among the instruments for maintaining a state of being qualified, and there is no doubt that this is the way things are going to develop. Yet the initial certification of a young professional is and will remain an especially important event in the continuum of a professional career.

Generally speaking, there are four kinds of requirements that need to be satisfied by those who aspire to any widely accepted accounting qualification. They are (1) educational requirements, (2) examination requirements, (3) experience requirements, and (4) a character investigation.

Most of the other sessions of this conference are being devoted to a discussion of accounting education, and therefore it seems appropriate to pass over the educational requirements here. Nor do I have anything of interest to say about character investigation. I shall therefore address the balance of my remarks to the two issues of professional examinations and the experience requirements.

What, if anything, distinguishes a professional qualification from an academic degree? The question is not an idle one, for if we were to find that our professional examinations were not materially different from academic examinations, and if the other requirements (notably the experience requirement) were to be progressively whittled away, we might have to ask ourselves whether professional qualifications served any purpose which was not already being served by a university degree. I believe that a professional qualification should serve a different purpose from that served by an academic degree. It follows from that that we should be on our guard against any attempt to make them virtually interchangeable.

This question—what distinguishes a professional qualification from an academic one?—clearly reflects on the nature of professional education itself. If I may be allowed to quote from myself here, I would say:

> What makes professional education different from mere education (if such a pejorative is permissible) is that it has to combine knowledge and skill in a subtle way. From this combination, with the maturity that comes with experience and given the essential personal quality of integrity—a quality which can be nurtured by professional experience but which has to be implanted by earlier upbringing—comes the rounded professional man. More than "mere education" is involved.[7]

As a canny Scot put it a few years ago, "the graduate knows 'about' things, the professional trained man can 'do' things—and employers prefer to engage those who can do things in preference to those who know about things."[8] Essentially the same idea is expressed by G. L. Bach when he says: "The professional man asks 'what tools do I need to solve the problem I face?'—not 'how do I do my stuff by using the particular tools I happen to know?' "[9] These ideas obviously have a bearing on the case for an experience requirement for those aspiring to be professionally qualified, and I shall return to that matter shortly. But these thoughts are also relevant to the nature of professional examinations, for they point in the direction of an examination which will test both knowledge and skill.

I do not want to overemphasize this distinction. Many academic examinations, especially in accounting, already do test skills as well as knowledge. It is really a matter of balance. Academic examinations will tend to emphasize knowledge rather than skill, and it is appropriate that they should do so. Even for the professional man, skill without knowledge will prove to be a barren gift, for though he may be able to deal expertly with a familiar situation, he will be at a grave disadvantage in confronting a new and unfamiliar one. To put the need for balance between knowledge and skill into perspective, you have only to ask someone whether he would rather be operated on by a surgeon with a penknife or by a layman with all the latest tools and skill in their use, but with no knowledge of anatomy.

The CPA Examination and Some Alternatives

Although professional examinations in our field have not themselves gone unexamined, the studies I have found do not help us to evaluate them, nor do they lead to recommendations for improvement. For example, the report of the 1973-74 and 1974-75 Committees on Professional Examinations of the American Accounting Association contains an elaborate analysis of the content of the CPA, CMA, and CIA examinations.[10] But "because it would not contribute to project goals, the Committee did not examine the *adequacy* or *relevance* of content and coverage in either professional examinations or accounting curricula."[11] One may expect more in the way of evaluation from the "ongoing audit of the Uniform CPA Examination" which the AICPA has engaged the NASBA to perform. This audit, which began early in 1976, is examining the purpose, scope, and level of the examination, its security and administration, the grading and regrading of examinations, and the performance of candidates. I shall not be surprised if the audit group finds itself more concerned with problems of equity and administrative feasibility than with the more fundamental question of whether the scope and form of the CPA examination at the present time is the best kind of testing instrument that we can devise for our profession. Frank Weston, one of the discussants of this paper, is a member of the audit team, and I am hoping that he will be able to bring us up to date on the status of this project.

One of the most important things to note about the CPA examination, unfortunately, is that it is conducted on a vast scale. With some 42,000 candidates taking the examination twice a year in over one hundred centers, ease of administration and grading is bound to rank high on the list of criteria which those responsible for the examination will set for themselves. This alone will explain why multiple-choice questions constitute such a large part of the examination. Using the mean estimated time suggested on the papers for each question as an indication of the weight allotted to it by the examiners, the table below shows the relative weight of multiple-choice questions, questions calling for quantitative answers, and questions requiring verbal answers in four of the five papers which constituted the November 1976 examination. I have not analyzed the questions in the business law paper. Where a question consisted of two or more parts, each part was classified separately, using my own subjective weighting of the several parts.

What I was looking for was the amount of weight given to skill in problem recognition and the exercise of professional judgment in dealing with a problem once it had been diagnosed. While one cannot say that multiple-choice questions do not call for any professional judgment, they are by their very nature constructed to permit one right answer. This cannot leave much room for judgment. The questions classified as quantitative are also for the most part designed to be either clearly right or wrong. There was very little room for judgment, and they were designed to give the candidate an unambiguous signal as to the nature of the problem. One might have expected to find more scope for judgment in the verbal questions, but I was disappointed even there. Of the four verbal questions in the auditing paper, one required the candidate to list the items to be included in the typical engagement letter and to describe the benefits derived from preparing such a letter. Another called for a list of audit procedures. At most 20 percent of this paper could be said to call for the exercise of judgment. I would assign the same percentage to judgment in the theory paper. These are generous estimates. That means that for these four papers taken together, for which a total of 960 minutes were allowed, something less than 10 percent of the candidate's time and effort was to be devoted to material on which he or she might exercise some judgment.

CPA Examination, November 1976

Percentage of total mean estimate of time to be devoted to multiple-choice, quantitative, and verbal questions

	Multiple-Choice	Verbal	Quantitative	Total Minutes Allowed for Paper
Accounting Practice				
Part I	37	59	4	270
Part II	37	63	—	270
Accounting Theory	48	5	47	210
Auditing	54	—	46	210

We could do better than this, although it would involve a considerable effort. I had an opportunity a year ago to study a promising Canadian experiment. One of the four papers which make up the Uniform Final Examination for the Canadian Institute of Chartered Accountants is devoted to a single long and complex case study, for which four hours are allowed. The case presents a situation which poses many different kinds of problems—tax, financial analysis, managerial decision making, internal control, and possibly several others. Though of course the candidate is instructed as to the general scope of the report he is to write, he is not told what problems are present in the situation, but is left to make his own diagnosis. This part of the candidate's task carries heavy weight. The case will also require him to perform a considerable amount of quantitative analysis, and he will finally have to come up with recommendations. This begins to look like a real-life professional situation. Of course, this kind of paper is difficult to grade equitably, and it is more costly in time and money to administer. But there is evidence that it does test qualities in the candidate which are not adequately tested by the more traditional papers, and it comes closer than they do, in my opinion, to what a professional examination ought to be like.

The accountancy profession will do well to monitor the progress of an important project which has now been embarked on by the Educational Testing Service for the legal profession. This project is being supported by the American Bar Foundation, the Association of American Law Schools, the Law School Admission Council, and the National Conference of Bar Examiners.[12] The project is divided into four phases. *Phase 1:* determining the statistical relationship among the measures constituting the steps a person must take en route to becoming a practicing attorney. These measures include law school admissions criteria, law school grades, and bar examination scores. *Phase 2:* studying what lawyers do. To what extent do they perceive their legal education as preparing them for those roles? How do large organizations evaluate lawyers at the present time? *Phase 3:* developing tests of professional competence. The methods to be used will cover tests of knowledge, rating scales, and situational tests approximating actual tasks but carried out under standardized conditions in order to permit equitable scoring. *Phase 4:* reexamining the relationships among the various methods taken to select entrants to the legal profession, and the relationship of those measures to measures of performance in legal practice. I know of no inquiry of comparable scope in our own profession. I hope that those responsible for our own professsional examinations will follow this project with the care that it obviously deserves. Phase 1 was reported on at the June 1976 Annual Meeting of the Law School Admission Council.

An Experience Requirement for Certification?

The attitude of the profession to the question of whether a period of work as an accountant should be a prerequisite to certification has undergone and is still undergoing change. In 1956 a majority of the members of the Commission on Standards of Education and Experience for Certified Public Accountants (the Perry Commission) reported in favor of the eventual elimination of experience requirements, although there were powerful dissenting voices in this report. In May 1959 the Council of the AICPA decided not to accept this recommendation, but adopted instead a resolution which affirmed:

> That an experience requirement be retained; that with the baccalaureate degree with or supplemented by evidence of study of accounting [to the extent set forth in a prior resolution] the experience be not less than two years; that as education is extended beyond the baccalaureate degree, the length of experience should be reduced but should not be less than one year; that the experience should be under the guidance of a CPA and some of the experience should be in the area of third party reliance; and that a committee of the AICPA should prepare a statement as to what in general should be an acceptable type of experience for the CPA certificate.

In 1960 this resolution was amended to state "that at least one year of the required experience was to be in the public practice of accounting." In accordance with these resolutions, a Committee on Qualifying Experience was appointed, under the chairmanship of George Hansen, and reported in April 1961. It reaffirmed that "the CPA certificate is evidence of demonstrated competence for the practice of public accounting," and that "beyond the desired educational level a specific type of experience is needed to enhance the technical competence and develop the personal qualities of a person desiring to become a CPA."

The high point of the attack on an experience requirement was reached in the report of the Committee on Education and Experience Requirements for CPAs (the Beamer Report), the recommendations of which were adopted by the Council of the AICPA in May 1969. Recommendation 3 stated: "at least five years of college study are needed to obtain the common body of knowledge for CPAs and should be the education requirement. *For those who meet this standard,* no qualifying experience should be required" (italics added). It should be noted that another of the committee's recommendations stated: "student internships are desirable and are encouraged as part of the educational program."[13] The reasons adduced by the committee for their view that an additional year of education justified elimination of the experience requirement are set out in the following passage from their report:

> The recommendation that no qualifying experience should be required of those who complete five years of acceptable college study is made as a consequence of our study of the issues. . . . The reasons for our recommendation are summarized as follows:
>
> 1. We have concluded that the common body of knowledge delineated by *Horizons for the Profession* can best be obtained through college study.
> 2. We recognize a clear-cut distinction between the value of experience and the value of an experience requirement. There can be no question about the value of experience but there is serious doubt about the value of present-day experience requirements.

3. It is unreasonable to require a period of qualifying experience for which uniform standards cannot be set and which cannot be effectively policed.
4. Experience requirements imply apprenticeship which is inappropriate for a learned profession.
5. The continuing dilution, reduction, and elimination of experience requirements is positive evidence of their ineffectiveness and of the trend toward eventual elimination of all experience requirements.
6. There is no evidence that CPAs obtaining their certificates in jurisdictions without experience requirements are more often guilty of infractions of the rules of professional conduct or substandard practice than those with extensive experience.
7. A fifth year of college study is of greater benefit to the CPA than a year or two of experience as a junior staff member of a CPA firm. While the first years of appropriate experience may enhance certain qualities such as professionalism and technical competence, a college program of at least five years permits the attainment of both breadth and depth of knowledge that is unlikely to be obtained from a four-year program and satisfying an experience requirement.

While the foregoing reasons are the bases for our recommendations, there are two practical considerations which further support our position:
1. Most CPAs who plan to practice independently will take a position with an established CPA firm for a few years.
2. Even in the absence of an experience requirement, the time needed to pass all parts of the CPA examination will provide most candidates with a period of practical experience.[14]

I believe that the committee was misguided in its view that education is a complete substitute for experience. It is true that as accounting has become more sophisticated, the balance between formal education and experience as instruments of learning has changed in favor of education. As analytical techniques for problem solving in business have developed, the role of formal study has increased, and the need to rely on the judgment that comes from experience has somewhat diminished. But it is quite another matter to assert that to become professionally qualified a person should be required to show no more evidence of his ability to function effectively in a professional capacity than can be gained from his performance in the classroom. A committee that did not question the value of experience but had serious doubts about the value of present-day experience requirements might have been expected to look for ways to make the requirements more effective, but this is a challenge which it did not accept. Some of the arguments used by the committee are strange indeed. It uses the word "apprenticeship" as a term of opprobrium. Name-calling is hardly evidence of the rightness of the committee's views. Nor is the "continuing dilution, reduction, and elimination of experience requirements" positive evidence of their ineffectiveness. It may simply be evidence that it takes trouble to make them effective, and that we can make life easier for everybody if we do away with them. But who said that it was the committee's job to make life easy? The practical consideration mentioned by the committee in further support of their position, that "most CPAs who plan to practice independently will take a position with an established CPA firm for a few years," had been effectively answered in 1956 by Richard Claire and J. S. Seidman in their dissent from the majority report of the Perry Commission. They said, in relation to the same argument, that "the Commission is relying on the fact that its own disavowal of an experience requirement will not be taken seriously by many prospective practitioners. We think this exposes the weakness of the majority position."[15]

The fundamental issue raised by the Beamer Committee's recommendations relates to the significance which one attaches to a professional qualification. The two conflicting views on this matter were again expressed succinctly by Claire and Seidman: "Ours is a 'practicing' not an academic profession. The public looks upon the CPA certificate as a mark of competence in practice, not a license to learn how to practice. To the public, the CPA, young or old, denotes finished goods, not raw materials."[16] This issue has again been looked at more recently by the Committee on Qualifying Experience which reported to the NASBA Board of Directors in October 1976. A committee vote on the question "Should experience be required for a permit to practice public accountancy?" was a unanimous yes. The committee's position in relation to an experience requirement for CPAs who do not engage in public practice is not clear from their report. However, they do explicitly recognize that while education may provide the technical know-how to pass the CPA examination, there are other attributes necessary for successful professional performance which qualifying experience can help to provide. Important among these, I believe, are a sense of professionalism and what the committee calls "the judgment required to be able to apply the technical knowledge gained by education to practical everyday situations."

Perhaps the most important conclusion reached by the NASBA Committee on Qualifying Experience is that "if experience requirements are to be used to protect the public user of accounting services, the quality of the experience must be emphasized, and means must be developed to measure and verify the experience on a uniform basis." It is probably the problem of equivalence which has caused the state boards more trouble than anything else in implementing experience requirements, and has no doubt led many of those who have had to grapple with this problem to favor their elimination as one way of getting rid of the problem. Everyone agrees that experience in public practice is an acceptable form of experience, but what about experience in industry, in financial institutions, in the Internal Revenue Service, and in other branches of government? The seriousness of this problem is diminished if the experience requirement calls for a minimum period of work in public practice under carefully monitored conditions, and this I believe to be desirable.

I believe that our profession can learn something from the experience gained by the Institute of Chartered Accountants in England and Wales in monitoring the quality of experience of those aspiring to membership of the Institute under training contracts. Under the English system, a formal training contract is entered into between the trainee and his principal, and this contract is registered at the Institute. I do not believe that this legal contract is itself important. What is important is that the Institute requires the trainee and his principal to keep a training record showing week by week what kind of experience has been gained. This is examined periodically by the Institute, and if it does not meet the required standards, the length of experience necessary for admission to membership may be increased until the standards have been met. Other features of the English Institute's system make it easier to control the quality of training. These include the requirement that the training shall be carried out in the office of a chartered accountant, and that the right to take trainees shall be granted only after the Institute has satisfied itself that the practitioner can provide the trainee with reasonable opportunities for gaining satisfactory experience.

A Two-tier System?

There is much support for a so-called two-tier system as a way around the equivalence problem in connection with the experience requirement. There is no experience requirement for the CPA certificate itself under such a system, but a prescribed amount and kind of experience must be gained to obtain a license to practice. It is not surprising that this system finds favor with many members of state boards, for it gets rid of one of their major difficulties. Yet in my view it downgrades the CPA certificate. By substantially making it simply another academic qualification, it raises a serious question as to what its significance might be. However, if such a system were to be adopted by all states, by lowering the value of the nonpracticing

CPA certificates the way might be cleared for its gradual replacement by other qualifications, of a more specialized character and better adapted to meet the needs of those not in public practice. The Certificate in Management Accounting is alive and well and waiting in the wings to take on such a role. The Certificate in Internal Auditing, in its more limited field, is also already available.

How Do Good Accountants Get That Way?

So far as I know, no one has asked, "How do good accountants get that way?" If we knew the answer to this question, we should really know something about the relative importance of education, experience, and the other ingredients of preparation for the profession, and what kinds of education, experience, and so forth were likely to be most productive. In the medical profession, such a question has been asked about doctors with somewhat surprising results.[17] In one study, eighty-eight family doctors in North Carolina were intensively studied to evaluate their clinical skills. Each practitioner was followed by one or more members of the research team through three or four days of office, hospital, and house calls.

> Each doctor was graded on six activities: history taking; physical examination; use of laboratory aids for diagnosis; therapy; preventive medicine; and keeping of clinical records. Then his clinical skill, as rated by the researchers, was stacked against his medical school record, internship, patient-load, medical society and hospital affiliations, family background, office facilities, and so on.

The result was to prove false many common assumptions about what makes a good doctor. There was no connection between the doctors' clinical ratings and their Medical College Aptitude Test scores, the type of medical school attended, the type of hospital they trained in, or the length of hospital training in pediatrics, surgery, and obstetrics and gynecology. There *was* a relationship between the clinical ratings and medical school grades (for doctors under thirty-six), the length of hospital training in medicine, the quality of office accommodation and equipment, the number of medical journals subscribed to, and adherence to an appointment schedule. The relationship between clinical skill and the number of hours a year spent on refresher courses was unclear. The researchers were aware of most of the criticisms that could be leveled at their study, but even if it were flawed, they were at least asking the right question. When we eventually ask it about accountants, we too may get some surprising answers.

Notes

1. Milton Friedman, *In Capitalism and Freedom* (Chicago: University of Chicago Press, 1962), pp. 144-45.
2. Ibid., p. 145.
3. Davis v. Allen, 307 S.W. 2d 800 (Tenn. Ct. App. 1957).
4. *Report of the AICPA-NASBA Committee on Professional Recognition and Regulation* (1973), p. 3.
5. Ibid., p. 12.
6. Ibid., pp. 49-50.
7. David Solomons, *Prospectus for a Profession* (London: Gee & Co. Ltd., 1974), p. 101.
8. John C. Shaw, "Recruitment and Training—Possible Developments," in *Tomorrow's CA in the Making* (Institute of Chartered Accountants of Scotland, 1970), p. 27.
9. G. Leland Bach, "Education for the 1980s," in *The Future of Accounting Education* (Carnegie Institute of Technology, 1960), p. 11.
10. *Accounting Review* 49 (Supplement, 1976): 1-37.
11. Ibid., p. 4.
12. See Alfred B. Carlson, "Research Will Lead to Performance Test for Lawyers," *Findings* 3, no. 2 (1976).
13. There are those who think that internships, if made part of the student's formal education, provide a satisfactory substitute for an experience requirement. This view is expressed by Maurice Moonitz in his "The Beamer Committee Report—a Golden Opportunity for Accounting Education," *The Journal of Accountancy* (August 1973), pp. 64-69. While an internship can be a valuable adjunct to formal education, I do not believe that short periods of work experience (i.e., less than a year of continuous experience) will enable the trainee to be given anything but low level tasks.
14. *Report of the AICPA Committee on Education and Experience Requirements for CPAs* (March 1969), pp. 12-13.
15. *The Perry Commission Report,* p. 145.
16. Ibid., p. 144.
17. Lois Hoffman, "How Do Good Doctors Get That Way?," in *Patients, Physicians, and Illness,* ed. E. Gartly Jaco (New York: The Free Press, 1958), pp. 365-81.

View from an Educationist D. Solomons

We are concerned, in this session, with the development of financial managers, not necessarily with the education and training of chartered accountants. Hitherto the senior positions in financial management in this country have typically been filled by chartered accountants. Michael Julien's paper has raised the question whether that is likely to continue to be true, and it is most appropriate, as we enter the Institute's second century, to press for an answer to that question. Do we want the leaders in the field of financial management to continue to be chartered accountants? If we do, is the Institute's present education and training policy likely to secure that result? Financial managers, broadly defined, do, after all make-up about half of the Institute's membership. The question is therefore not an unimportant one for the size and status of the Institute in the years ahead.

An "Ideal" Education for Financial Managers

Consider the education, general and professional, that you would like a young financial manager that you were hiring to have. In framing your answer, disregard initially all questions of practicality, all considerations of the cost and the time required to complete this "ideal" preparation for a career in financial management. It is time enough to think about what is feasible once you have a good idea of what you would like the perfect candidate for your job to have in the way of education if there were no constraints of time and money. I am looking only at his or her education, not the personal qualities that are such important ingredients of success. Of course, personal qualities are developed, or thwarted, or changed by the education that a person undergoes; and the kind of education that he or she chooses to obtain is not independent of the inherent characteristics of that person. So education and character interact on each other, and neither can really be considered separately. Nevertheless, we have to try to do just that if we want to draw up a general purpose specification of the ideal preparation for a financial manager.

What would that preparation include? I would want:

- University-level study of a broad liberal arts curriculum, including some work in the humanities, natural sciences and social sciences. Although this curriculum would be non-vocational, the foundation for later vocational study would be laid, including an introduction to economics and enough mathematics to provide a base for later work in statistics and quantitative methods.

This would be followed by:

- A broad study of business administration, including further work in economics, and study to a respectable level of the legal environment of business, statistics, marketing, production, labour relations, organisational behaviour, quantitative methods, information systems and international business. Accounting and finance are considered separately next.

- Study of the elements of financial management, including accounting (financial and managerial), financial institutions, financial planning models, taxation, internal auditing and control, and international finance.

- Finally these academic studies would be integrated by a course in business policy, in which the disciplines studied earlier would be brought to bear on complex business situations.

That would complete the academic education. It would be full-time education, but not necessarily continuous. Indeed, it would be better if it were interrupted, in the later phases, with some periods of work experience, so that the world of business that was being studied was not encountered only in the classroom. But the kind of integration of study and experience that I would like to see is not easy to achieve, and it has rarely proved to be successful. I am not talking about the mixture of work and part-time study that we are all too familiar with. What I would like to see is closer to the "sandwich" idea; but the limited success of "sandwich" schemes to date is evidence of the difficulty in practice of effectively combining academic study and work experience.

Separate from the academic study of concepts and separate also from "learning on the job", I see a need for what I have called "practical instruction". This already forms a part of good training schemes, both in some professional firms and in industry. It is the "how to do it" type of instruction for which professors have little patience but which constitutes an important element in preparation for a profession, and it can usually be done more efficiently under controlled conditions in a classroom than in the stressful conditions of the workplace.

These prescriptions go well beyond what all but a few well-educated financial managers in the UK now have at the outset of their careers, and well beyond anything that can be regarded as practical politics as a requirement for Institute membership in the foreseeable future. The prescribed studies would take at least seven years of higher education - more probably eight. In a British setting, this sounds like a long time. However, to put it in perspective, it may be noted that lawyers in the US spend seven years at the university and physicians spend eight. The periods are divided between four years of undergraduate pre-professional study followed by three years (for lawyers) or four years (for physicians) in a professional school. For physicians, there will be further specialised study beyond that.

The Proposals in the Solomons Report

Because the above prescriptions go beyond what is presently practical, they are only distantly related to the proposals put forward in 1974 in the Solomons Report "Prospectus for a Profession". Those proposals did not require (though they looked favourably on) a base of liberal studies. They did not focus on financial managers but attempted to cater for a broad spectrum of accountants. They recognised Britain's limited resources and were stripped down to the bare essentials. Even so, they were well in advance of what was then (and still is) expected of prospective chartered accountants.

Briefly summarising my main proposals, I recommended the following:

- For non-graduates, two years of full-time study of a prescribed curriculum at a university or polytechnic, leading to a Diploma in Higher Education. The curriculum was designed to provide the professional education needed by an entrant into the accountancy profession. I would now wish to modify this proposal, as I shall explain later.

- For the so-called non-relevant graduates (i.e., those taking degrees in arts or sciences not specifically related to the accountancy profession), full-time study through one calendar year of the same curriculum designed for the Diploma in Higher Education. At the end of the year, those graduates would be awarded a special graduate diploma. This proposal also now needs modification.

- As all candidates, including the relevant graduates who had already followed an approved curriculum at a university or polytechnic, had already been examined at their educational institution, there seemed to me to be no need for a further Institute examination of the usual academic type. However, I proposed a different kind of test at a later stage.

- Theoretical study would be followed by three years of work experience, not necessarily under a training contract, in a "recognised training establishment" which would have to meet specified standards. My 1974 proposals called for at least one year of work experience in public practice, one year in industry, and one year in either, chosen by the candidate to suit his or her career plans. I shall come back shortly to this proposal, which I would now also wish to modify.

- During the period of work experience, there would be four

or five months of practical instruction, of a kind I have already described. This might be obtained in the training department of a professional firm, an industrial company, in a polytechnic, at one of the private tutorial establishments, or perhaps in a new, specially designed institution, which I called a Practical Instruction Centre, to be set up by the profession itself.

- After the practical instruction had proved its value, I would be willing to reduce the required period of work experience to two years.

- As a final condition for Institute membership, I proposed that there be a test of professional competence. There is not time now to go into this proposal. The Institute has so far judged it to be impractical. The Chartered Institute of Public Finance and Accounting on the other hand , has been demonstrating, during the last few years, that is is quite practical and can be implemented successfully. However, one does have to recognise that their numbers are smaller than our Institute's.

- There were proposals for a fellowship qualification and a continuing education requirement. I shall not discuss these matters here, although continuing professional education, the form it should take and whether it should be mandatory, are matters of great importance. Preparation for professional responsibility is increasingly thought of these days as a life-long process. The attainment of a professional qualification is important only because people think it is important. The attainment of the status of chartered accountant does not itself change a person's capacities. Personal growth should continue throughout most of one's working life; and it is the purpose of continuing education to promote this process of maturation. The problem is to know how to make it effective.

In light of hindsight, and speaking six years after the publication of my proposals, it seems to me that there are three, and only three, major changes and I would make if I were writing my report today. First, it is clear that the Diploma of Higher Education, a two year diploma, has not been well received by British educators; and in any case I now question whether it was realistic to expect to cover all the things that I wanted to cover in my model curriculum in the space of two academic years. I would therefore now press for an all graduate profession, and my two-year Diplomas in Higher Education would become a three-year degree programme. With the recent demographic changes and the consequent reduction of pressure to gain entry into the universities or polytechnics there is nothing visionary or impractical in this proposal. In any case, only about 30% of persons entering into new training contracts are now not graduates.

As a corollary to the extension of the two-year diploma programme to a three-year degree, I believe that the one calendar year of the graduate diploma should be extended to 18 months for those non-relevant graduates who have covered none of the ground previously - virtually an MBA degree with a concentration in accounting. Partial exemption could be given to graduates with semi-relevant degrees.

The third modification that I would make to my 1974 proposals is to provide for more flexibility in the type of work experience that would qualify for Institute membership. I would now allow a candidate to divide the three-year training period between professional practice or industry and commerce in whatever way seems best for the candidate so long as the training was obtained in a recognised training establishment.

The key proposal is the one calling for a considerable increase in full-time professional education for all entrants. The present one year foundation course, which non-relevant graduates now need not take, would become either a full relevant degree or (for non-relevant graduates) a graduate diploma requiring 18 months of full-time study. At present, a non-relevant graduate who has had no professional studies before entering into a training contract can, if he chooses, spend twenty-six weeks of study leave (the maximum allowed) in classes, though I am sure that few, if any, trainees do that. Typically the amount of full-time study will be much less. I do not want to discount part-time study too heavily. It has its place. But however good it is, it is a second best.

The Education and Training Directorate's Policy Statement

I believe that the crucial test of whether chartered accountants belong to a learned profession - and this is regardless of whether they are destined to become financial managers or practitioners - is to ask how much study is expected of them as they prepare for entry into their profession, and how broad those studies are required to be. With respect to both of those dimensions, length and breadth of study, I find the Institute's recently published "Review of Education and Training Policy" (January 1980) disturbing and profoundly disappointing. In a list of seven areas of what the Education and Training Directorate call the "basic technical knowledge" of a chartered accountant (Paragraph 5(a)) only one refers to anything beyond accounting, taxation and auditing. No wonder that the document goes on to say that "this (i.e., the basic technical knowledge) can be imparted in a comparatively short period of time in an academic environment and is readily assessed by examination". If you are prepared to accept the Education and Training Directorate's blinkered view of what a chartered accountant needs to know as we prepare to enter the Institute's second century, you will no doubt share that judgement. I think it is an invitation to the Institute to become a second-rate institution.

A Convergent or Divergent Profession

It is time now to focus on those prospective Institute members who are preparing to become financial managers. My 1974 proposals were designed for what I hoped would shortly become an integrated profession. I provided for a limited amount of differentiation in the syllabuses and examination subjects to be taken by those going into public practice, the public sector or financial management and, as I have already indicated, I allowed a degree of choice between training in a practising office or in a business enterprise. But I wanted, as far as possible, to maintain a unified profession, while allowing to a limited degree for the special needs of its separate branches.

In "Prospectus for a Profession" I argued that the forces causing the two main branches of our profession to converge were more powerful than those causing them to diverge. Looking ahead, I saw three forces making for convergence:

- Auditing would increasingly use a "systems approach", causing auditors and management accountants to think more alike.

- Auditors would become financial advisers to small clients, and would therefore increasingly use the same skills as financial managers.

- The expansion of the management advisory services side of public practice and the increasing involvement of auditors with forecasts would also bring the two branches closer together.

I believe now that I overestimated those forces and underestimated the forces making for divergence. The most powerful of those forces is the auditor's tradition of independence from his clients as compared with the financial manager's commitment to his company and his industry. The simple fact seems to be that the two branches, though they may sometimes use the same skills, still for the most part have different interests and different objectives.

If financial management had been recognised as a separate profession in 1880, it is inconceivable that preparation for it would have been identical with that for the auditing profession and in particular that the experience requirement for a financial manager would have called for three-years work in an auditor's office. Yet the Education and Training Directorate believes that what was good enough in 1880 is good enough today and will be good enough tomorrow. In the Policy Review already referred to, they say (paragraph 6 (d)):

"The Directorate believes.... that personal professional qualities can best be developed from experience in a practising office. It has considered the special need to provide for the many members who turn to commerce or industry, but believes that the fundamental qualities looked for in chartered accountants, wherever they may work, are those developed during the period of training in the practising office;...."

I can only say that if that remains the Institute's policy, I would be surprised if the financial managers of the future continued to find the Institute a congenial organisation to represent them. Since 1974, the other accounting bodies in this country have developed their curricula along specialised lines to meet their special needs, and the Institute's undifferentiated curriculum looks increasingly ill-adapted to serve the needs of financial managers.

Educating Financial Managers in America

You can usually learn something about the nature of a problem in one country by looking to see how it is handled in another country, though differences in the environment make it dangerous to suppose that one country's methods can quickly be transferred elsewhere. I am familiar with the American scene, and though Britain and America are in many ways so alike, the differences are also significant. There, financial managers are almost invariably graduates. Most will have taken a bachelor's degree (requiring four years of study) in business administration, and many of those will have followed it up by taking an MBA degree, sometimes by part-time study in an evening programme of a kind that many universities offer. Those with bachelor's degrees not in business administration will probably have chosen economics or engineering as their major subject at the undergraduate level, though it may also have been in some field quite unrelated to business. It should be remembered, in any case, that in America the curriculum for a bachelor's degree, no matter what the major field is, will generally be much broader and less specialised than a bachelor's degree typically is here.

Those with a bachelor's degress in non-business subject are more likely than the business graduates to go on to take an MBA, requiring two years of full-time study or its equivalent in part-time study.

Although many financial managers gain the CPA qualification after graduation, and CPAs are found at the very top of several giant American corporations, it is less common over there for financial managers to get a professional qualification after a degree than is the case here. Two of the most important organisations of financial managers, the Financial Executives Institute and the National Association of Accountants, do not hold examinations or give qualifications. However, the latter body (NAA) has fairly recently established an affiliate, the Institute of Management Accounting, for the purpose of holding examinations leading to the award of a Certificate in Management Accounting (CMA).

The Future of Business Education in Britain

The oldest collegiate school of business in the world, the Wharton School of the University of Pennsylvania, will celebrate its centenary next year. There is no business school, graduate or undergraduate, in the UK that is nearly that old. Both the London and Manchester Business Schools were established only in 1965. What American universities were doing for business education from 1881 onward had to be done here, for much of the past century, by the accounting profession. There is no reason why a chartered accountant's office and a training contract should continue to be a principal entry into the world of managemnet, whether financial management or any other; and I do not believe that it will for much longer.

But we should be cautious about making predictions. A comparison of Britain in 1880 and Britain in 1980 leaves one in no doubt that a financial manager then would have had a hard time foreseeing the world we live in. In 1880 prices were falling at the rate of 2% per annum, in 1980 they are rising at an annual rate of 19%. Then, the bank rate was 3%. Now the minimum lending rate is 17%. Then, the standard rate of income tax was 5d (old pence) in the £ or roughly 2%. Now the basic rate is 30%. The telephone had just been invented and was regarded as a curiosity. Today there are over 23,000,000 telephones here. Perhaps there were some wiseacres around in 1880 who could have foretold some of these changes though I doubt it. My long range inquiry into education and training of the accountancy profession would have benefited from a crystal ball in 1973. I didn't have one then; and I don't have one now.

D. Solomons, BCom, DSc(Econ), FCA
Professor of Accounting,
Wharton School, University of
Pennsylvania

ACCOUNTING EDUCATION: AN INTERNATIONAL PERSPECTIVE

DAVID SOLOMONS
WHARTON SCHOOL, UNIVERSITY OF PENNSYLVANIA

Empirical research in accounting has changed the nature of our subject in recent years and has added much to our knowledge. But one question that it has notably avoided is the one that should underlie all educational planning, national or international. What goes into the making of a good accountant? Or, putting it another way, how do good accountants get that way? Formulating an educational program without an answer to that question is like buying a map before you have decided where you want to travel.

WHAT MAKES A GOOD ACCOUNTANT?

The Long Range Enquiry into Education and Training that I conducted for the British accountancy profession between 1972 and 1974[1] took that thought as its starting point. Much more time and money than we had would have been necessary to pursue it to the bitter end, and even now no one has really studied empirically what makes a good accountant. Of course, accountants are not a homogeneous species, and the qualities and skills that go to make a good tax practitioner are no doubt different from those exhibited by a good auditor and even more different from those that make a good financial manager. So to the question "What makes a good accountant?" there must be several answers, none of them simple. And while accounting education still has a common core, the divergences between the various specialties are probably becoming more important rather than less.

Introducing an international dimension complicates the question further, for accountants do not have the same responsibilities in all countries, and therefore the criteria by which a "good" accountant is to be recognized will vary somewhat from place to place. This poses difficult questions for a body like IFAC's Education Committee, when it attempts to draft a universally acceptable set of guidelines for the development of accounting education and training around the world.

At one of the discussions I held during the Long Range Enquiry, I asked a group of British accountants what qualities they looked for in prospective recruits to their firms. Most of the answers I got put integrity first. An ability to communicate and general intelligence were also frequently cited. But of course these qualities are not peculiar to accountants. They are found in all professions. The one quality, it seems to me, that distinguishes accountants from other professionals is numeracy. Yet no member of the group I interrogated mentioned it. Presumably it was too obvious to be noted - yet it is the only quality I can think of that separates accountants from other professionals. As I said in my 1974 report, "an accountant without numeracy...is like a musician who is tone-deaf."

But anyone who presumes to offer an educational plan for accountants must be able to say more than that. If an accountant does not have more than average skill in handling numbers or, more generally, quantitative data, he has probably chosen the wrong profession. But computational skill alone may mean no more than adroitness in using a pocket calculator. The qualities that one looks for in a good accountant cannot stop there.

In an inquiry I conducted a few years ago for the Canadian Institute of Chartered Accountants into one aspect of their examination system, I addressed a questionnaire to a number of accounting educators, training directors of professional firms and others (including three recent examinees), asking them among other things what qualities or skills (other than book knowledge) a professional examination should seek to test. Presumably those qualities are the same as the qualities that distinguish potentially successful entrants into the profession from those who have less potential for success. From the collective wisdom of the respondents to my questionnaire, the following list of skills emerged - skills that a professional accountant needs and without which he will fail, however much book knowledge he has.

1. The ability to sift relevant from irrelevant information.

2. Diagnostic skill, i.e., the ability to recognize the problems most deserving attention in a complex situation and to rank them in some rough order of priority.

3. Capacity to analyze data both to aid in the diagnosis and to point the way to recommendations for action.

4. The capacity to bring book knowledge drawn from diverse subject areas to bear, in an integrated manner, on a problem situation.

5. The ability to formulate proposals in a logical and realistic manner.

6. The ability to communicate results to a client succinctly and coherently.

Of course, this is a list of necessary, not sufficient, skills, making for success in an accounting career. There are personal qualities as well that a successful accountant must have, such as integrity, industry, and an ability work with others, that are different in kind and generally not less important than the qualities just listed. These personal qualities, if they can be tested at all, would have to be tested by some quite different means from those with which educators are at present familiar. They are also qualities that are either inborn or are derived from family or social environments or from early education. Higher education, I suspect, can contribute little to them.

The skills listed above are skills that higher education can help to develop, and it is by its contribution to those skills that its success should be measured. Presumably anyone entering upon tertiary education would have them to some degree already, so that it is a matter of cultivating them rather than implanting them in an empty seedbed, so to speak.

It is worth mentioning here a study that has recently been conducted by the Educational Testing Service, of Princeton, NJ, (ETS), for the

American Institute of Certified Public Accountants into the need for a test for admission to accounting programs.[2] The test would be comparable with the Graduate Management Admission Test (GMAT), but would focus on accounting rather than management. The ETS inquiry has elicited opinions from a large sample of accounting educators about the skills that are thought to be necessary for successful performance in accounting programs (i.e., educational programs in accounting).

A questionnaire survey of that kind should not be confused with an inquiry into the really interesting question—what makes a good accountant—for they are two stages apart. One stage away from the important question would be to ask knowledgeable people what they *think* makes a good accountant. The ETS inquiry asks what people think makes a good accounting *student* - a question that cannot do much to improve accounting education, for before an admission test can be devised, it is obviously necessary to make assumptions about the kind of education to which the student is to be admitted.

One manifestation of the wide gap that separates success in accounting from success in accounting programs can be seen by contrasting the great importance invariably attached to communication skills by persons working in the profession and the low priority attached to those skills in accounting education. It would be unrealistic for an admission test to give much weight to verbal aptitude, for few accounting courses, or courses in related subjects, at the present time offer much reward for verbal skills. Yet, paradoxically, ETS's respondents did attach weight to communication skills as a predictor of success in accounting programs.

ENQUIRIES INTO CURRICULUM CONTENT

Until more is known about what it takes to make a good accountant, an empirical foundation is lacking on which accounting educators can base prescriptions. I am not referring to enquiries that have asked various groups of respondents to rank or rate the importance of different subject areas for the purpose of constructing a curriculum. That kind of enquiry has been conducted over and over again. *Horizons for a Profession* did it in 1967 in the United States. William Vatter did it in 1964 in Australia. More recently it has been done on a considerable scale again in the United States by Richard Flaherty in his 1979 American Accounting Association study, *The Core of the Curriculum for Accounting Majors.* These studies are useful (I hope) for educators.

But they do not tell us anything about how good accountants get that way.

My own 1974 study for the British profession did not seek opinions about the content of accounting curricula. It did ask a large sample of working accountants of all kinds about the importance they attached to each of a long list of techniques, subject areas, and job responsibilities. For each topic, respondents were asked (a) in respect of their principal activity to rate the importance to them of having a working knowledge of that topic in their present work and (b) to indicate whether they thought that the probable importance of the topic to whomever would be doing their present job or its nearest equivalent ten years hence would have increased, decreased, or remained the same. It may be of some interest for this conference to recall that, focusing first on the English chartered accountants, who were the largest group, the only topics, in a list of over eighty, that were expected by more than 50% of the respondents to be more important ten years hence were accounting for inflation, audit of computer systems, foreign languages and international accounting, and comparative accounting methods. Interestingly, the cost and management accountants differed little from this assessment, though they expected slightly less growth in importance (to them) of computer auditing and slightly more in the importance of appraisal of management performance.

THE INGREDIENTS OF SUCCESS

Before leaving the question "How do good accountants get that way?," we might take note of two U.S. studies that came closer to addressing that question, one in the public accounting field and the other in financial management. Hans Johnson, of the University of Texas at San Antonio, mailed questionnaires to 365 persons who became partners in the U.S. of the "Big Eight" in 1973 and got responses from 229 of them.[3] His questions were designed to elicit the new partner's rankings of various skills as factors contributing to success in their fields. The ranking he obtained put technical proficiency first, leadership and supervision second, ability to deal effectively with client-related problems third, decision-making fourth, followed by oral and written communication. The relatively low ranking given to communication skills is curiously at odds with another answer that rated English as the most important non-accounting college course contributing to their professional development, with economics as a distant second and then mathematics. Information about personal characteristics that were thought to be important contributors to success was also obtained in this study.

Note that though Johnson's enquiry was concerned with success in accounting, not with academic success, it did rely on *opinions* about the factors contributing to success rather than on a study of the actual differences, in education and personal characteristics, that separated successful from unsuccessful accountants. A study carried out for the Financial Executives Institute in the U.S. by the consulting firm of A.T. Kearney & Co. and reported on in 1970 did try to uncover the sources of success of financial managers.[4]

In any study of the ingredients of success, there will always be debate about the definition of success, and the use of a money measure is almost inevitable. The Kearney group used total annual cash compensation judged against norms or averages for the job classification, age, type of industry (durable goods manufacturing, non-durable goods manufacturing and non-manufacturing) and size of company measured by annual sales. The job classification provided for three levels:

First level	top financial officers
Second level	controller
Third level	budget and general accounting executive

At each level, subjects were divided into the more successful and the less successful, and the characteristics that differentiated the two groups were examined.

As our primary concern in this session is education, we need not linger over the personal characteristics that were found to contribute to success. However, there is no clear cut line between what is and what is not acquired through education. Education can presumably take some credit for analytical and communication skills, which were found to be among the more important ingredients for success for financial managers, as well as for technical skills, which were placed among the less important ones. In this last respect, incidentally, the Kearney study is at variance with Johnson's study of partners.

The educational differences that were found between the successful and the unsuccessful financial managers will give more satisfaction to some accounting educators than to others. Some of the significant results are summed up in the following table.

Percentage of Each Category Rated "Highly Successful"

	Non-business Undergraduate Degree	Finance/Accounting Undergraduate Degree	Other Business Undergraduate Degree
With MBA	28%	14%	N/A
Without MBA	21%	14%	10%

In other words, this research suggests that a non-business undergraduate degree followed by an MBA is more likely to produce a successful financial executive than any other kind of education. But it is disturbing (to those of us who teach in undergraduate business programs) to find that, without an MBA, a non-business first degree is more likely to lead to success in this field than a business degree, whether accounting oriented or not. However, these labels no doubt cover a wide variety of curricula, with different mixtures of business and non-business subjects in what is finally labeled as a business degree. Moreover, the non-business first degrees will have included degrees in engineering and economics. They must not be assumed all to have been in the humanities.

The successful group believed more strongly than the others that a financial executive would benefit from a broad education in the liberal art. However, when asked which discipline they would regard as very important if they were to repeat their education, all respondents ranked accounting and control as most important, and gave high ratings also to English composition, finance, economics, human relations, mathematics and statistics, a fairly high rating to law and low ratings to literature, history and political science, sociology and psychology and also to production and marketing.

The FEI study is a start in a direction where much more work is needed. We should be devoting less time to polling opinions and more time to analyzing the facts. Identifying the relevant facts is itself no small task.

EDUCATIONAL SURVEYS

I turn now to look at some different approaches to accounting education in different parts of the world. Most of my attention will be directed to the differences between the United States and the United

Kingdom, for the simple reason that those are the two countries I know best, though I shall not ignore the rest of the world. In any case, British and American ideas on professional education exercise a strong influence on much of the rest of the world, and the differences between them are of some importance when considering the prospects for international harmonization.

A survey of accounting education around the world is already under way under the aegis of the Education Committee of IFAC, working through IFAC's regional organizations.[5] Thus UEC in 1977 published a report of its Main Committee IX entitled *Training for the Profession: A Comparative Study,* in which a great deal of information about the education, training, and certification of accountants in 15 countries of western Europe was summarized. A survey is being conducted by the Confederation of Asian and Pacific Accountants (CAPA) of education in its area, and a paper was presented on this subject at the 9th CAPA Conference in October 1979 in Manila.[6] The Inter-American Accounting Association (IAAA) is also committed to the preparation of a survey of education in its area.

Having myself had the task of trying to present a coherent picture of the education and training arrangements of six professional bodies within the tiny area of the British Isles, I have nothing but sympathy for those responsible for the IFAC surveys. Responses to questionnaires are slow coming in or do not come in at all. Because regulations are consistently changing, some of the information is obsolete before it can be collated. National institutions and their regulations vary in so many respects that reducing them to a pattern may defy ingenuity. And changes in the composition of a committee charged with a task of this kind may rob the inevitably protracted work of all continuity.

These surveys are a necessary step towards harmonization; and it is indeed true that a journey of a thousand miles starts with a single step. But for reasons that I shall consider below, I do not believe that rapid progress towards educational harmonization is likely. I am not even sure that, in the short run, we are moving towards it rather than away from it. Before explaining this gloomy prognosis, some discussion of the meaning of the harmonization concept is necessary.

WHAT DOES HARMONIZATION MEAN?

Harmonization is a word with a warmly comforting sound, but its meaning is not clear. In the present context it can mean:

1. uniform minimum standards of *quality* of education and training (E & T) delivered by E & T systems

2. the universal adoption of a uniform E & T system

3. uniform minimum standards of professional competence

4. uniformity of qualifications to practice, or their acceptance as equivalent for purposes of mutual recognition.

The first two of these meanings are concerned with inputs to the educational process, the last two are concerned with outputs; the first and third meanings contemplate a diversity of process leading to uniform results; while the second and fourth meanings look more to a uniformity of system, which is assumed to lead to uniform results.

The two principal initiatives that are going forward at the present time to secure harmonization in any of the above senses are to be found within IFAC and within the EEC. The IFAC initiative is the broader of the two, both geographically and in its objective, and will therefore be discussed first.

THE IFAC GUIDELINES ON EDUCATION AND TRAINING

The International Federation of Accountants (IFAC), which has only been in existence since 1977, is an organization of organizations. It has at present 75 member bodies representing 750,000 accountants in 57 countries. The Council of IFAC expects, in 1980 or 1981, to approve a set of guidelines on education and training on which the Federation's Education Committee has been working for some time. These guidelines have as their main purposes:

(i) establishing the essential elements on which education and training programs for all accountants should be founded, whether they are destined to exercise their profession in public practice, in industry or commerce or in government services, and

(ii) recommending the minimum standards and conditions of professional education and training that an accountant should successfully complete in order to obtain membership of his professional body and to exercise his profession.

These two objectives do not correspond neatly to any of the four meanings of harmonization given above, but the first objective straddles the first two meanings given, while the second objective straddles the last two meanings.

In seeking to achieve its educational objectives, IFAC is attempting to prescribe minima for:

(i) the standard of general education that should precede professional education

(ii) the theoretical content of professional studies and examinations

(iii) the standards of examinations leading to qualification

(iv) the practical experience requirement in education and training.

The Federation, however, is not finding it easy to reconcile the many differences that exist among the approaches of the member countries to these matters.

The differences are the result of different economic conditions, cultural outlooks, governmental influences, the organization and role of the accounting profession, the availability of higher education, national traditions concerning the role of apprenticeship, and the relationship in each country between its institutions of higher education and the professions. Just to contrast the positions in the U.S. and the U.K. on some of these matters, in the U.S. the CPA certificate is granted by the several states, in the U.K. professional qualifications are granted by private institutions; higher education is more widely available in the U.S. than in the U.K., the professions and the universities are closer to each other and the importance attached to practical experience in relation to theoretical study, especially at the prequalification stage, is much less. Other national differences elsewhere may be cited, such as the protracted study of economics that precedes professional study in the Netherlands, the more legalistic approach to accounting in Germany than in the Anglo-Saxon countries, and the simpler demands (in some respects) made on the profession in the developing countries than in those that are more developed.

In light of these and many other national differences, the difficulty that IFAC is having in securing agreement even on *minimum* guidelines is easy to understand. It must further be remembered that even when agreement has been reached, the guidelines will be merely hortatory; they will have no sanctions behind them; and as they will have to accommodate almost everything that any member country is already doing, there is little prospect that they will have an elevating influence on educational standards in the near future. In the longer run, it may be hoped, the outlook is more encouraging.

HARMONIZATION WITHIN THE EEC

In relation to the education and training of auditors, the European Economic Community is concerned with harmonization in the third and fourth senses of the word mentioned above. The EEC is concerned with the products of the educational process, not with the process itself. This is forthrightly expressed in an explanatory memorandum accompanying the Commission's draft Eighth Directive that was issued in December 1979. In its commentary on article 4 of the Directive, the memorandum states (p. 4):

> Education systems differ profoundly in the various member States, and there is not the slightest need to alter this state of affairs. What matters is the end result: the obtaining of a high qualification to be able to carry out statutory audits, in a way which provides all the necessary guarantees.

Elsewhere, the memorandum (p. 17) explains the objective of the Directive as "to create a Community framework guaranteeing that, in all the member States, persons authorized to carry out statutory audits of the accounts of limited liability companies have equivalent minimum qualifications." Work on the Directive has been proceeding for some eight years, and it may be two years more before it receives final approval. It is concerned with the protection of investors. It is not to be confused with other EEC proposals to give mutual recognition to professional qualifications of the member States. Those proposals are broader in scope and are at a much less advanced stage.

Much of the December 1979 draft of the Eighth Directive is concerned with matters outside the scope of this paper, such as establishing the auditor's independence and the recognition of auditors who are not natural persons. In fact, only articles 4, 5, and 6 are germane to our present purpose. Those articles are reproduced as Appendix A to this paper.

Article 4 states the educational requirements in broad terms, and implies that there shall be a two-part examination covering theory and practice. Article 5 specifies in more detail what the test of theoretical knowledge shall cover, and calls in addition for a test of the candidate's ability to apply his knowledge in practice. The relationship of the two tests to each other is the source of some confusion in some parts of the Community, and it is likely that the final Directive will differ somewhat from the December 1979 draft on this point (and no doubt on others also). The British accounting bodies are pressing for the substitution of an "assessment" of the candidate's training in place of a test of his practical ability.

The Eighth Directive is relatively narrow in its scope; it is concerned only with the qualifications of persons authorized to conduct statutory audits, so that many accountants within the EEC will not be touched by it. On the other hand, whereas the broader IFAC guidelines have no teeth, so to speak, the EEC Directive, when finally issued, will have the force of the Treaty of Rome behind it. Still, like almost all international standards, it represents a lowest common denominator. Virtually no present national practices will need to be changed. The effect of the Directive on the protection of investors will be visible, if at all, only in the distant future.

THE PROSPECTS FOR HARMONIZATION

It is not surprising that international harmonization proceeds so slowly and so superficially. What right have we to expect harmonization on a world scale when contiguous areas that speak the same language and answer to the same governments have not succeeded in securing internal harmonization? The public accountants of the 50 states of the United States have achieved uniformity on nothing except the use of a uniform CPA qualifying examination. The British Isles have six distinct professional organizations of accountants, each with its own educational requirements: there are even important educational differences between England and Scotland. The ten provinces of Canada, though they use a uniform final examination for chartered accountants, retain a number of educational requirements peculiar to each province. And Australia has two separate organizations, rather different from each other in character and both of them different from the accounting organization in New Zealand. And all of these territories (except for the province of Quebec in Canada) speak the same language and enjoy the same legal traditions.

DIVERGING DEVELOPMENTS IN THE U.S. AND THE U.K.

Professional organizations naturally reflect, at least in part, the characteristics of the nations to which they belong; and this is well exemplified by the accounting professions of Britain and the United States. Two years ago I surveyed the educational systems of the two countries in a paper published in the Netherlands. As it is unlikely that many participants in this Roundtable will have seen that paper, and as it is not in any important respect yet out of date, I am reproducing it, as background material, as Appendix B to this paper.

Instead of moving closer together, it seems as though, in the immediate future, British and American accounting education will move further apart. My reason for holding that view lies in the contrast between the current policy of the AICPA, as expressed in the Institute's statement, *Education Requirements for Entry into the Accounting Profession*, issued in May 1978, and the Review of Education and Training Policy issued by the Education and Training Directorate of the English Institute (ICAEW) in January 1980. The AICPA statement (pages 3 and 4) asserts that

> At least 150 semester hours of college study are needed to obtain the common body of knowledge for CPAs and should be the education requirement. For those who meet this standard, no qualifying experience should be required to sit for the CPA examination.[7]
>
> The scope and content of the educational program should approximate what is described in *Academic Preparation for Professional Accounting Careers*§ and should lead to the awarding of a graduate degree.

A sample program of the kind just described is set out in Table 4 of *Academic Preparation for Professional Accounting Careers*, and is reproduced as Appendix C to this paper.

Contrast the AICPA statement of 1978, which is still that Institute's policy, with the recent statement of the ICAEW's Education and Training Directorate. Paragraph 5(a) of that statement summarizes what is described as the accountant's "basic technical knowledge" under seven heads, all of them relating narrowly to accounting topics except one that calls for an ability to "understand the environment in which business organizations function, and the particular forces which can affeet that structure." This basic technical knowledge "can be imparted in a comparatively short period of time in an academic environment and is readily assessed by examination." So much for accounting education.

Most of the E & T Directorate's review is concerned with examinations rather than with education. There is, however, also a reaffirmation of the role of training contracts (the modern name for apprenticeship) in the Institute's scheme of things, and an adherence to the view that "training contracts should continue to be served in practicing accountants' offices." This in spite of the fact that one half of the Institute's 70,000 members are not engaged in public practice. If this policy statement does in fact represent the English Institute's best thinking on education and training, it seems likely that the Institute will enter its second century with an educational system that, at least as regards its non-accounting graduates, now a very important segment of its new recruits, will not be too different from that with which it began its existence in 1880. The gap between the British and American approaches to accounting education will have widened. That is one reason for thinking that we may be moving away from harmonization rather than towards it.

THE THIRD WORLD

Another reason for thinking that educational differentiation rather than harmonization may mark the remainder of this century is to be found in what is happening in the developing countries. As the American Accounting Association's 1978 Report, *Accounting Education and the Third World,* showed, countries that were formerly colonies of the imperial powers used educational material developed in the mother country and appropriate to that country rather than to its colonies. Accounting education in the former British colonies in Africa and Asia is still, to a considerable extent, held back by dependence on irrelevant subject matter and irrelevant methods unsuited to local conditions. This situation will no doubt change, as indigenous material and native teachers who have learned to think for themselves substitute ideas that better fit the needs of those countries. But by doing so, they will bring, for some time to come, more diversity and more disharmony rather than less. It will be part of the price we shall have to pay for the emergence of the Third World from the shadows of colonialism.

The Committee on International Accounting Operations and Education of the American Accounting Association, which was responsible for the preparation of *Accounting Education and the Third World*, presented a plan to help the developing countries to raise the level of accounting and of accounting education. The chapter of the report in which those recommendations are made is short, and it is reproduced as Appendix D to this paper.

IMPLICATIONS FOR INTERNATIONAL ACCOUNTING PRACTICE

On the educational front, there is not likely to be, in the near future, any considerable diminution of the impediments to international practice that are being discussed in other sessions of this conference, except perhaps within the EEC. Each country thinks its own arrangements are best, and develops them along its own lines. The influence of IFAC should be salutary, but I do not expect to see rapid and dramatic results. Too often the only way to get agreement is to settle for a collection of whatever common elements can be found within numerous conflicting systems, leaving each country free to develop on its own beyond the minimum set by the standards. But in the search for agreement, something valuable may be learned—that the way a country currently handles its problems may not be the only way or even the best way. And with that knowledge, the road to progress may be opened.

APPENDIX A

THE EUROPEAN ECONOMIC COMMUNITY'S EIGHTH DIRECTIVE (DRAFT OF DECEMBER 5, 1979), ARTICLES 4, 5, and 6.[9]

ARTICLE 4

1. A natural person may be approved to carry out the activities referred to in Article 1 only after having attained university entrance level, followed a programme of professional education and training and passed an examination of professional competence at graduate level which is organized or recognized by the State.

2. Such examination, the general content of which is set out in Article 5, shall guarantee in the most appropriate manner a good level of theoretical knowledge of subjects relevant to the auditing of accounts and the ability to apply such knowledge in practice.

ARTICLE 5

1. The test of theoretical knowledge included in the examination shall cover in particular the following subjects:

- auditing,
- evaluation and critical appraisal of balance sheet and profit and loss accounts,
- general accounting,
- problems relating to group accounts,
- cost and management accounting,
- internal control,
- accounting standards and method of evaluating balance sheet items and of determining results,
- company tax law,

- company criminal law,
- company law,

In so far as they are relevant to auditing:

- principles of law (civil, commercial, and social law),
- information and computer systems,
- business, general and financial management of business undertakings,
- mathematics and statistics,
- basic principles of financial management of business undertakings.

2. By way of derogation from paragraph 1, holders of a university degree or equivalent qualification in one or more of the subjects referred to in paragraph 1 may be exempted from the test of theoretical knowledge in the subjects covered by such degree or qualification.

3. The test included in the examination of ability to apply the theoretical knowledge in practice shall take place after a minimum of three years' practical training with an auditor approved pursuant to this Directive and involving principally the statutory audit of the annual accounts of companies.

4. By the way of derogation from paragraph 3, such practical training may take place after the test of theoretical knowledge referred to in paragraph 1.

ARTICLE 6

1. Member States may authorize persons to sit the examination of professional competence provided for in Article 4, notwithstanding the fact that they have not attained the level of study required under Article 4 if they can show:

(a) that they have for fifteen years engaged in activities enabling them to acquire sufficient experience in the field of finance, law and accountancy; or

(b) that they have for seven years engaged in such activities and have also undergone the practical training referred to in Article 5 (3) or (4) and are at least 25 years of age.

2. Member States may deduct periods of professional training in the subjects referred to in Article 5 (1) from the years of activity referred to in (a) and (b) above.

APPENDIX B

ACCOUNTING EDUCATION IN BRITAIN AND THE UNITED STATES: A SURVEY

BY DAVID SOLOMONS
ARTHUR YOUNG PROFESSOR OF ACCOUNTING
THE WHARTON SCHOOL
THE UNIVERSITY OF PENNSYLVANIA
Reproduced from: *Maandblad voor Accountancy en Bedrijfshuishoudkunde, May 1978.*

Anyone who looks at the accounting professions of the United States and of Great Britain with the eyes of an educator must be struck by the distance that now separates the systems of education and training in the two countries.

Starting from a common heritage, the two systems have diverged markedly. Many of the leaders of the American profession in the latter part of the nineteenth century had come to the U.S. from Britain to audit the accounts of enterprises financed by British capital, and had settled there. The first truly national organization of accountants, the American Association of Public Accountants, was founded in 1887, and these immigrant accountants were among its founders. They naturally brought with them the British notion of relying on apprenticeship as the principal method of preparation for entry into a profession. Yet within a few years this idea was eclipsed by a growing emphasis on formal education rather than on learning from experience. In Britain the idea of apprenticeship—a pupil learning his trade from a master has remained the basis of the professional education of accountants. The terminology has changed somewhat, so that what was formerly a contract of apprenticeship (in Scotland)[10] or articled clerkship (in England and Wales) has now become a training contract. But this is simply a new term for an old concept.

One must be careful about using the term "system" for either America or Britain in this context, for there is great diversity on both sides of the Atlantic. In the U.S., under its federal form of government, education and the regulation of the professions is largely in the hands of the states and as a consequence variations of every kind from state to state are the rule rather than the exception. More will be said about this later. In the United Kingdom, there is a different kind of diversity. There are different systems in England and Wales and in Scotland, and the two jurisdictions in Ireland introduce a further element of complexity. Moreover, throughout the British Isles, though the Institutes of Chartered Accountants are the oldest and most prestigious bodies of accountants which conduct examinations and grant qualifications, there are several other such bodies, somewhat to the confusion of the general public which has difficulty in finding its way among the plethora of designatory letters.

No system of accounting education can be understood without understanding the profession which the student of accounting will enter. In Britain it is a profession which is regulated by private organizations, and in which the state plays a minimal role. It does not grant qualifications and it is slow to interfere with the profession's conduct of its own affairs. These matters are handled by private voluntary bodies, under powers conferred by royal charters and by by-laws made thereunder, or under rules agreed to by the members. This is in marked contrast with the situation in the United States, as will be seen later.

THE INSTITUTE OF CHARTERED ACCOUNTANTS IN ENGLAND AND WALES

The largest though not the oldest body of accountants in the British Isles is the Institute of Chartered Accountants in England and Wales, which received its royal charter in 1880 and which at the end of 1976 had 64,000 members. This comprises about one half of all the qualified accountants in Britain. The Institute's membership is divided more or less equally between those in public practice and those engaged in industry, commerce and finance, public administration, education and other activities. It is particularly noteworthy that with some 30% of its members working in industry, the English Institute has more members working in that sector than does the Institute of Cost and Management

Accountants, a body which caters specifically for industrial accountants.

In spite of its large industrial membership, the English Institute is still thought of by most people outside the accounting profession as being primarily a body of practitioners, and its power structure and training requirements provide justification for this impression. The one characteristic that distinguishes a chartered accountant from other qualified accountants in Britian is that he or she must have entered into a training contract *with a chartered accountant in public practice* and have served in the practice for three years if a graduate or for four years if not a graduate. Theoretically, it is possible for the trainee to spend up to six months of this period on secondment to an industrial concern[11] to get first-hand experience of management accounting, but only in a minute number of cases has advantage been taken of this provision, for most practicing firms discourage their trainees from doing so. The chartered accountant's training, therefore, whatever work he may subsequently take up, is obtained in public practice, which for most trainees means predominantly in the field of auditing.

THE ENGLISH INSTITUTE'S EDUCATIONAL ARRANGEMENTS

Historically, the preparation of an English chartered accountant for his professional career has placed more emphasis on training than on education, and this emphasis is changing only slowly.

For a non-graduate, the minimum period of full-time study of accounting and related subjects (specifically law, economics and statistics) is one academic year of nine months. This is the period required for the so-called Foundation Course, which is typically taken at a polytechnic or college of further education before the start of the training contract. No further *full-time* study is required, although in the course of preparing for the two professional examinations which must be passed on the way to qualifying as a chartered accountant, short periods of full-time study may be pursued. Preparation for these examinations normally proceeds concurrently with the training contract, and under the terms of the contract, leave for full-time study may not exceed 26 weeks. Part-time study by correspondence or evening classes, still plays an important part in the professional education of chartered accountants.

It was not till 1970 that the English Institute's intake of graduates into the ranks of new trainees reached the 20% level. Since then the percentage has increased rapidly. By 1972 it had reached 30% and by 1974 it was over 50%. This does not mean, however, that over half of the new recruits into the Institute now devote a considerable amount of time at the university to the study of accounting and related disciplines. In 1972, only 16% of the total graduate entry and only 5% of entrants of all kinds into training contracts held "approved" degrees, corresponding roughly to what in America would be called accounting majors. Since 1972, these percentages are thought to have remained fairly stable. The picture is confused somewhat by the substantial number of overseas graduates who may have studied acounting but whose degrees are not recognized as "approved" degrees for the purposes of the Institute's statistics. But even taking these into account, it is probably safe to say that well over half of the graduates now entering the profession have degrees which include little or no accounting, though many of them will have degrees in economics or business studies. There will also be many with degrees in arts and science subjects. It should be remembered that neither Oxford nor Cambridge, whose graduates are held in the highest esteem, offer degrees in accounting or even in business administration. In setting the tone for the relations between higher education and the accounting profession in Britain, this fact has an importance which goes beyond the numbers of graduates involved. It is also important to remember that it is much less common in Britain than in the United States for arts and science graduates who seek a career in accounting or business to go on a second (master's) degree in those fields after completing their undergraduate studies.

Graduates holding degrees with enough profession-related study to be classified as "approved" degrees (in the technical sense only, for this does not mean that the Institute disapproves of other degrees) follow a slightly different path into the profession from other graduates, though considering that the "approved" graduate may have spent three years or more studying accounting, law and economics and other business-related subjects while the "non-approved" graduate may have spent no time at all on any subject related to business, the difference in treatment is not great, being limited to the Foundation or pre-professional stage. The graduate who holds an "approved" or "relevant" degree is given exemption from this stage and can proceed directly to preparation for the two professional examinations. The graduate with a non-business degree normally takes a "graduate conversion course" which, when satisfactorily completed, gives exemption from the Foundation examination. Conversion courses are offered by a number of polytechnics and by several private tutorial establishments. They usually consist either of full-time study of accounting, economics, law and statistics for a period of three months or two short periods of full-time study (typically one of 2-3 weeks and one of five weeks) with part-time study in between.

Most candidates prepare for the two professional examinations which all would-be chartered accountants have to pass, after the completion of or exemption from the Foundation stage, by taking courses with private tutorial establishments. These courses again are organized into short blocks of full-time study interspersed with guided reading and other part-time studies. A minority of candidates look to public-sector institutions, such as the polytechnics, in preparing for these examinations. There, the instruction is generally given in the evenings or by day-release spread out over a period of eighteen months for each examination. Incidentally, no exemptions from these examinations are given in recognition of prior study at a university or elsewhere.

THE SCOTTISH INSTITUTE

The oldest body of professional accountants in the British Isles is the Institute of Chartered Accountants of Scotland, the Edinburgh component of which received its Royal Charter in 1854, twenty-six years before the English Institute. It has over the years provided a somewhat more congenial climate for the academic study of accounting than has been found south of the border, and the Scottish Institute has always had closer links with the universities than its English counterpart. This led in 1960 to the introduction of a prescribed "academic year" in Scotland, whereby all non-graduate trainees were required to interrupt their practical training to devote one academic year to the full-time study of accounting, law and economics at a Scottish university.[12] The importance of this development lay in the fact that this was the first time that any British body of accountants had required all of its trainees to have spent some period of full-time study at a university (though, ironically, it was only trainees not studying for a degree who were required to pursue profession-related studies while there).

The "academic year" experiment in Scotland lasted until 1973, when it was replaced by the present system. Now, entrants into the Scottish Institute must hold a degree (in any field) or an accounting diploma requiring two years of full-time study. Graduates in fields other than accounting must complete a one-year diploma course in accounting and related subjects in an institution of higher education. These arrangements correspond to the Foundation stage in the English Institute but are more rigorous in their requirements.

Unlike the English Institute, which provides no instruction itself directly for prospective chartered accountants, the Scottish Institute does provide its own classes in Edinburgh and Glasgow in preparation for its professional examinations, and attendance at them by trainees is compulsory. Instruction (full-time) is provided in blocks of two or three weeks at a time, amounting in total to about 15 weeks of instruction. Though this is less in total than English Institute candidates typically spend in preparing for their professional examinations, it must be remembered that considerably more time will have been devoted in Scotland to study at the pre-professional stage.

The Scottish Institute, like its English sister, attaches great importance to on-the-job training. Graduates must serve under a training contract with a practitioner for three years, non-graduates for four. No part of these periods may be spent in industrial or commercial employment, even though a great many Scottish chartered accountants leave public practice soon after qualifying and spend the rest of their working lives in such work.

OTHER BRITISH QUALIFICATIONS

To get a complete picture of the British profession's educational arrangements, one would have to look at the requirements of the Association of Certified Accountants, the Institute of Management Accountants and the Chartered Institute of Public Finance and Accountancy. This would take more space than we can spare. Only the first of these three bodies has members in public practice as auditors. The other two are more specialized, as their names imply. Many accountants in Britain are members of more than one body. In general, these institutions give graduates exemptions from certain of their examination requirements, usually on a subject-for-subject basis. They all have experience requirements for admission to membership. Preparation for their examinations is generally by part-time study in the evening or by day-release at a polytechnic, or by means of correspondence tuition.

A concerted effort to integrate the British accounting profession was made ten years ago and failed when it was rejected by a vote of the members of the English Institute. Since then the various bodies have gone their own way educationally as in other matters. As a result, educational institutions are faced with a diversity of curricula which confront professional students, and this naturally adds to the burdens placed on them. Though in the economic marketplace generally competition may be expected to lead to product improvement, there is little evidence that that has been the result of the fragmented state of the British profession. Probably most British accounting educators would agree that the educational outlook would be brighter now if the vote on integration had gone differently in 1970.

THE C.P.A. QUALIFICATIONS IN THE U.S.A.

It is curious that in Britain, while post-secondary education is in the hands of the state in accounting as in other fields (except for the private tutorial establishments that have been referred to above), the conferment of professional qualifications is wholly in private hands. In the United States, on the other hand, private and public institutions share in the educational process while the principal professional qualification is granted by state bodies. This is the certified public accountants certificate (C.P.A.) which is conferred by 54 State Boards of Accountancy - one in each of the fifty states and four others covering other territories. Since each state is largely autonomous in matters of professional regulation, there is plenty of room for diversity in the requirements for becoming a C.P.A. Fortunately, this diversity has not for a good many years now extended to the C.P.A. examination, for since 1952 all the State Boards have used the uniform C.P.A. Examination administered for them by the American Institute of C.P.A.s. But there are other requirements to be satisfied by a prospective C.P.A besides passing an examination, and it is these other requirements that exhibit considerable variation from state to state. Most states require a college degree but some do not. In some states, the degree curriculum to be followed is specified in great detail, in other it is not. Most states have an experience requirement which must be satisifed before a C.P.A. certificate will be granted, though a few do not; and there are many variations in detail among those that do. The newest area for variation in the C.P.A. regulations among the states concerns continuing professional education after the certificate has been issued. Though a similar diversity of regulations afflicts other professions such as law and medicine, in none is it so serious as in accountancy, for large accounting firms have nation-wide practices and local variations in the right to practice can cause particular inconvenience. It is not surprising that there is considerable support for the idea that the C.P.A. certificate should be a national, not a state, qualification; but it does not seem likely that this change will come about soon.

THE ROLE OF AMERICAN UNIVERSITIES IN ACCOUNTING EDUCATION

When a British accountant refers with satisfaction to the increasing number of graduates who are entering the profession, he is not necessarily referring to graduates who have studied accounting or closely related subjects as part of their degree studies and it is probably fair to say that the British profession still does not look to the accounting departments of the country's universities and polytechnics as its major source of recruits. This fact is reflected also in the scanty representation of accounting educators on important committees within the professional bodies and the very modest financial support which accounting departments receive from the large professional firms. In all of these respects, the situation in America is very different.

In the first place, the typical C.P.A. has graduated, probably from a state university, with a degree in which accounting was a major constituent. In 1977-78 it is estimated that over 46,000 accounting graduates will leave the universities with bachelor's degrees and over 6000 more with master's degrees[13] and that 28% of these graduates will enter the public accounting profession (though of course they will not all stay there). These figures alone show what an enormous impact *accounting* graduates have on the accounting profession in the United States. It is not simply that virtually all new C.P.A.s are graduates. They are graduates whose university studies, either at the undergraduate or graduate level and sometimes at both have been oriented towards professionally relevant subjects.

The reference above to a "typical" C.P.A.'s education may given an impression that the accounting programs that are available to students entering the universities and colleges are marked by a high degree of uniformity. Such an impression would be quite misleading. The fact that many accounting students will later take the C.P.A. examination and will look for a university curriculum that will help them to prepare for it does tend to impose limits on the degree of diversification to be found. Nevertheless, the choice of educational institutions which confronts the prospective student in America is a rich one indeed — richer, perhaps, than in any other country. He or she has a choice between state schools,[14]) private non-denominational schools and church-affiliated schools; between co-educational schools or schools admitting only males or females; between universities with large graduate programs and colleges with no graduate programs at all; between schools with traditional four-year programs and "cooperative" schools that alternate periods of study and employment; between schools that emphasize scholarship and those that emphasize athletics or narrow vocationalism. These are the more important choices. They do not exhaust the list.

THE C.P.A. EXAMINATION AND OTHER QUALIFICATION REQUIREMENTS

For would-be accountants, the main force drawing these many strands together is the C.P.A. examination. As was explained earlier, this examination is conducted by the American Institute of C.P.As on behalf of the 54 state boards of accountancy. It is held twice a year in over 100 examination centers throughout the country, and each examination attracts over 40,000 candidates. The examination covers accounting theory, accounting practice (two papers), auditing and business law. Clearly an examination conducted on such a huge scale presents formidable problems of administration and of ensuring equity in grading. For this reason, the examiners make extensive use of multiple-choice questions. In this and other ways, the examination is designed to secure ease and fairness of grading. To anyone who believes that a professional examination should above all else be a test of professional competence and judgement, the C.P.A. examination leaves much to be desired.

Perhaps because of the shortcomings of the C.P.A. examination, many of the states have not been content to rely on it alone to select those who are to be granted the C.P.A. certificate, but have in addition stipulated, sometimes in great detail, the nature and extent of the professional education that the candidate must have received. Perhaps the most important example is to be found in the state of New York, the first state to have required C.P.As to hold a college degree. New York has for many years had rigorous standards, defined in terms of the number of hours of formal instruction that a candidate must have received in accounting, finance, economics, law and other subjects (including general educational subjects) at the collegiate level before he can take the C.P.A. examination in that state. Now New York is considering raising its educational requirements still higher in the early 1980's to a level where they can be satisfied only with a master's degree in accounting. One or two other states have already gone down this road.

Side by side with this piecemeal regulation of accounting education by the separate states, a more coordinated approach is now being attempted through the joint efforts of the AICPA and the American Accounting Association. The latter body speaks for accounting educators throughout the country. A joint committee set up by the Institute and the Association, and now joined by other accounting bodies, is working on plans for a national accounting accreditation scheme. The details of the scheme have yet to be worked out, but its purpose is unambiguously to maintain and eventually to raise standards of accounting education by withholding the stamp of approval from programs which do not meet the standards. It seems possible that at some future time admission to the C.P.A examination might be open only to candidates who have graduated from accredited programs. A set of well thought-out national standards, if the fifty-four juriisdictions would agree to accept them, would seem to be preferable to the present patchwork of regulations by the several states.

EXPERIENCE REQUIREMENTS FOR C.P.A.s AND CHARTERED ACCOUNTANTS

By contrast with the situation in Britain, where the professional organizations attach great importance to a period of work experience under more or less carefully monitored conditions as a prerequisite to obtaining some of their qualifications, in the United States there has been a steady movement towards substituting education for experience in preparing for entry into the profession. In Britain, at least for chartered accountants, not only must the candidate have had at least three years experience, but he must have gained it under a formal training contract with his employer in public practice. In America many states require two years of experience for those holding bachelor's degrees and one year for those with master's degrees. But there are a few states which do not require any experience at all, and some others that allow a master's degree to be substituted for experience. However, in those states which have dispensed with an experience requirement for the C.P.A certificate, a distinction is generally drawn between being "certified" and being "licensed to practice", and a period of experience is still required before a license to practice as an independent practitioner will be issued.

There has been a lively debate for many years in the U.S. over the value of experience requirements. Those who do not think it valuable —and this is the official position of the American Institute of C.P.A.s — argue that less of value can be learned from a short period of low level employment than could be learned from a corresponding period of formal education. They argue, moreover, that the quality of experience obtained by a trainee cannot be standardized and cannot be controlled by the State Board which issues the certificate. Nevertheless, most State Boards still do have an experience requirement, though the one year generally required of those holding master's degrees can have little more than symbolic value.

The effort that has been made by the English Institute in recent years to tighten its control over the quality of the experience gained by its trainees contrasts markedly with the defeatism which surrounds this subject in America. In England a detailed training record has to be submitted to the Institute by the trainee and his employer periodically, and if the experience gained does not meet the Institute's standards, the deficiencies must be made good. It must be a matter of judgement as to how effective this system is. Certainly the value of an experience requirement cannot rationally be dismissed until some such determined effort to make it work has been tried.

PROFESSIONAL EDUCATION AS A LIFELONG ACTIVITY

The most important development in the field of accounting education in recent years has been the extension of the period of education from the preparatory period preceding entry into the profession to the whole of an accountant's working life. Continuing education on a voluntary basis has been around for a long time, and all professional organizations have offered opportunities for self-improvement to their members. The new feature in the situation now is that what has been a voluntary activity by some is becoming a required activity by all. Following the lead of Iowa, the first state to make continuing education obligatory in 1969, more and more states are doing so and it seems certain to become a nationwide requirement before long in the U.S. More recently, Florida, Maryland and Michigan have gone further still in the direction of the periodic re-testing of the knowledge of its C.P.A.s. They do not yet require all C.P.A.s to submit themselves to re-examination, but an opportunity for re-examination is offered as an alternative to the attendance at courses which its mandatory continuing education law requires.

The British professional bodies still rely on voluntary self-improvement. The argument against voluntarism is, of course, that those most in danger of obsolescence will be least likely to rectify this situation unless they a.e made to do so. On the other side, those who are sceptical about compulsion, at least in its present form, point out that it concerns itself only with the number of hours devoted to professional development courses and similar activities, not to their quality nor to how much is learned from them. Periodic retesting of professional competence as a condition for the retention of a professional qualification would be one way of satisfying the sceptics. It may not be so far away.

APPENDIX C

Reproduced from: *Education Requirements for Entry into the Accounting Profession,* A Statement of AICPA Policies, AICPA, May 1978.

TABLE 4 A SAMPLE PROGRAM

	Semester hours
GENERAL EDUCATION	
Communication	6-9
Behavioral sciences	6
Economics	6
Elementary accounting	3-6
Introduction to the computer	3
Mathematics and statistics	12
Other general education	24-18
	60
GENERAL BUSINESS EDUCATION	
Economics (theory and the monetary system)	6
The legal and social environment of business	3
Business law	6
Marketing	3
Finance	6
Organization, group, and individual behavior	3-6
Quantitative applications in business	6
Written communication	3
	36-39
ACCOUNTING EDUCATION[a]	
Financial accounting theory	
Applied financial accounting problems	15
Contemporary financial accounting issues	

Cost determination and analysis	
Cost control	6
Cost-based decision making	
Tax theory and considerations	
Tax problems	6
Audit theory and philosophy	
Audit problems	6
Computers and information systems	6
	39[b]
ELECTIVES	15-12[b]
Total semester hours	150

[a]Includes accounting for both profit-oriented and not-for-profit entities.
[b]Three semester hours of the thirty-nine hours of accounting education and six hours of the twelve to fifteen hours of electives, or both, might be alloted to an area of specialization, as described on page 26.

APPENDIX D

CHAPTER XV
SUMMARY AND CONCLUSION

Reproduced from: *Accounting Education and the Third World, (American Accounting Association, 1978).*

A. THE ACCOUNTANCY EDUCATION INVENTORY AND DEVELOPMENT PLAN

The main purpose of this monograph by the Committee on International Accounting Operations and Education of the American Accounting Association (AAA) has been to outline in an integrated frameowrk (1) *the scope, methods, and vehicles* available for improving accounting education, knowledge and practices in Third World countries and, (2) the role of educational institutions, e.g., the AAA, in providing accounting assistance.

In presenting this framework the Committee relied upon both its own extensive international experience and the comments and presentations from educators and practitioners in several Third World countries. The Committee feels it has been able to present a clear "pattern for action" which warrants due consideration by accounting educators and practitioners, public agencies, international and regional accounting institutions, economic development bodies, and other interested entities. However, the study is not a "cookbook" for each country or region. It is important that each country assess its own developments and requirements, based upon an accounting "inventory and plan," and portray its activities and demands in a carefully prepared accounting development report. This, in our opinion, should be submitted to governmental agencies, foreign accounting educational institutions, and international and regional accounting and economic development agencies (such as the World Bank, IMF, UN, Asian Development Bank, etc.). The Committee is convinced that if the needs of each country or region are reflected in well-prepared "accounting educational requirement study," along the lines conveyed in this monograph, the prospect of obtaining considerable international, regional and local assistance of various kinds will be greatly enhanced international and regional development agencies, such as the World Bank, UN (e.g., UNESCO), and regional development banks (Asian, African, Latin American), tend to be quite receptive in (a) helping to design and present such feasibility reports and (b) assisting in finding ways and means to implement the requests outlined. It is important that such requests be based upon carefully delineated "inventories and plans," as conveyed in this study, with adequate inputs from all parties concerned.

B. REGIONAL AND INTERNATIONAL COORDINATION AND COOPERATION

The Committee also believes that such accounting educational layouts and efforts could and should be better coordinated regionally and internationally. An international "accounting clearing house," or international accounting education federation, or other vehicle, might be the most effective means to spur accounting development activities.

The American Accounting Association could play a part in channeling such efforts, by helping in the preparation of accountingg requirement studies and by othrwise assisting countries in their accounting educational efforts. In the Appendix (item A) an outline is given of the extent to which the AAA itself could be helpful. But in the interests of better international and regional coordination in the accounting field, such activities might be better directed by an International Association for the Advancement of Accounting Education, (see Appendix - item B). Such a body would have as one of its principal objectives the promotion of knowledge and the provision of assistance between accounting educators and institutions. It should be a truly international association, working in close cooperation with international agencies such as the World Bank, IMF, UN, etc. and the newly established International Federation of Accountants (IFAC), the international body of accounting practitioners.

C. CONCLUDING RECOMMENDATION FOR ACTION

While the ultimate aim of this study has been to develop greater awareness of the potential role of accounting in economic development, and to find means to foster assistance, a more direct objective is to search for specific vehicles to accomplish this. The International Committee of the AAA, therefore, invites a detailed response from recipients of this study concerning:

1. the ideas outlined in this monograph.

2. the ways and means that recipients conceive how accounting education, training, and practice can and should be improved in their country.

3. the role of national accounting educational associations (e.g., AAA), national accounting institutions, international and regional accounting bodies, (e.g., IFAC) and international development agencies in promoting more effective accounting education and the spread of accounting knowledge.

Based upon the responses received, the AAA Committee intends to prepare a followup report for circulation to parties reflecting their ideas, and the steps required for action on an international or regional scale. Essentially the Committee visualizes this monograph as a basic framework for potential international implementation to help improve accounting in Third World countries.

FOOTNOTES

1. *Prospectus for a Profession*, the Report of the Long Range Enquiry, was published in London in 1974 by the Advisory Board of Accountancy Education and was distributed by Gee & Co. (Publishers) Ltd.

2. It may be necessary to explain, for the benefit of participants from countries where entry into the accounting profession is not invariably through the universities or equivalent institutions of higher education, that the accounting programs referred to here are degree programs (either graduate or undergraduate) with a major accounting content.

3. Hans V. Johnson, "A Survey of New Partners," *Journal of Accountancy,* July 1975, pp. 87-90.

4. Schiller, Felden, Files, and Wortzel, *The Development of Financial Managers,* (New York, Financial Executives Research Foundation, 1970).

5. I am indebted to the following, among others, for help in obtaining information for this section of my paper:

> Associate Professor J. Harrison, Head of the School of Accountancy, South Australian Institute of Technology, and formerly chairman of an IFAC Working Party on the theoretical content of professional studies and education.
>
> Dr. J. Keuzenkamp, of the Netherlands, chairman of the Education Committee of UEC.
>
> Professor John R. Small, of Heriot-Watt University, Edinburgh and chairman of the Education Committee of IFAC.

6. "Academic Preparation and Continuing Education of Accountants," by John O. Miller, Caulfield Institute of Technology, Melbourne, Australia.

7. The AICPA is probably the only accounting organization in the world that totally discounts the need for qualifying experience.

8. This is Appendix I to the AICPA's *Education Requirements for Entry into the Accounting Profession.*

9. Official Journal of the European Communities, No. C 317, pp. 10-12, December 18, 1979.

10. In Scotland trainees were still called apprentices until 1970.

11. Consideration is now being given by the Institute to the possibility of extending this period to twelve months.

12. As many trainees for the Scottish Institute work in London, special provision for comparable classes had to be made there.

13. *The Supply of Accounting Graduates and the Demand for Public Accounting Recruits,* Spring 1977, A.I.C.P.A.

14. Whereas in Britain the term "school" is generally applied to eduational institutions up to but not beyond the secondary level, in the U.S. it is used for any type of educational institution.

Management Accounting

Cost Accounting and the Use of Space and Equipment*

By David Solomons

DAVID SOLOMONS, B.COM.(London), Chartered Accountant. Born 1912 in London. Reader in Accounting in the University of London since 1949.

After graduating at the London School of Economics in 1932, Mr. Solomons qualified as a Chartered Accountant and then worked with a London firm of Chartered Accountants until the outbreak of war. After war service abroad and a short period with the Control Commission for Germany, he returned to the accountancy profession in 1945. He became Lecturer in Accounting at the London School of Economics in 1947.

He is the author of *The Monthly Statement as a Management Tool*, and of articles in *Economica*, *Accounting Research*, etc.

The Problem

In a well-known West End department store the whole of one floor is devoted to the restaurant. One section of the restaurant is a "help-yourself" cafeteria. In the other section, normal service is provided at tables. The two sections of the restaurant are separated from each other by a partition of movable screens. It was recently observed that the screens had been moved, so as to give more space to the cafeteria at the expense of the restaurant proper. It is the object of this article to examine the principle on which space ought to be allocated between the two sections of the restaurant. Any principle which can be formulated should then be applicable to the allocation of space between any competing uses in merchandising or factory premises. The allocation of machinery and other equipment between competing uses raises a number of difficult questions, some of which are here only briefly indicated, but the principle which is examined below undoubtedly has an important bearing on that problem also. We shall be looking at what is admittedly a "test tube" example. But in a discussion of principles, the test tube has an honourable part to play.

* [Reprinted, by permission, from *The Accountant*, March 27 and April 3, 1948.]

The problem presented by our restaurant is one which, in a slightly different form, has recently been exercising accountants in the course of discussions on the rationale of allocating overhead expenses between different products or jobs.[1] Many of the reasons usually put forward for the allocation of overheads are at least open to question. Nevertheless, it can be claimed, as against the exponents of marginal costing who deny altogether the usefulness of overhead allocation, that a costing system which stops short at direct or chargeable costs does not give management any guidance in accurately assessing the relative profitability of two jobs, one of which puts heavy demands on factory space and equipment, and the other of which can, say, be handled entirely by manual labour, unassisted by machinery, and on the customer's site, thus making no demands on the entrepreneur's own factory space.[2] The normal procedure of the anti-marginalists would presumably be to apportion the fixed expenses, including depreciation, between all the jobs passing through the works, on bases which seem most appropriate to each expense (*e.g.*, rent might be allocated in proportion to floor-space used, depreciation in proportion to machine value and running time, etc.). They would then claim that jobs making heavy demands on space and equipment had been loaded with a correspondingly heavy burden of fixed expense, and the relative profitability of different jobs could then be judged by comparing the margins between the total cost thus ascertained for each job and the price obtainable for each.

The point may be put in another way. It has for long been one of the economist's most uncompromising criticisms of costing practice that cost accountants measure profitability by comparing prices with historical costs, whereas it is not historical costs (*i.e.*, past expenditures) which are relevant, but " opportunity " costs, *i.e.*, the incomes or satisfactions given up by adopting one course of action rather than another. It must be admitted that, so far, this criticism has made remarkably little impression on the approach which cost accountants make to their problems. In so far as the force of

---

[1] See W. T. Baxter, "Should Cost Accounting ignore Overheads?" *The Accountant*, June 21, 1947. The question which Prof. Baxter poses, "Can objective cost figures show whether potential earnings are being maximised?" is precisely the question which it is here proposed to examine.

[2] See, *e.g.*, "The Pros and Cons of Marginal Costing," by G. C. Stone, F.C.W.A., in *The Cost Accountant*, January-February, 1948. Mr. Stone's article appeared after this paper was written. He expresses the objection here dealt with thus: "Marginal costing obscures the demands of individual products on capital and other services represented by fixed expenses."

the criticism has been appreciated at all, it has been countered with the argument that the " opportunity " cost of two jobs, both of which make certain demands on factory space and equipment, can be adequately compared by comparing the overhead allocations with which they would be charged in any normal job costing system. Thus the job which required more factory space or more machine hours would be charged more for factory rent and expenses and plant depreciation and these charges would approximately represent the income which could have been earned by the space and equipment in alternative uses. If, then, the job still shows a profit over its direct costs plus the overhead allocation, it can be regarded as showing a profit over its opportunity cost.

Now the entrepreneur's real problem is, of course, not " Are overheads being recovered? " but " Are earnings being maximised? "[3] Perhaps if we turn back to the problem presented by the restaurant and the cafeteria, we shall be able to judge how far " objective cost figures " can " show whether potential earnings are being maximised." We may also be able to judge whether, if they can do this at all, they will best do it by accepted methods of overhead allocation, or by much more refined methods than those commonly in use.

Measuring Demands on Space

Returning, then, to the problem of the department store restaurant, let us ignore for the moment the existence of other departments in the store. In considering the allocation of space between the restaurant proper and the cafeteria, what we first need is a ready means of converting units of floor-space occupied into numbers of meals served. The number of customers who can be served per 100 square feet of floor-space, at any one time, in the restaurant and the cafeteria respectively will be determined by such technical considerations as the size of tables used, the room required by waitresses to manœuvre, and so on. On the other hand, the length of time for which tables are occupied by customers will depend largely on consumer habits, though it will also vary to some small extent with the composition of the meal. The demand which the average customer makes on space must therefore be a function of these two factors, and it can be conveniently expressed in

[3] Even if the entrepreneur's objective is not the maximisation of earnings, he ought to know what his actual objective is costing him in terms of sacrificed income; and to know this, he must know where the point of maximum income lies.

terms of square-foot-hours—one square-foot-hour signifying the occupation of one square foot of space for one hour.

It is to be expected that the average figure of square-foot-hours per customer for the restaurant will be higher than for the cafeteria—customers will tend to linger longer over meals, and waitresses will require more space than will a "help-yourself" service. Suppose, then, that in the restaurant proper, customers take, on the average, 30 minutes to pass through, and can be seated at a density of 16 per 100 square feet. We then get $\frac{100 \times 30}{16 \times 60}$ or 3.125 square-foot-hours as the measure of the demands on space made by each customer. Similarly, in the cafeteria, the average time per meal might be 20 minutes, and the density 20 customers per 100 square feet, giving $\frac{100 \times 20}{20 \times 60}$ or 1.66 square-foot-hours per customer.

Given the area which is to be devoted to catering, and given the length of time available for serving meals (we shall simplify the problem by assuming that customers arrive in a steady stream throughout this period), it is now a simple matter to compute the number of meals which can be served, on any given assumption as to the way the total space is divided between restaurant and cafeteria. Thus, suppose the total available space to be 7,000 square feet, and that meals are to be served only between noon and 2.30 p.m., then there are available 7,000 × 2½ or 17,500 square-foot-hours, and this can be converted into terms of restaurant meals by dividing by 3.125, or into terms of cafeteria meals by dividing by 1.66. Thus, with no cafeteria, 5,600 restaurant meals could be served. If the space were divided equally between the two sections, we could get 2,800 meals in the restaurant as well as 5,270 in the cafeteria.

Normal Costing Procedure and the Maximisation of Revenue

With this somewhat lengthy preamble, we are in a better position to consider our original question, "Can objective cost figures show whether potential earnings are being maximised?" The maximisation of revenue from the catering department will depend on many factors, but one of the principal factors which it is within the competence of the management to control is how the total space is divided between restaurant and cafeteria. What guidance can normal costing procedure give to the management to help them reach a sound decision on this question?

Presumably, in the first place, there would have to be some arbitrary decision as to how the total floor space was to be divided between restaurant and cafeteria. We will assume that it is, in fact, decided to divide the space equally between them. This, using the foregoing data, would give 3,500 square feet to each section, in which, between noon and 2.30, and given the same technical conditions of supply, 2,800 restaurant meals and 5,270 cafeteria meals could be served.

The cost of these meals would then be computed, in the light of what is known about the variable costs (*i.e.*, the direct costs of food, service, etc.), the fixed costs of the departments for equipment, supervision, etc., and the rent of the whole floor, suitably apportioned between the two sections. Assuming the direct costs of food and service to be 1s. 8d. in the restaurant and 1s. 5d. in the cafeteria, separate fixed costs to be £150 and £100 respectively, and the total rent to be £40, we would have :—

	Restaurant	*Cafeteria*
Direct cost of meals :	£	£
2,800 at 1s. 8d.	233	
5,270 at 1s. 5d.		373
Separate fixed costs	150	100
Rent apportionment (in proportion to floor space)	20	20
Total cost	£403	£493
Average cost per meal	2/11d.	1/10d.

Now suppose that market conditions do not permit the restaurant to sell 2,800 meals at 2s. 11d., and/or that 5,270 cafeteria meals cannot be sold at a price of 1s. 10d. In that case, the above computations give no assistance to the management in deciding whether the catering department ought to close down altogether (even though the rent might still be payable for the space, for which no other use might readily be found). And even if these costs can be covered, no indication is given as to whether the equal division of space between restaurant and cafeteria is the *best* division, from the point of view of maximising earnings. The management is presumably left to fall back on trial and error.

It looks, then, as though objective cost figures drawn up on a conventional basis will not point the way to a maximisation of earnings. Yet such a pointer does exist in the form of a comparison of earning power per physical unit of space or equipment as between different prospective employments of these resources. It is to the development of this idea that we shall now turn.

An Alternative Approach

In the department store restaurant which we have been discussing, the catering manager wants just that allocation of floor space between his two sections which will maximise earnings from his floor. This ideal allocation will clearly be achieved when nothing is to be gained by transferring space from one section to the other, *i.e.*, when the transfer of one square-foot-hour of space adds no more to the gross margin of the transferee section than it subtracts from the gross margin of the transferor section. In other words, the ideal allocation of space must be that which gives *equal additional gross margin per additional square-foot-hour of space* for the two sections.

Such an allocation of space can be ascertained only by an examination of a number of possibilities as to the selling price which could be charged for varying numbers of meals in the two sections, and as to the costs which these meals would entail. The various possibilities for the restaurant and the cafeteria can be set out in the form of two combined cost and demand schedules. These schedules can then easily be made to incorporate certain additional information, which is derived from the basic information relating to costs and prices. Once that has been done, the ideal allocation of space can practically be read directly from the schedules.

We shall assume, then, that for the two types of restaurant service, demand and cost schedules can be constructed, however approximately, so that at each possible price, the number of customers for each service can be estimated, and the corresponding costs of providing that number of meals can be ascertained. The costs to be included in these schedules are those costs of each service which would cease if the service were discontinued. Thus general establishment charges, such as any apportionment of the rent of the whole store, can be excluded. So, for this limited purpose of dividing one floor between the two services, can fixed costs which are incurred for the two services jointly—*e.g.*, the fixed costs of running the kitchen, where this serves both the restaurant and the cafeteria. We need, for our present purpose, to concentrate on the separate " avoidable " costs of the two sections.

The schedules are set out opposite.

RESTAURANT

Price per meal (1)	*Number of meals sold* (2)	*Total receipts* (3)	*Separate fixed costs* (4)	*Total variable costs* (5)	*Additional revenue* (6)	*Additional costs* (7)	*Additional gross margin* (8)	*Square-foot-hours* (9)	*Additional Square-foot-hours* (10)	*Additional Gross Margin per add'l square-foot hour* (11)
		£	£	£	£	£	£			£
5/–	1,000	250	150	100	250	250	—	3,125	3,125	—
4/9	2,000	475	150	184	225	84	141	6,250	3,125	·045
4/6	2,500	562	150	219	87	35	52	7,812	1,562	·033
4/3	3,000	637·5	150	250	75·5	31	44·5	9,375	1,563	·029
4/–	3,500	700	150	276	62·5	26	36·5	10,937	1,562	·023
3/9	4,000	750	150	300	50	24	26	12,500	1,563	·017
3/6	4,500	787·5	150	337	37·5	37	0·5	14,062	1,562	·001
3/3	5,000	812·5	150	375	25	38	–13	15,625	1,563	—

CAFETERIA

(1)	(2)	(3)	(4)	(5)	(6)	(7)	(8)	(9)	(10)	(11)
		£	£	£	£	£	£			£
3/6	2,000	350	100	150	350	250	100	3,320	3,320	·030
3/3	3,000	487	100	225	137	75	62	4,980	1,660	·037
3/–	4,000	600	100	300	113	75	38	6,640	1,660	·023
2/9	5,000	687	100	360	87	60	27	8,300	1,660	·016
2/6	6,000	750	100	410	63	50	13	9,960	1,660	·008
2/3	7,000	787	100	437	37	27	10	11,620	1,660	·006
2/–	8,000	800	100	455	13	18	– 5	13,280	1,660	—
1/9	9,000	788	100	470	–12	15	–27	14,940	1,660	—

Drawing Up the Tables

The tables set out the conditions of demand and cost, for the restaurant and the cafeteria, which the management expect to encounter in the course of business, ignoring for the moment the limiting factor of space. It must be emphasised that, at least so far as columns 1 to 5 are concerned, they are no more than estimates of probabilities, made before any action is taken, and in the light of which future action can be planned. Column 2 shows the number of meals which it is believed can be sold at the corresponding prices shown in column 1. Column 3 is of course obtained by multiplying column 2 by column 1. Column 4 shows those costs which are specific to each service, and which do not vary with the number of meals served. Cleaning and supervision will serve as examples. It is not suggested that, in fact, many elements of cost are as fixed as those shown in column 4; in any case, they are included in the example partly to illustrate the now well-established point that fixed costs do not enter into short-term decisions as to price and output, once it is decided to produce the products in question at all. Column 5 shows the total of those costs which vary with output, and will include such items as food and waitresses' wages.

All the remaining columns are derived from the basic information in columns 1 to 5. Column 6 simply shows the increase which each line of column 3 represents over the previous line of the same column. Column 7 is similarly derived from column 5. Column 8 shows the difference between columns 6 and 7. The term " gross margin " is used here to mean the total income of the section subject only to the deduction of sectional fixed costs. Column 9 is obtained by converting the number of meals in column 2 into square-foot-hours by multiplying by the factor already obtained, *i.e.*, 3.125 for the restaurant and 1.66 for the cafeteria. Column 10 is derived from column 9 and is simply the increase shown by each figure in that column over the preceding figure therein. Column 11 is obtained by dividing column 8 by column 10. It represents the additional net income to be obtained by using an additional square-foot of floor space in that section for one hour, on the assumption of course that the demand for meals is spread evenly through time.

Using the Tables

It can be seen from the tables that, given unlimited space, profits would be maximised with a supply of just over 4,500 restaurant meals and just over 7,000 cafeteria meals, since up to these points each addition to the number of meals sold increases the total gross margin and, of course, the sectional net profit. In such circumstances, there is no problem of space allocation. But suppose, as before, that the space available on the whole floor is limited to 7,000 square feet, giving 17,500 square-foot-hours. Then profit will be maximised when the available space is allocated between the two sections in such a way that the additional gross margins per additional square-foot-hour are equal. The tables indicate such an allocation directly—it is achieved when the values in column 11 are equal in the two sections, and the values in column 9 add up to 17,500. It is achieved, that is to say, when approximately (by reason of the incompleteness and discontinuity of the tables) 3,500 restaurant meals and 4,000 cafeteria meals are supplied. This calls for an allocation of about 10,900 square-foot-hours, or 4,360 square feet, to the restaurant, and about 6,600 square-foot-hours, or 2,640 square feet to the cafeteria. The conversion of square-foot-hours to square feet is, of course, simply a matter of dividing by 2½, the number of hours during which meals are served. With this allocation of the total available space, each section is yielding about £.028 of additional gross margin per additional square-foot-hour, and no alternative allocation of space which did not involve the complete closing of one section could result in a higher total net profit.

Continuing to ignore, for the moment, the existence of other departments, let us suppose, as before, that a separate rent of £40 is paid for the whole floor which houses the restaurant and cafeteria. The results of the whole catering department may then be summarised thus:

	Restaurant	*Cafeteria*	*Total*
	£	£	£
Total receipts	700	600	1,300
Separate costs	426	400	826
Sectional net profits	£274	£200	474
Rent of whole floor			40
Total net profit			£434

Setting out the results in this way, it is clear that, having maximised sectional net profits, the allocation of space between these two sections cannot be affected by any change in the rent of the floor as a whole nor by any consideration of the way in which the management may decide to apportion the rent of the whole building between different floors. As a joint fixed cost, rent is irrelevant to our problem. Whatever allocation of the available space maximises profit in the absence of rent still maximises profit when rent is charged, and however it is apportioned between the two sections.

In certain circumstances, however, it would not be enough just to equalise the additional gross margins per additional square-foot-hour, because there exists the possibility that the complete closing of one section, and the transfer of its space to the other, would increase the total net profit of the store. It might do this through the saving in fixed costs which, together with the increments of gross margin accruing from the expanded section, might more than compensate for the loss of gross margin from the closed section. Thus, in the above tables, suppose that the restaurant fixed costs had been not £150, but £380, and that there had been no cafeteria fixed costs at all; and suppose further that the variable costs were unchanged (these assumptions are, of course, unrealistic and are merely illustrative). These changes in the assumptions make no difference to the other columns of the table (except for the first line), and so long as both restaurant and cafeteria are to be kept open, the best allocation of space will be exactly as before. This will give sectional net profits, subject to rent, etc., of £44 (total receipts £700 minus fixed costs £380 and variable costs £276) and £300 (total receipts £600 minus variable costs £300) respectively, a total of £344; and this cannot be improved on so long as both sections are to be kept open. But it can be improved on by closing the restaurant completely and expanding the cafeteria until it is supplying 7,000 meals—beyond this point additional gross margin is negative. By closing the restaurant we save (it is assumed) the fixed costs of £380; and the cafeteria, with no fixed costs, makes a profit of £350 (receipts of £787 minus variable costs of £437) compared with £344 from the two sections together.

In these somewhat unusual circumstances, therefore, the principle which has been enunciated needs to be modified by adding a further condition which must be satisfied if the apparently best allocation of space is to be consistent with the maintenance in operation of both sections. This condition is that it must not be possible to increase the total net profits of the business by closing one section altogether. Such a possibility arises if, having arrived at the allocation of space which equalises the additional gross margin per additional square-foot-hour, it is then found, by examining the figures, that the closing of either section and the devotion of its space to the other results in an increase of total gross margin.

Some Modifications

When we began our consideration of this problem, we assumed that the space required per customer and the time taken per meal were determined by technical considerations and by consumer habits. We can now easily make the conditions of the problem more realistic by dropping these assumptions. It is, for instance, possible that if prices are lowered, customers will accept a certain amount of crowding. Another possibility is that by reducing prices and also reducing the size of meals, the time taken by the average customer in the restaurant or cafeteria can be reduced. These possibilities can be reflected in the tables by estimating the number of meals which can be sold under these less attractive conditions at each price, and then applying to the number of meals at each price a revised factor (lower than 3.125 or 1.66 respectively for the two sections) to convert meals into space-hour requirements. Column 9 of the tables will reflect this change. If the meals are reduced in size, the variable costs per meal will also presumably be reduced, and this, too, will be reflected in column 5 of the tables. None of these changes in the contents of the tables will, however, in any way affect their use.

There is one particularly serious criticism that may be levelled at this analysis. It is that we have made the unwarranted assumption that conditions of costs and demand can be forecast for the two sections independently. On the demand side in particular, there can be no doubt that the number of meals demanded in the restaurant at any particular price will be to some extent determined by the price which is being charged in the cafeteria. To attempt to modify the argument to provide for this point would be out of the question here. All that can be said is that it is doubtful if the conclusions already reached can be invalidated by the simplified assumptions which we have made.[4]

Generalising the Results

In fact, in our department store, there are other departments, actual and potential, which are competing for the space occupied by the restaurants. Whether or not the whole floor

[4] For a theoretical solution of this problem, see R. H. Coase, "Monopoly Pricing with Interrelated Costs and Demands," *Economica*, November, 1946.

at present allotted to the latter ought to remain so allotted must depend on whether a transfer of one square foot to other uses would yield a higher additional gross margin than it does at present. In most other uses in this store, space can be occupied for, say, eight hours a day, and not merely for two and a half hours, as we have assumed is the case with the restaurants. Consequently, in considering transfers of space from catering to other uses, it is the comparative additional gross margins per square-foot-day, not per square-foot-hour, which are relevant. Thus the return from the restaurants is £.023 × $2\frac{1}{2}$ or £.057 per square-foot-day at the margin, and it will pay to transfer space from the restaurants to other departments if the transfer of one square foot will add more per day to the total gross margin of the store than this figure. Only by a comparison of the above schedules for the restaurants, modified, however, to give yields per day instead of per hour, with similar schedules constructed for other departments, can a rational allocation of space be made—even though the schedules be no more than a series of conjectures in the mind of the store manager.

Here again, however, we must recognise that the equalisation of additional gross margins per square-foot-day may give only an *apparently* best allocation of space, and that because of the incidence of fixed costs the closing of one department altogether and the sharing of its space among other departments may increase the total gross margin of the store. This situation will not be disclosed merely by an examination of the figures in column 11 of the tables, which must therefore be subject to this further test before a final allocation of space is made.

There remains one further consideration, which is that transfers of space cannot be made without incurring costs. In the case of the restaurant, these would probably take the form of the costs of moving the screens. It is obvious that any movement of the screens, in order to be worth while, must result in an addition to gross margin greater than the cost of the move. It follows that an allocation of space which did not equalise the values in column 11 of the tables as between two departments could still be a perfectly rational allocation so long as the difference between the two values, multiplied by the length of time which is expected to elapse before a change in any of the basic data makes reallocation of space necessary for other reasons, does not exceed the cost of a reallocation.

The costs of reallocation may be of even greater importance in practice in connection with the use of machines and equipment referred to in the next paragraph, than they are in relation to the use of space. The costs of reallocating space will include such items as the re-erection of screens and partitions and the movement of stocks from one department to another. The cost of reallocating machinery will normally take the form of retooling and resetting. The costs of making such changes are easy to under-estimate.[5]

The Use of Equipment

The analysis which has been developed in terms of space (or more precisely, space-hours) is equally applicable to the allocation between competing uses of plant and other fixed equipment. Indeed, its use in this connection is in some respects simpler, since we can work directly in terms of machine-hours, a less complex unit than space-hours. Specific machines, or machines which can be treated as broadly interchangeable, will be allocated between lines of product or jobs in such a way that the additional gross margin per additional machine-hour of a particular machine from each product or job is the same.

Yet there are many difficulties arising from the allocation of plant and equipment which do not present themselves in the course of allocating space in a department store. For instance, in an industry where jobs pass through a series of operations, only the final price for the completed job will be known. How, then, is the gross margin per machine-hour to be ascertained for individual processes? There is, too, a difficulty raised by the possibility of varying the intensity with which machines are used. These questions need further consideration, which they cannot receive here. It must be sufficient to state the principle. Its detailed application can come later.[5] Nevertheless, even in the crude form in which it is here stated, the principle is not without its practical applications. It could be applied to the allocation of items of plant, such as vehicles, industrial X-ray plant, and other specialised equipment for whose services a separate price can be quoted, distinct from the price of the work to which they are ancillary.

---

[5] Some of these problems are more fully discussed in "Some suggestions for measuring the relative profitability of competing uses of floor space and fixed equipment," by C. L. Paine, *Accounting Research Association Publication No.* 2, to the whole of which excellent paper this article owes a great deal.

Conclusion

The method of determining the "best" allocation of space and equipment which has been under discussion has little in common with currently accepted costing methods, or with what most people would regard as accounting in any sense. It is, however, none the worse on that account. Viewed as a method of reflecting in the cost accounts the "opportunity" costs of space and equipment, the procedure of overhead allocation is a poor second best. It conveniently but unjustifiably identifies these "opportunity" costs with apportionments of past expenditures. The main defect of this procedure is that it throws no light on possible improvements in the use to which resources can be put. What is needed is a method which relates the physical resources used with the probable income resulting from such use and from possible alternative uses. The original money costs of these resources, once incurred, are of very secondary importance.

The objection may be raised that many different kinds of physical resources are involved in any form of economic activity, and whereas the approach developed in this article relates only one kind of resource at a time (*e.g.*, space or machine capacity) to the income produced, more normal costing methods take account of the costs of all these resources at once, by allocating a proportion of rent, depreciation, etc., to each of the operations which are being carried on. This, however, is not a virtue but a defect of that procedure. We are right to concentrate on one kind of resource, one factor of production, at a time. The factor to concentrate on is the one which constitutes the bottleneck limiting our operations at the present moment. This may be space, machine capacity or some other factor. Whatever it is, it is the additional gross margin per additional unit of the "bottleneck" factor which should determine the allocation of resources. In our restaurant example, we assumed that space was the limiting factor. It might, in fact, have been not space but the shortage of staff which limited operations. In that case, the calculations would have had to be made in terms of additional gross margin per additional man-hour instead of per additional square-foot-hour. The principle is not affected.

It may well be that in practice we should encounter a series of bottlenecks, one after the other—space, staff, equipment and so on. But it is still almost certainly true that these factors will operate as the *effective* bottlenecks one after the other—only one at a time. And it is the limiting factor of the moment that should be the subject of our calculations. By trying to take them all at once, the procedure of overhead allocation may give an entirely wrong distribution of resources.

Accepted methods of cost accounting have given rather scant attention to this problem of the use of resources. It is one which demands a budgetary approach, and although it has received some attention from exponents of budgetary control, this has usually meant concentrating on the relation of gross margin to turnover from different products, from which the conclusion is drawn that production should be directed to those lines which give the highest ratio of gross margin to turnover. This seems to me to ignore the important relationship, which is not that of gross margin to turnover but rather gross margin to the physical volume of resources utilised for different products. This is essentially a question of a choice between alternatives—a choice between possible future courses of action. Such questions do not lend themselves to treatment by customary accounting methods, especially when these methods are applied to exclusively historical information. Certainly to devote attention to the apportionment of overheads is to introduce a factor which, though it might conceivably be relevant to some problems, is not relevant to this.

Uniform Cost Accounting—A Survey

By David Solomons

Part I

In much that has been spoken and written about post-war industrial reorganisation in Great Britain, frequent references can be found to the desirability of promoting the development of uniform costing schemes in industries for which none have yet been devised, and of getting them more widely adopted in industries which already possess them. Perhaps no other excuse need be offered for attempting at this time to survey and evaluate the existing uniform costing schemes in this country than that a study of them may help to put into perspective some of the current discussion about their further development.

What Uniform Costing Is

Uniform Cost Accounting has been defined by the United States Chamber of Commerce in terms which have gained wide acceptance:

"Uniform Cost Accounting comprises a set of principles and in some cases of accounting methods which, when incorporated in the accounting system of the individual members in an industry, will result in the obtaining of cost figures by the individual members of the industry which will be on a comparable basis."[1] The trouble with this definition is that it says too much. It is by no means self-evident that the cost figures which different firms show, under a uniform costing system, really are on a comparable basis. I shall return to this point later. But because it is easier to agree about what uniform costing is than about what it does, it seems preferable to define it simply as the formulation of an agreed set of cost accounting definitions and conventions for adoption by all the firms in a particular industry.

This definition, of course, answers one question only to raise another—what is an "industry"? If it is true that

[1] *Uniform Accounting Activities of Trade Associations* (Dept. of Manufacture of the U.S. Chamber of Commerce, M.A. 801–804).

" product differentiation robs the concept of industry of both its definiteness and its serviceability. Outside of the limiting cases of pure monopoly and pure competition, the substitutability between any two products, the competitiveness between any two firms varies only in degree. The grouping of firms into industries cannot be based on any clear-cut criterion . . . "[1], then a good deal of doubt must at once be cast on the value or validity of cost comparisons between firms, or of the possibility of devising any single accounting system for an " industry " which will meet all the accounting needs of all the firms in it. In point of fact, if one looks at the groups of firms for which uniform costing systems have been devised in this country one finds that the common characteristic which binds each group together is not so much that all the firms in the group are producing substitutable products, but that they are using the same raw materials and subjecting them, broadly, to the same processes. However fatal product differentiation may be to the validity of the concept of an industry in the field of value theory, the concept is not without meaning for our present purpose. At the same time it must be recognised that that meaning is not at all precise. Technological differences between firms, like product differences, are matters of degree. Technologically, the differences between firm A and firm B, between B and C, C and D, may in each case be small, yet the difference between A and D may be great enough to make it difficult to recognise them as members of the same industry. Curiously, hardly any uniform costing schemes start by defining the range of firms to be comprehended by the system. Often a scheme deals with a process rather than an industry as commonly understood. In the case of iron and steel, for instance, there are in fact three schemes, not one. These deal separately with blast furnaces, open hearth steel furnaces and rolling mills. And specialised schemes have developed for other sections of the industry. In the plastics industry again, the three main sections—the moulders, the injection moulders and the fabricators—have distinct though similar systems.

The Beginnings of Uniform Costing

The uniform costing movement—it is not too much to call it a movement, for its exponents have often used the

[1] R. Triffin, *Monopolistic Competition and General Equilibrium Theory*, I. quo., p. 188.

language of the crusade—is at least 60 years old, and seems to have made its first appearance in the United States in the iron stove trade. The National Association of Stove Manufacturers, which had been formed in 1872, had by 1889 developed a uniform "formula" for ascertaining the costs of individual articles. In 1891, the President, in his Presidential address, was able to say that "an excess of capacity now exists in about the same ratio as it did in 1872, but it is not as dangerous as then, because of the greater intercommunication of stove men and the consequent greater facilities for adjusting the production to the demand and because of the automatic regulation of a uniform cost system."[1]

Among the printers in America, local typothetæ associations were at work on problems of cost finding before 1887 but it was not until 1910 that the Standard Uniform Cost Finding System for Printers was formally approved for general adoption by the United Typothetæ of America.[2] The activities of the printers in America are of particular interest for their bearing on the subsequent development of uniform costing in Great Britain, for the Master Printers in this country were taking a lively interest in what was going on in America. When the Federation of Master Printers set up a committee in 1911 to consider the question of "increased cost of production and the consequent necessity of increasing charges", one of its duties was to visit America to study costing methods in use there. The main result of the committee's work was the appearance in April, 1913, of the Printers' Cost Finding System. This system, while not the earliest uniform costing system to appear in this country, is the oldest of those which are still actively being used.

It is, however, not among the printers but among the makers of iron bedsteads that the most notable English pioneer of uniform costing is to be found. This was E. J. Smith, the champion of the New Trades Combination Movement, who in a series of articles in the *Birmingham Daily Post* in 1895 and in his book[3] published in 1899 set out his scheme for ensuring that industrial competition should not

[1] *The Iron Age*, 14th May, 1891, p. 933.

[2] For a detailed account of these develpoments see "Typothetæ Experiments with Price Maintenance and Cost Work", by Leona M. Powell, in *Journal of Political Economy*, February, 1926, pp. 78–99.

[3] *The New Trades Combination Movement*, by E. J. Smith, 1899.

result in losses to producers. This was to be achieved by ensuring, by agreement within each industry, that all producers should fix their prices by adding to their ascertained costs an agreed percentage for profit. "It is part of my scheme", he writes, "to establish in every trade a system of cost taking which, while it may not be all that could be desired when tested by the special circumstances of any individual business, is still all that is needed for the purpose of fixing throughout an entire trade a selling price for each manufactured article which will bring a legitimate and reasonable profit to each maker without unduly taxing the purchaser".[1] It is far from clear whether Smith wanted a uniform price to be charged by all producers as well as the adoption of uniform costing. In one passage, he says that the scheme does not involve uniform prices. "All that would be insisted on would be that, whatever the selling price, it bore the proportion of profit on dead cost agreed to."[2] But Mr. W. A. Addinsell, in a paper on "A new system of cost taking in trade" reprinted in Smith's book, and of which, presumably, Smith therefore approved, speaking of two producers making the same article by different processes, one cheap, one dear, says: "... any saving by the cheaper process which turns out as good an article as the dearer one is regarded as a question of management only, and the benefit must be retained by the maker instead of being given away in the selling price. Each member is at liberty to adopt whichever process he pleases, but the one he selects must be charged at the rate provided by the schedules."[3] It is interesting to find, at so early a stage in the development of uniform costing, justification of a later comment by a trade association secretary that "when you find uniform cost accounting systems, you find uniform figures".[4]

The relation of uniform costing to uniform prices has not always been one of cause and effect. In some cases the order of development was the other way round. The pottery industry provides an example. In April, 1901, a book was issued by the Earthenware Manufacturers' Association containing a number of schedules showing estimated costings of a large variety of goods for the guidance

[1] *Op. cit.*, p. 30.
[2] In a reprint of his *Birmingham Daily Post* articles, p. 12.
[3] Smith, *The New Trades Combination Movement*, p. 45.
[4] Federal Trade Commission, *Report on Open-Price Trade Associations*, 1929, p. 175.

of manufacturers in fixing prices. It was not until 1921 that anything that could be called a uniform costing system for the industry was produced. And the Federation of Master Printers which, as has already been mentioned, published their Costing Scheme in 1913, had in 1907 published a booklet entitled '*Profit for Printers*' or '*What is Cost?*', which set out cost rates for hand and machine composition, said to be based on returns made to a London accountant by a number of printers. These figures were recommended for general adoption in the industry, for pricing purposes.

The Extent of Uniform Costing in Great Britain

In Great Britain very little information is available about the activities of Trade Associations, and it is impossible to say how many Associations engage in costing activities or regard this as one of their functions. The possible range of such work is of course very wide. At one end of the scale, an Association may employ a permanent staff of cost accountants, publish an elaborate costing manual for the industry, install the recommended system for its members on request, deal with costing queries as they arise, regularly collect and tabulate cost statistics and circulate the information obtained among members. At the other end of the scale, an Association may do little more than undertake to establish contact between members seeking advice and some selected professional accountant with special knowledge of the industry. In Great Britain, at least, at the present time, though there are some notable exceptions, whose number is increasing, there is a tendency for Associations to approximate more to the latter extreme than to the former.

What is usually understood as uniform costing involves, as a minimum, the publication of a costing manual setting out a recommended costing system for adoption throughout the industry. In Great Britain about 26 such systems have appeared since 1913, from which year the earliest existing British scheme, that of the British Master Printers' Federation, dates. Seven schemes (pottery, paper box, paper bag, bakers, india-rubber manufacturers, tin box and electrical manufacturers) appeared between 1920–1930, and five (iron and steel, laundries, cocoa and confectionery, hosiery, and wholesale clothing) during the period 1931–39. Fourteen schemes (plastics, steel wire, cotton weaving, iron foundries, drop forgers, paint and varnish, black bolts, wholesale and manufacturing opticians, fertilisers, steel fabrication, dyeing and cleaning, brushes, gowns and millinery, and steel foundries) are the products of the war or post-war years.

If the progress of uniform costing could be measured by the rate at which new schemes have appeared it could fairly be described as being in a flourishing state. The true picture, however, is less impressive. The printing scheme certainly retains the interest of a substantial percentage of the firms in the industry. Of the seven schemes which appeared during the 1920's, however, not one now has anything more than a historical interest, and one industry (paper boxes) has recently started again with a new scheme. The systems prepared during the 1930's have fared better: those for iron and steel and laundries in particular have at least created an interest in costing among firms in the industry, and the iron and steel scheme has played a not unimportant part in determining the price structure in the industry. But although the hosiery scheme dates from 1936, the Hosiery Working Party found that until 1944–5 few manufacturers kept records of material usage and wastage, and it was rare for the wages charged in the unit costs to be reconciled with the total wages paid for a given period, overheads were seldom divided between factory overhead and general administration, and selling and distribution expenses were often lumped together under the general heading of overheads. The existence of uniform schemes in the pottery and clothing industries does not protect these industries from strictures on their standards of costing by their respective Working Parties. For the rest, it is perhaps too early to judge. Of the wartime and post-war schemes certainly none has yet proved itself. Of the potentially most important scheme among these, that for cotton weaving, issued as recently as 1947, a well-informed member of the industry said two years later that he knew of only one or two firms that had actually begun to use the scheme and that it had not received general acceptance by the industry.

The Position in the United States

In the United States, many more uniform costing schemes have made their appearance than in Great Britain but it seems doubtful whether they really play a more important part in industry. According to the Temporary National Economic

Committee's "Trade Association Survey",[1] out of a total of 1,244 Trade Associations in 1938–39, 560 engaged in accounting activities and worked on cost statistics and studies. Of these Associations, 269 included such work among their major activities. 348 Associations included the establishment of uniform accounting among their activities, 158 of them regarding this as one of their major activities. This and other evidence points to the effective existence of about 150 uniform costing schemes in the United States. Such a figure suggests that we are here confronting a major force in the organisation of American industry and many writers on this subject have given the same impression. Yet, apart from these figures, the available evidence does not unequivocally support such a view.

From a report on cost accounting in industry, published by the Accounting Department of the U.S. Office of Price Administration in 1946, it is possible to obtain some idea of the extent to which cost information is available in a wide range of industries which were subject to investigation by O.P.A. accountants during the period 1942–1945. The experience of the O.P.A. in this connection is summed up by Mr. Paul M. Green, at that time Deputy Administrator for Accounting in O.P.A., in the following words: "Our summary shows that there is a great variation in cost-accounting methods. It shows that cost records in some industries are far better than those in others, as would be expected. . . . It is difficult to judge exactly the percentage of all companies in all industries that can supply cost data on a product basis. The only completely accurate statement is that many of them cannot. Probably 85 per cent. of all industrial companies do not allocate cost on a product basis and 15 per cent. are readily able to produce such information."[2] Compare this with the view of the Federal Trade Commission in its Annual Report for 1916[3] that "10 per cent. of our manufacturers and merchants know the actual cost to manufacture and to sell their products. Forty per cent. estimate what these costs are, and 50 per cent. have no method". Even making full allowance for the fact that the O.P.A.'s figure of 15 per cent. relates to "all industrial companies," while the Federal Trade

[1] T.N.E.C. *Monograph* No. 18, Washington, 1941. 76th Congress, 3rd session. Pp. 373–374.
[2] O.P.A. *Report on Cost Accounting in Industry*, p. iii.
[3] At p. 15.

Commission's 10 per cent. relates to "our manufacturers and merchants", the spread of cost knowledge in the 30 years which separates the two reports is not impressive. And when due credit is given to the educational efforts of the National Association of Cost Accountants, the increased use of mechanised accounting methods and other factors which have operated during the period in the direction of a more widespread use of cost accounting, the achievements of uniform costing in the United States would seem to have been rather modest. It is perhaps significant that in the O.P.A. report, uniform costing gets only one reference, in connection with the rubber industries.

Another light on uniform costing's uncertain hold on American industry is thrown by J. H. Foth, who in 1930 wrote about the experience of the American Photo-Engravers' Association, which had adopted a simple cost system as long ago as 1913: "The need for continuous cost education and the results of such efforts are well illustrated in the American Photo-Engravers' Association . . . after many years of educational work and perfecting of the system, the Association recently found it necessary to take vigorous steps to interest its members in cost accounting."[1] The experience of this Association in having to "interest its members in cost accounting" is typical of what has happened many times on both sides of the Atlantic, once the initial interest evoked by the appearance of a new uniform scheme has subsided.

THE WORKING PARTIES AND UNIFORM COSTING

Enough has been said to suggest that uniform costing has not been strikingly successful in winning support from industry. Yet at the present time there is no lack of advocates for its extension, and many advantages are claimed for it. Most of the claims commonly made are to be found in one or other of the reports of the Working Parties appointed by the President of the Board of Trade in 1945 and subsequently, as the following quotations will show:

(1) "Not until such a [uniform costing] system is in general operation will there be a reliable yardstick by which to

[1] J. H. Foth, *Trade Associations*, p. 263. But it should also be noted that according to S. J. Lengyel ("Standardised Accountancy Considered Internationally," in *Accounting Research*, July, 1949, p. 135) "The Photo Engravers reported in 1938 that 323 of 511 member plants used the Association's uniform system".

measure efficiency or a basis for understanding between the individual manufacturers." (Domestic Glassware Report).

(2) "We regard the keeping of expenses and production records in a uniform manner as important in itself . . . If . . . all firms in the same section do the work in the same way, and use the same terms with the same meaning, there is a ready means available at any time for pooling information for the benefit of all, without any need for disclosure of business secrets to business rivals." (Cotton Report).

(3) "Whilst a standard [costing] system would not be easy to develop it would amply repay the time and trouble involved, and its development would increase the effectiveness of the costing itself. Once developed and commonly operating, it would allow a free and voluntary interchange between members of the industry of information that would incite valuable comparison. Instead of the best brains being confined to their own immediate field, they would receive stimulation from such comparisons and the contacts that would inevitably follow. . . . Efficient costing systems are not cheap to run and for this reason some manufacturers are tempted to use over-simplified systems. . . . If, however, the initiative were taken by the Council of the Heavy Clothing Industry to formulate a sound costing system the initial cost would be borne by the industry as a whole and the best system would thus be brought within the means of every member." (Heavy Clothing Report).

(4) ". . . there has been no effective attempt on the part of the industry to educate itself about costing or to introduce a uniform costing system so as to enable sufficient statistical information to be available to throw a clear light on the fortunes of the industry." (Jewellery and Silverware Report).

(5) "[A uniform system] would also enable comparison to be drawn between one manufacturer and another and provide more reliable information than is available at present for the purpose of the industry's price fixing arrangements." (Linoleum Report).

(6) "If the market is turning against the trade as a whole, joint action can be better planned and initiated, based on

known cost factors. When all are using the same system, the trade is insured against the damage that an individual manufacturer, through erroneous costing, can innocently engage in uneconomic trading and start a phase of weak selling." (Rubber Proofed Clothing Report).

It will be noted that the arguments for uniform costing which are advanced above are of two distinct kinds. The first set of arguments suggests that uniform costing will raise industrial efficiency, the second that it will limit price competition. Unfortunately, this latter tendency is likely to counteract any beneficial effect on efficiency which uniform costing might otherwise have. There is also running through the reports a tendency to confuse demands for *more* costing with a call for *more uniform* costing. These two objectives are, of course, distinct—they may even be contradictory, in the sense that a more widespread use of costing may lead to more, not less, diversification. But what most of the Working Parties want is both more costing and more uniformity.

Before proceeding to examine the arguments for and against uniform costing, some more adequate description of it needs to be given than is contained in the bare definition with which this article began. To such a description we shall now turn.

Contents of a Representative Uniform Cost System

Some uniform cost systems, especially some of the earlier ones, have been sketchy in the extreme, and have fallen far short of the minimum degree of precision in instructions to users which is essential if any uniformity of practice is to be secured. Other schemes have been worked out with great care, so as to provide for almost every possible contingency. There is, therefore, really no *typical* system. But it is possible to specify a number of matters which will usually be dealt with in any scheme which purports both to be practical and to provide an effective degree of uniformity.

1. It is necessary to define for each industry what it is that is being costed, i.e., the product or process unit or units the cost of which is being ascertained by the cost system. Other general characteristics of the system also need to be clearly described. To what extent, if at all, are the total

costs shown in each firm's cost statements to be "tied in" with the total expenditure recorded in the firm's financial accounting system? Does the system provide for a comparison of actual costs with standard costs computed on the basis of what management regards as a desirable and attainable level of efficiency and productive activity? An examination of the existing British systems shows that, in general, they do not provide for such comparisons of actual and standard costs: they do place considerable emphasis on the value of relating the cost figures closely to the figures in the financial books.

2. Definitions of all elements of cost must be given. The content of prime cost—direct materials, direct labour, direct expense—and of each subdivision of overhead expenses, i.e., works, selling and administrative overhead, must be defined precisely, so as to eliminate any possibility that different firms might record and subsequently report the same costs under different heads. At the same time, certain expenditure will usually be specifically excluded from costs, e.g., taxation, debenture interest, etc., and these exclusions need clearly to be set out.

It is becoming common for all modern schemes to include a code of accounts. All assets, liabilities, expenditures and incomes are listed and numbered, and the content of each account is specified. The accounts for expenditure and income are arranged in groups so that the content of such group totals as prime cost or works overheads is automatically also specified. Quite apart from the gain in clarity and precision which this system brings, the numerical code greatly facilitates the adoption of mechanical methods of accounting.

Uniformity of definition within an industry is of the essence of uniform costing. A comparison of the definitions used by different industries shows, on the other hand, a remarkable lack of uniformity, in spite of the efforts of the Institute of Cost and Works Accountants to secure a standardised costing terminology. Almost any costing term could be taken as an example, but "direct materials" will serve. The definitions of this term to be found in the British uniform systems fall into two groups. One group, which includes the definitions used by the printers, iron founders, and steel fabricators, consists of variations on the theme that direct materials are those which can be charged direct to the job, or customer, or specific cost unit. The other group of definitions, which includes those of the steel wire makers and drop forgers, takes as the test of " directness " in materials that they should actually enter into the body of the finished product. There are, too, many variations on this formula. The different ways in which different industries define " direct materials " are partly explainable by reference to each industry's specific problems. Thus, for chocolate or hosiery manufacture, boxes are important enough to be included in direct materials, whereas in some other industries packing is a distribution overhead. But if differences of definition as between industries are to be explained by reference to their different needs, it seems perhaps possible that, in view of the difficulty of defining an " industry ", different firms in the same " industry " may also find their interests better served by some diversity of definition rather than by uniformity. Any justification for diversity of definitions between industries may to a considerable extent also justify diversity between firms in the same industry.

3. Wherever the value of resources is liable to change between the date of their purchase and their consumption in a productive process, the basis on which they are to be valued for inclusion in the costs needs to be defined. More specifically, the basis of valuation of raw material issues and the basis for computing depreciation of fixed assets ought to be laid down.

What is deemed important for uniform costing is that all firms in the industry should adopt the same valuation bases. Yet, surprisingly, an examination of the existing British schemes shows that remarkably few of them contain any precise directions on either of these important sources of disuniformity. And those which do by no means agree on the manner in which these problems are to be dealt with, as the following tabulation of a random selection of schemes shows :

Scheme	*Basis of Valuing Material Issues*	*Basis of Calculating Depreciation of Plant*
Printers	Not specified	By diminishing balance method on " working value " of plant (which is not necessarily book value)
Iron and Steel ..	At current values	Depreciation not included in costs
Plastics	First-in-first-out	Not specified

Scheme	*Basis of Valuing Material Issues*	*Basis of Calculating Depreciation of Plant*
Cotton Weaving ..	.. At standard price	By straight-line method, on "replacement value" of plant
Steel Wire ..	.. At Trade Association's list price ..	At Income Tax wear and tear rates on diminishing balance
Laundries ..	.. Not specified	At 15 per cent. on written down value
Cocoa and Confectionery	.. Actual cost, if ascertainable, or average cost	At 7½ per cent.—15 per cent. according to life of plant
Steel Foundries	.. Average cost	At 120 per cent. of Income Tax wear and tear rates

It is, of course, not a mere difference in depreciation *rates* which is here in question. That would be sufficiently explained by the different conditions in different industries. But these differences are not sufficient to explain the extraordinary variety of *methods* which have just been listed.

4. Since uniform costing schemes, as at present conceived, always aim at computing average total cost, the method of apportioning overheads has to be specified. This involves answering many questions. What productive departments are to be distinguished within the firm? Are departments to be further divided into cost centres?[1] What service functions are to be treated as separate departments? Are overheads to be subdivided into such categories as works, selling and administration overheads, and in what way? And how is each kind of overhead expense to be apportioned to departments and ultimately to units of product?

As might be expected, a great variety of methods for dealing with these questions is to be found among the existing uniform systems. Here, too, many of the differences between methods in different industries are naturally due to real differences between the industries. But some at least of the variations are no more than reflections of the essentially arbitrary nature of any method of allocating "common costs".

5. A fundamental aspect of the problem of allocating overheads concerns the treatment of idle capacity. Are full overheads to be charged to current output even when this represents substantially less than full capacity? Or is a separate "cost of idle capacity" to be ascertained and

[1] Defined as a production unit, within a department, for which separate running costs can be ascertained.

written off as unproductive expenditure? The following tabulation shows how this problem is dealt with by 16 British uniform schemes:

Scheme	*Treatment of Idle Capacity Costs*
Iron and Steel, and Black Bolts	Temporarily idle plant is to be charged with due proportion of charges which continue to be incurred and which would have been charged to production if plant had been working. Permanently idle plant is to be charged only with amounts directly incurred on it. Both sets of charges to be written off as unproductive losses
Plastics	Labour "idle time" to be charged as indirect labour
Cotton Weaving	Fixed and variable costs are distinguished, so that effect on costs of changes in capacity usage can be seen
Iron Foundries	Standard overhead rate is recommended, so that effect of idle capacity will be reflected in under-absorption of overheads
Brushes	Full overheads charged to current output, even when this is below normal
Fertilisers	Proportion of overheads pertaining to idle plant to be written off as unproductive loss only in exceptional circumstances, e.g., where plant is surplus to requirements. Otherwise, costs of idle capacity, if above normal, to be noted for information, but to be left in cost records as current running costs (Idleness above normal means idleness due to seasonal shut down, major repairs, planned shut down of excess capacity, etc.)
Dyeing and Cleaning ..	Value of information as to costs of idle capacity is mentioned, but the system does not give the information
Printers, Steel Wire, Steel Fabricating, Laundries, Cocoa and Confectionery, Drop Forging, Hosiery, Opticians	Not specified

6. Besides the materials and services which have to be paid for by current disbursements, there may be other factors of production employed in the business which, because they are owned by the proprietors, give their services "free". Freehold buildings are occupied rent-free. The proprietors' capital involves no outlay of interest. A sole trader's business or a partnership will be managed by the proprietor(s), whose remuneration will emerge as profit rather than as a cost. Even in a private limited company, the directors' salaries, which are fixed at will, may bear no relation to the market value of the managerial services which the directors render. In any cost comparison between a firm which hires all its factors and one which owns some, costs have to be "imputed" to the owned factors in order that the recorded costs of the two firms may be truly comparable.

Here again, there is a valuation problem. How are the proprietors' managerial services (if any) to be valued?

How is the occupancy of freehold buildings to be assessed? And in the case of interest on capital, there is, besides, the whole vexed question (at least it vexes cost accountants if not economists) of whether this should be included in costs at all, even when the capital is borrowed and interest on it has actually to be disbursed.

It will, by now, not be surprising to find a great variety of approaches to these questions in the British Uniform Systems which have been examined. The following tabulation will give some idea of the variety of methods recommended:

	Treatment of Interest on Capital	*Proprietor's Services*	*Owned Buildings*
Printers	Charge interest at 5 per cent. on all capital employed	Allow a "reasonable" salary	Charge interest on the capital value of buildings, a "fair" amount for depreciation, and all maintenance costs
Iron and Steel, Cotton Weaving, Iron Foundries, Black Bolts	Interest not to be included in costs	Not dealt with	Not dealt with
Steel Wire	Interest is regarded as an appropriation of profit, not as a cost	"Reasonable" remuneration to be charged	Not dealt with
Laundries	Interest is not regarded as a cost, but is to be entered on cost sheets as a memorandum entry	A "proper" allowance to be made for proprietor's services	Charge annual rateable value in lieu of rent
Cocoa, Chocolate and Confectionery	Not dealt with (but see last column)	Charge a "reasonable" salary for managerial services and usual rates for other services	Mortgage interest, if any, to be treated as rent of mortgaged building
Hosiery	Interest to be omitted from costs but to be considered when fixing price, as part of the profit	Not dealt with	Charge gross Schedule A Assessment
Brushes	Interest to be omitted from costs	Charge a "reasonable" salary—what an employee would have to be paid	Charge depreciation at 2 per cent. p.a. on original cost, or net Schedule A Assessment
Clothing	Inclusion of interest in costs is regarded as theoretically correct, but it is to be excluded to avoid "controversy and confusion"	Partner's actual salary to be charged	Not dealt with

	Treatment of Interest on Capital	*Proprietor's Services*	*Owned Buildings*
Opticians	Only interest on short-term bank overdraft to be included in overheads. Long-term interest to be treated as appropriation of profits	To be treated like directors' remuneration	Charge gross Schedule A assessment
Fertilisers	Interest not to be included in costs	Charge a notional amount "appropriate to the services rendered"	Nothing is to be included in costs for occupancy of owned buildings
Steel Fabricating	In general, interest should be excluded from costs but it should be included where: (1) work on job goes on over extended period without commensurate progress payments (2) money is borrowed to finance a specific contract (3) materials require maturing — interest then to be included in the materials charge	Not dealt with	Charge expenditure, on repairs and maintenance, and depreciation of buildings in lieu of rent
Dyeing and Cleaning, Plastics, Drop Forging	Not dealt with	Not dealt with	Not dealt with

It would be tempting to look for profound explanations of the striking lack of uniformity in the treatment advocated by different industries of the specific costing problems which have just been examined. Yet such evidence as there is suggests that no such profound reasons exist. The methods incorporated in an industry's costing scheme tend to be those already widely adopted in the industry, or it may happen that a particularly forceful member of the costing committee charged with the preparation of the scheme is able to press his views on his more pliable colleagues and get them written into the scheme. One of the oddities of British uniform costing—the complete exclusion of depreciation from costs in the iron and steel industry—has no more profound explanation than that the costing committee which drew up the original scheme left depreciation for special subsequent consideration but has never in fact filled this gap in the scheme.[1]

7. If the system is to appeal to all or most of the firms in an industry, it must endeavour to meet the differing needs of large and small firms. It is, perhaps, to a failure to do this that the demise of a number of schemes can be attributed. In the main, two methods have been used to permit diversity in costing schemes without abandoning their essential uniformity. Sometimes two or three versions of the scheme have been prepared, all basically similar but introducing into the versions adopted for larger firms more detail and complexity than is permitted in the small-firm versions. In other cases, only one scheme is prepared, but within the broad outlines applicable to all firms, additional detail is introduced by the subdivision of main account heads for adoption only by the larger firms.

(*To be concluded*)

The London School of Economics.

[1] "DEPRECIATION AND OBSOLESCENCE. It is recognised that provision for depreciation and obsolescence is a proper charge against cost, and that the basis for the determination of the provision for inclusion in the cost requires thorough investigation.

Pending such investigation it is recommended that costs shall not include any provision for depreciation and obsolescence, but that for statistical purposes the provision might be entered as a footnote."—*The Iron and Steel Industry Uniform Cost System*, p. 14.

.Uniform Cost Accounting—A Survey

By David Solomons

Part II[1]

Uniform Costing's Objectives

In the first part of this article, an attempt was made to give some idea of what uniform costing is. We can now turn to a consideration of its objectives, of the social consequences of achieving these objectives, and of how far its actual achievements fall short of its aspirations.

The objectives of uniform costing can be summarised under four heads. They are:

(1) To improve each firm's knowledge of its own costs so that it can

(a) seek out sources of inefficiency and waste, and

(b) base its prices on true cost information rather than on mere conjecture.

(2) To provide a uniform basis of price fixing as between firms, and so to eliminate competition based on imaginary cost differences.

(3) By facilitating an exchange of cost information within the industry, to improve each firm's knowledge of its competitors' costs, so that each producer will be stimulated to effect economies by profiting from the experience of the most efficient.

(4) To facilitate enquiry into specific cost problems of the industry. The enquiries may be carried out by, say, a Research Association with a view to ascertaining which of two methods of production is more efficient: or they may be made by a Trade Association to provide a factual basis for negotiation with a Government department. This is to say nothing of the use of standardised accounting as an instrument of control in a planned economy such as Nazi Germany.

[1] For Part I see *Economica*, August 1950, pp. 237—253.

Many other claims have been made for uniform costing from time to time, but they are usually little more than variants on the four points set out above. Let us now subject these to closer examination.

The first claim mentioned is, in effect, that the spread of uniform costing means the spread of good costing, and that this is in itself a good thing. The discussion of uniform costing within trade association circles helps to make member firms cost-conscious : and the preparation of a single system for the whole industry represents an important "external economy" which substantially reduces the cost of costing for each firm. There is, therefore, an increase in the demand for costing and a reduction in its price, a combination of circumstances which can usually be relied upon to result in an increase in consumption of the service in question.

It is, of course, impossible to prove or disprove that the uniform costing movement has resulted in a wider recourse to cost accounting than there would have been without it. Evidence has already been adduced which suggests that progress in this direction has been less impressive than is commonly supposed, and that in some cases uniform schemes have been short-lived and have left little mark on the industries which sponsored them. Nor is it at all self-evident that the Heavy Clothing Working Party is right in thinking that, as the result of the work of some central body, "the best [costing] system would be brought within the means of every member". The essence of a uniform costing system is, after all, that it should be widely adopted. It must therefore be kept within the reach of those firms who are worst equipped and staffed to handle complex records. The industry is liable to have to go at the pace of the slowest, and the firms with advanced or novel methods of cost ascertainment and cost control are at least as likely to be held back by a uniform scheme as are those with more rudimentary costing systems to be helped forward. It is no answer to this charge to say that the uniform scheme is a minimum scheme which does not preclude elaborations or developments of it, for such a contention is not generally true. For instance, firms which might wish to adopt standard costing methods, by which costs are analysed by processes and functions rather than by products, would certainly find such methods incompatible with a uniform costing system designed to give

B

continuous information about "actual" product costs. Again, a firm which desired its costing system to give information about incremental costs would be hard put to it to extract such information from a uniform system which was designed, as most existing systems are, to provide figures of average total cost per unit of product. One result of these conflicts may be that, where the uniform costing scheme is the basis on which a trade association collects and circulates cost statistics, member firms who wish to continue to support the scheme, but who also want cost information of a kind different from that provided by the uniform system, are driven to keep two sets of records or at least to prepare two sets of cost statements, one set to meet the requirements of the trade association, the other giving the information which they require for their own purposes.

Again, there is a danger that, a uniform scheme having once been adopted as the "one best scheme" for the industry, its very existence will encourage resistance to change. Uniform schemes are often revised in detail, but it is unusual for a new edition to embody any fundamental departure from the original scheme. Thus each scheme tends to crystallise the state of costing practice which existed when it was first devised. It is noteworthy, for example, that no British scheme published before 1936 introduces cost standards as an integral part of the system.

Turning now to the problem of competitive price fixing, there are two distinct but related aspects of uniform costing which need to be considered. One of these is concerned with providing the entrepreneur with accurate information about his costs so that prices can be rationally based. This is generally agreed to be desirable. But one need not therefore agree with the Rubber Proofed Clothing Working Party when it argues that one advantage of systematic cost accounting is that "no individual manufacturer can damage the whole trade by engaging in uneconomic trading". Such a statement is, of course, not true if, as seems likely from the context, "uneconomic trading" here means selling below average total cost, for such a phenomenon will certainly be possible and may be advisable, whatever costing system is being operated. A good system, in fact, will emphasise the distinction between those costs which tend to be fixed and those most likely to be variable with changes in output and so will facilitate selling at less than "full cost" where this is justified by the state of the market.

The other contribution which uniform costing is said to make to the elimination of "unhealthy" competition is not so much that it provides entrepreneurs with an *accurate* basis for price fixing as that it provides them with a *uniform* basis for it. The point has often been illustrated by some such example as the following. Two producers, A and B, each produce hooks and screws. A charges the two products with overheads by adding a percentage on prime cost. B charges overheads by adding a percentage of direct labour cost. The costings of the two products, when prepared, look like this (the figures, of course, are quite fictitious):

		Producer A		*Producer B*
		£		£
Hooks (per cwt.)				
Material		10		12
Labour		6		4
Prime Cost		16		16
Overheads	100 per cent. on prime cost	16	200 per cent. on labour	8
		£32		£24
Screws (per cwt.)				
Material		18		12
Labour		14		20
Prime Cost		32		32
Overheads	100 per cent. on prime cost	32	200 per cent. on labour	40
		£64		£72

If we assume that A and B each make 1 cwt. of each product, both producers incur total prime costs of £48 and total overheads of £48. On both products each producer's prime costs are the same. For a total expenditure of £96, each can produce 1 cwt. of hooks and 1 cwt. of screws. So far as real factors go, competitively there is nothing to choose between the two firms. Yet simply because they adopt different costing procedures, B will drive A out of the market for hooks, and A will drive B out of the market for screws, with dire results for both of them. So much, runs the argument, for un-uniform costing.

The point has been succinctly expressed in general terms by two American writers as follows: "The greatest advantage to be derived from uniform cost methods is that of ensuring a more uniform selling price. This object would be attained, even if the uniform system were not as scientific as it should be, for if errors were made through the method established, all manufacturers would at least be figuring the same way, all would be making the same mistakes, and unfair and ignorant competition would be eliminated."[1]

Now, so far from this being an argument in favour of uniform costing, it is a strong argument against it. If it is true that uniform costing can lead to the perpetuation of a system of prices based on erroneous cost information, we shall be much better off without it: for with normal competition, firms will jostle each other out of their errors. To revert to our numerical example above, we can surely expect that when Producer B finds that he is monopolising the market for hooks but is being driven out of the market for screws, he will take advantage of the opportunity to push up the price of hooks: and if he has unused equipment because of the loss of screw sales he would be foolish indeed if he preferred to leave this idle rather than accept orders for screws at some price which, while it might be less than £72, still made a useful contribution to fixed costs. And with producer A acting similarly but in reverse, their errors of price fixing would soon be eliminated. And when we add that this jockeying for position will be going on between not two but many firms, the chances of such errors persisting for long seem slight indeed—unless a uniform costing system perpetuates them for us.

In general, trade associations both in Great Britain and in the United States which have prepared uniform cost

[1] Nicholson and Rohrbach, *Cost Accounting*, p. 12; quoted by the Federal Trade Commission in their report on Open Price Trade Associations, 1929.

schemes have made no secret of the fact that one of their primary motives in so doing was to eliminate "uneconomic competition", by which is usually meant selling below average total cost. Some of the British schemes, for example, make the point quite explicitly. Thus, the fertiliser industry's scheme states that "lack of costs or fallacious costs may innocently cause unfair prices—either under control or under competition". In the view of the Council of Ironfoundry Associations, "the principal advantage of the adoption of uniform costing methods is the elimination of unhealthy competition in an industry due to lack of cost information or lack of comparability in the methods employed in finding the cost of individual jobs". In cotton weaving, "uniformity in the ascertainment of cost data and the application of sound principles will be vital to the industry in the future. Co-operation is imperative for price management. . . ." Mr. E. Victor Amsden, who prepared the chocolate and confectionery scheme, wrote in *The Accountant* that "in the cocoa, chocolate and confectionery industry a system was produced to encourage cost keeping of an improved kind with the idea that sound costing methods would reduce price cutting".[1] There is much other evidence of the same kind that, whether it is called "price management" or "orderly selling" or "the elimination of unhealthy competition" or the "maintenance of price stability", the prevention of price cutting is usually well to the fore in the minds of those who advocate uniform costing.

There is, of course, nothing inherent in uniform costing to prevent real price competition, and some trade associations have recognised this. Thus, the Wholesale Clothing Manufacturers' Federation, in the introduction to its costing scheme, says: "It should be clearly understood that the Costing System makes no attempt to fix prices. What it aims at is to enable a manufacturer to arrive at his true cost . . . if there are special circumstances which compel or influence him in selling at a lower rate of profit or even for no profit at all, the Costing System enables him to do this with his eyes open and with a full knowledge of the lowest figure which may be quoted without entailing a loss".

[1] "Uniform Costing Systems", by E. Victor Amsden. *The Accountant*, 24th October, 1942, pp. 255–257. Mr. Amsden also prepared a uniform costing scheme in 1923 for the National Association of Master Bakers, Confectioners and Caterers.

And the Dyeing and Cleaning scheme even goes so far as to recognise that " among certain members of the Industry some apprehension may exist that the installation of costing systems will throw into bold relief the low processing cost of certain lines handled, and result in extensive price reductions to the disadvantage of the trade in general ". The fact is that a scheme designed to distinguish clearly short-run incremental costs might well stimulate price competition rather than the reverse, since it would show how far prices could safely be cut.

The effect of uniform costing is, nevertheless, usually to obscure short-run cost differences between the firms in an industry and by eliminating so-called " uneconomic " competition much of the sting is, at the same time, taken out of price competition altogether. The obscurement of cost differences is effected by concentrating attention on average total cost, which will usually be less dissimilar for different firms in the industry than will their variable costs. There are a number of reasons why this should be so. For instance, new firms will tend to be more highly mechanised than old firms. Their fixed costs will therefore probably be higher and their variable costs lower. Thus for a short period they could undercut their older rivals if they were content to cover only their variable costs : and if their fixed equipment is not fully employed and there is in the short run no alternative use to which it could be put, it would seem to be in their best interests to do so. But such action will clearly be discouraged by costing methods which focus attention on average costs, including full overhead allocations. Again, the inclusion of " imputed " costs, such as a salary to the proprietor of the business or a notional rent for premises which are owned will swell recorded costs by amounts which, for short periods, do not represent any opportunity costs at all. Few business men would not prefer to forgo their remuneration for a short period rather than give up their businesses. A building specially adapted to one purpose cannot easily or quickly be switched to another, even if it could then command a high rent. And even if it is not highly specific, in reckoning its value in another use the cost of closing down the existing business and moving ought strictly to be taken into account.

Thus by including in costs items which do not at all times for all firms represent real sacrifices of producing, uniform costing may give no more than an illusion of uniformity, and it is for this reason that at the beginning of this article I preferred not to adopt the definition of uniform costing put forward by the U.S. Chamber of Commerce. But too much should not be made of this criticism, as some American critics of uniform costing have at times tended to do. It is true, as these critics have pointed out, that there are other ways in which this sham uniformity can be induced. Thus the inclusion in costs of interest on capital employed in the business will raise the apparent costs of highly mechanised firms more than the costs of those less mechanised even though capital, once sunk in specific equipment, has no opportunity cost in the short run. Again, some firms may produce a commodity as a by-product, while others produce it as a main product. This implies real cost differences as between the two types of producers. These differences can be seemingly eliminated by some arbitrary method of allocating costs to by-products. It is easy to multiply methods like these by which costs which may really be different can be made to look the same. In fairness it must be said, however, that many of these methods are seldom found in practice. Of the British schemes which have been examined, few do in fact advocate the inclusion of interest in costs, and none attempts to allocate costs (other than post-separation costs) to by-products. In the United States, too, "there is . . . by no means a wide acceptance of the proposition that interest is properly chargeable to cost. . . ."[1] Moreover, in the last resort, firms which are not prepared to give up their short-run competitive advantages by adopting the cost methods just described will simply not adhere to the system laid down for their industry. This, perhaps, more than anything else explains the insecure hold which uniform costing has on the loyalties of the members of the trade associations concerned with it.

Uniform costing has sometimes gone beyond merely recommending uniform *methods* of costing, and has laid down certain uniform *figures* and rates for adoption throughout an industry. Thus uniform rates of depreciation may be recommended. A uniform percentage of capacity usage may be laid down for adoption as a base for spreading overheads. These rates and percentages naturally do not always correspond to every firm's own experience. The substitution of

[1] *T.N.E.C.*, Monograph No. 18, p. 262.

uniform data for each firm's own is only a first step. It may be followed by the substitution of uniform " costing rates " for each producer's own costs. It is then only a short step to the adoption of uniform profit loadings and eventually to the enforcement of agreed selling prices throughout the industry.

Again, it would be wrong to tar uniform costing too freely with this brush. In Great Britain uniform costing rates are not common, and where put forward by a trade association they are intended for use only by firms which have no system of their own (uniform or otherwise) for ascertaining costs. Thus the British Federation of Master Printers issues a folder of Standard Hourly Cost Rates. These rates, says the folder, " are calculated from ascertained facts relating to printing offices generally. They . . . are issued for general guidance. They can, however, be used in conjunction with the Federation Costing System until figures for the individual business are ascertained by means of this system ". These costing rates, then, can be used in two ways—as a standard against which each firm can compare its own figures, and as a basis of costing by firms which have no costing systems of their own. They represent the cost per hour of printing, not the cost of doing any specified printing job. The printer is left to use his own judgment as to the amount of printing he can expect to do in an hour. It would be absurd, in the circumstances, to regard the Federation's folder as an instrument of monopolistic extortion. In other cases, such as the British iron and steel industry, uniform costing has followed rather than preceded agreed selling prices for the industry's products.[1] In America, the Hardwood Lumber and Maple Flooring Cases of 1925, brought under the Sherman Anti-Trust Law, have made trade associations circumspect about costing practices which might be interpreted as illegal agreements between producers.[2] The transformation of uniform costing into uniform pricing is a potentially dangerous development rather than a present evil. That it is, at least in Great Britain, a real danger is seen from the passage in the Linoleum Working Party's Report to the effect that uniform costing would facilitate the furnishing of

[1] And for a reference to the pottery industry see *Economica*, Aug. 1950, p. 103.

[2] For a careful study of the legal status of uniform costing and related practices in U.S.A., see Richard H. Lovell, " Sales Below Cost Prohibitions ", *Yale Law Journal*, Vol. 57, pp. 391–425 (January 1948).

"information on costs for the purpose of fixing minimum prices". And it has yet to be seen whether No. 17 of the functions of Development Councils set out in the Schedule to the Industrial Organisation Act, 1947, the "formulation of standard costings", is a step in the same direction.

Uniform methods of cost ascertainment, in their price-fixing aspect, are, as we have seen, open to criticism. As a pre-requisite to a scheme for an exchange of cost information within an industry or trade, however, the value of uniform costing can hardly be gainsaid, though it is, of course, no more than a pre-requisite. As such, its value depends on what the trade association concerned does with it. This would be too obvious to be worth mentioning if it were not for the fact that, in Great Britain at least, it is exceptional to find a uniform costing scheme which is actually used as the basis for an exchange of cost information.

Two advantages are claimed for a dissemination of cost data among the members of a trade association. "Most cost statistics serve the dual purpose of enlivening the member's consciousness of the relation of cost to price and of stimulating his interest in the better and more economical management of his business",[1] i.e., cost statistics educate members to sell above cost, and to get costs down. The first of these functions has already been fairly fully discussed, though it should here be added that there is an additional danger, when costs are reported to a trade association, that active pressure may be brought to bear on low-cost producers not to "spoil the market". The second, or cost-cutting function, is of a much more constructive character. The pioneer work of Sir Arnold Plant and Mr. R. F. Fowler on the costs of running department stores in Great Britain is worth recalling in this connection. "The opportunity for the first time", they write, "to compare its own operating experience with the general experience of stores which it believes to be comparable provides a store with new information of definitely substantial importance. It is not that any special virtue attaches to possessing or attaining to a cost structure corresponding to that of generalised experience, but simply that, until the opportunity for such comparisons presents itself, the firm has no ordinates in relation to which it can plot the figures of its own experience".[2]

[1] *T.N.E.C.*, Monograph 18, p. 285.
[2] "The Analysis of Costs of Retail Distribution", *Economica*, May 1939.

It is clear that to be useful, the firm's comparison must be made with the costs of other firms " which it believes to be comparable ". Thus to satisfy this condition at all, the cost tabulation must analyse the participating firms into groups which are homogeneous at least as to the firm's size, locality and general type of product. Then, if the product can be more accurately defined so as to ensure reasonable homogeneity (e.g., a ton of pig iron), the cost per unit of output can be compared. Otherwise, only the percentage which each item of expense bears to total cost or to turnover can usefully be studied. The smaller the number of groups into which the whole sample is divided, the less valuable the comparison will be, for the group figures become merely an average of dispersed data. Obviously, a single set of averages for the whole sample will be of very little value at all. Ideally, each firm in the sample should be listed separately, under code, together with as many data as possible, such as turnover, number of employees, and so on to indicate the kind of organisation to which the costs in question belong, stopping short, however, of actually disclosing its identity.

It is perhaps too easily taken for granted that a high-cost producer is helped to make economies by knowing what his competitors' costs are. Enquiries made of a number of trade association executives have not clearly established many instances of economies being made in this way, though there have certainly been a few. The competitive firms in an industry are perhaps not unlike the candidates in an examination. To know what one's fellow-candidates' marks are may be interesting, but it is not clear that such knowledge will be helpful in improving one's own position next time. To know the average mark of all candidates would be even less valuable. What one wants to know is how to answer the questions. So, in the industrial field, a knowledge of other people's costs will, probably, only be useful if it gives rise to discussion in trade circles of *why* cost differences exist, or if cost statistics are circulated in such great detail as to show not only where but also how savings are effected. Thus a high-cost producer will not be greatly helped by the knowledge that a competitor's costs under the heading " materials " are less than his own. But the knowledge that this saving has been effected by substituting a cheap alloy for an expensive metal may be very valuable indeed. Cost statistics seldom, if ever, give such detailed information.

When one turns to enquire what trade associations in this country have achieved in the field of cost comparisons and the dissemination of cost statistics, based on uniform costing schemes, the results are not at all impressive. Through the activities of their costing department's accountants, who periodically visit some 300 firms, the British Federation of Master Printers have accumulated a good deal of information about the average cost per £1,000 of turnover, costs per 100 square feet of space and per £100 of capital employed in the printing trade, and this information is said to be used by the accountants when advising firms as to possible economies. But it is not made generally available to the industry, or even to the firms from which the information has been gathered. The Institute of British Launderers Ltd., just before the war, did arrange for a voluntary exchange of cost information in which about 20 laundries participated. Each firm received, every four weeks, a detailed tabulation of the turnover and costs of all other participating firms (represented by code letters), turnover being given in actual money values while costs (in detail) and trading profit were shown as percentages of turnover. In addition, information was given for each firm as to the average weekly number of customers in the period and the average price per bundle, the number of employees (divided as between "productive workers" and others), the average sales value of output and average wages per productive worker per week, the average weight of fuel used per week, the number of vans, average mileage run per week and the cost per mile, the total floor space, and the total installed horse power of steam engines or electric motors. With such information the danger that wrong conclusions may be drawn from a comparison of the costs of what are, but are not known to be, very differently situated businesses is at least substantially reduced. It should be noted that this scheme did not attempt to compare product costs, i.e., the costs of laundering particular articles, but only total costs (by type of expense). Unfortunately this promising scheme of the Launderers lapsed with the outbreak of war in 1939.

In a related industry, the National Federation of Dyers and Cleaners has very recently organised a quarterly exchange of cost statistics, in which about 30 firms are at present participating. The first tabulation was made for the December 1949 quarter. It is too early to say whether this scheme is likely to command wide support in the industry.

The only other known existing scheme for exchanging cost information which is based on a uniform costing system is that organised by the Iron and Steel Federation. Data are collected separately for each of the main products (pig iron, soft basic billets, black sheets, railway rails, sheet bars, steel plates, and steel joists). For pig iron, summarised costs per ton for each producer (represented by a code letter) are circulated monthly to all members in that section of the industry, while for other sections only the average costs for all producers are circulated. This information is also made available to the Ministry of Supply and plays its part in the price-fixing arrangements for the industry.

No trace has been found of any other instances of a uniform costing scheme serving as the basis for an exchange of cost statistics within an industry in this country. Trade association officials who were asked why their own associations, which had sponsored costing schemes, did not promote such an exchange of information, usually said that firms in their industry were unwilling to make cost data available to competitors, even under code. In one case it was suggested that the information, especially so far as it related to management remuneration and profits, might be misused by the trade unions in the industry. This last suggestion perhaps throws some light on the much wider circulation of cost statistics in American industry, where trade unions take a more favourable view of profits than that common among British trade unionists.

Finally, it has been claimed, a uniform cost system may be a pre-requisite to the institution of *ad hoc* cost studies and enquiries by a trade association or similar body. On the face of it, it is here that the greatest scope exists for " external economies " in the accounting field, and for really constructive work by trade associations, perhaps in collaboration with the co-operative research associations in each industry. So far as British experience goes, however, this work has hardly started. Of interest as a pioneer effort in the field of efficiency studies is the work of Dr. L. H. C. Tippett, at the Shirley Institute, for the cotton industry.[1] It is, however,

[1] For an account of Dr. Tippett's work see his article, " Study of Industrial Efficiency, with special reference to the cotton industry ", in *Journal of the Royal Statistical Society*, Vol. CX, Pt. II, 1947.

worth noting that the cotton investigations have been based on physical facts such as loom stoppages rather than on costs. There is all too little evidence that such cost data based on uniform costing as have been collected by trade associations in this country have proved to be of value even as a starting point for studies aimed at reducing costs. The amount of information which firms can be asked to provide as a matter of routine is naturally severely limited, and any particular expense heading therefore almost invariably covers what is in fact a heterogeneous collection of costs. A total of expenses grouped under some such caption as "material handling costs" is of little use to an investigator who is trying to compare the costs of mechanical handling with the costs of using wheelbarrows. Inevitably he will have to go to the individual firms for his information, and although uniformity of expense headings in different firms may make his detailed enquiries a little easier, the advantages of uniform costing, at least in its present form, in this respect can hardly be put higher than that.

Conclusions

Uniform cost accounting has a real contribution to make to industrial efficiency, but it is not at present making that contribution. As an instrument for improving each firm's knowledge of its own costs, its achievement in making smaller firms cost-conscious has been small while larger firms may actually sometimes have been held back in their costing methods. Uniform costing may well have reduced competition by obscuring cost differences between firms, but this can hardly be accounted a virtue from the social point of view. Little has been attempted in the way of disseminating information among firms about their competitors' costs, and what has been attempted, while it may have directed thought to the possibility of cost reductions, has not clearly indicated where or how such reductions might be effected.

These shortcomings are due to a misplaced emphasis. Trade associations have unfortunately if naturally emphasised the pricing aspects of uniform costing, whereas the constructive aspects are those concerned with the raising of efficiency and the reduction of costs. The failure of uniform costing to establish itself can be traced, it may be suggested, to its attempt to be all things to all men. Cost accountants are coming to realise that no one kind of grouping of costs can serve all the needs of even a single business. Much less can it serve all the needs of a number of diverse businesses. With the recognition of this fact, and an acceptance of a more limited rôle than its exponents at present claim for it, uniform costing could justify its existence. It could do this by providing a starting point for cost studies, to be carried out perhaps by operational research sections of research associations rather than by trade associations. Such studies would aim at the development of cost-saving techniques; they could be substantially helped by a form of uniform cost accounting which was not preoccupied with price fixing. A further study, not limited like the present one to a survey and critique of British uniform costing as it exists at present, might well be devoted to the reforms necessary to bring such a state of affairs about.

The London School of Economics.

COSTING TECHNIQUES—THEIR EFFECT ON MANAGEMENT PRACTICE AND POLICY

By DAVID SOLOMONS, B.COM., A.C.A.

"No board would think of carrying on operations without a set of commercial books arranged by an accountant in whom they had confidence, yet the equally important technical records are nearly always treated in an amateur spirit . . . So far is this attitude carried that many otherwise experienced business men really and conscientiously do not believe that shop accounts are of any use at all." So wrote Alexander Hamilton Church a little over fifty years ago. There may still be business men who harbour similar doubts, but if there are they do not voice them in public. The battle for the recognition of cost accounting (a term which is surely destined, within a few years, to sound as archaic as Church's "shop accounts") as an essential tool of management has long ago been won. How and why did this remarkable change in the status of costing come about?

It was, of course, in the engineering industry that costing first won its spurs, and it was undoubtedly the growth of competition in that industry in the second half of the last century which created the need that costing was to meet. So long as easy conditions in the industry prevailed, quotations for jobs could be arrived at "by guess, and by God;" but, said an editorial in *Engineering* in 1891, "the present-day conditions of the engineering and manufacturing trades, as regards keenness of competition and consequent narrowness of profit, render this subject (*i.e.*, costing) of an increased importance." Estimates had to be based on reliable cost data, of a kind which could not be obtained from the ordinary financial books. So methods of analysis, as between one job and another, of the materials and labour costs incurred on the jobs passing through the works had to be developed, and a system of job accounts built up which would show the prime cost of each job undertaken. Overheads would then be added on some more or less arbitrary basis. These ascertained job costs could be compared with the estimates on which quotations had been based. Estimators were thus enabled to learn from their past mistakes, and to base future estimates, in part at least, on past facts rather than guesswork. *The Engineer* had noted in 1869 that "an estimate right within 20 per cent. of the actual cost is . . . regarded as a very good estimate, and one reflecting much credit on the engineer and all concerned." Estimating errors of this order could hardly be tolerated in the more competitive conditions prevailing at the end of the century.

A large range of engineering products, half a century ago, were "made to measure." Each customer's order was a "job," to be costed separately. It was a short step from the regular use of cost information for pricing such jobs to its use for pricing batch-produced and mass-produced articles. In the substitution of facts for guesswork as a basis of pricing, the influence of cost accounting on management has been almost wholly good—*almost* wholly good, but not entirely and always so; for management has sometimes been misled into thinking that the "cost of production" of an article, as ascertained and presented by the cost accountant, is objective and accurate in a sense and to a degree that cost figures simply cannot be. I am not merely referring to the human fallibility which cost accountants share with other men, but rather to the inherent limitations of the figures themselves.

Limitations of Historical Costing

There are many reasons why no one figure of historical cost of producing an article can be set up as the indisputably right figure. Stocks of raw materials will usually have been bought at several different prices for any one material, and it is seldom possible to say what was paid for the material embodied in any particular unit of output. Again, the incidence of overtime rates of pay as between one unit of output produced in normal hours and another physically identical unit made after normal hours may be quite fortuitous, so as to make it meaningless to say that the second had cost more to

---

Elsewhere in this issue will be found comments concerning future developments in the profession. It is therefore of interest to see an article written by Mr. David Solomons, which first appeared in the November issue of *The Manager*. The author predicts the simplification of costing procedures as a result of more widespread application of statistical sampling methods, and expects greater use of costing techniques in the field of selling and distribution.

The article is reproduced by kind permission of *The Manager* and Mr. Solomons.

produce than the first. Yet again, overheads cannot but be allocated between units of output on an arbitrary basis, the choice of which must therefore always be open to argument; and according as current overheads are spread on the basis of actual current output, full capacity output or normal capacity output, very different unit cost figures will emerge. For these and other reasons, any cost system which purports to provide a uniquely correct figure of the cost of any particular article produced is certainly promising more than it can perform. Where management has been led into over-estimating what the cost accountant can do, it has sometimes been led into under-estimating the importance of demand conditions in determining prices. " Cost plus 10 per cent." only looks like an objective method of arriving at selling prices until it is remembered that the figure of cost must have been based on some assumption about the volume of output to be achieved; and unless, at the price so fixed, that volume of output can be sold, no more and no less, the costing process will have pointed not to the right price but to one of a large number of wrong ones.

Former Cost Control

It is not only in relation to pricing that the serious limitations of the old type of historical costing have to be recognized, for they are no less serious in the field of cost control. Fifty years ago, where cost accounts were kept at all, such control of costs as was exercised was effected by comparing the cost of each product from month to month. No doubt such control was better than nothing at all, but it clearly left a great deal to be desired. In the first place, it did not of itself distinguish between fluctuations in cost caused by factors outside the firm's control—say, the prices of raw materials—and those for which the management could be held responsible, such as an increase in scrap. Again, the overhead element in the cost of a product was liable to fluctuate, not only because the level of expenditure on overhead services varied but also because the volume of output over which the overheads had to be spread fluctuated from month to month. Thus, an increase in product costs one month compared with the previous month might merely reflect a fall in output; and again, without some standard by which to judge the firm's existing efficiency, relative either to its competitors or to its own best attainable performance, it was almost impossible to know what significance to attach to any reduction in product costs from month to month.

Development of Standard Costing

In view of the serious shortcomings of historical costing in the field both of pricing policy and of cost control, its virtual supersession by budgetary control and standard costing during the last twenty years is not very surprising. By far the most important development in the sphere of accounting since the emergence of double-entry book-keeping itself in the fifteenth century, standard costing is a product of the first decade of this century.

In essence, it consists of a systematic recording of the actual costs of carrying on any specified operation or group of operations, and a systematic comparison of such costs with predetermined cost standards set for those operations on the basis of certain assumptions about the conditions in which they are to be carried on. These assumptions relate to such matters as the prices and the efficiency of the factors of production to be used, and the scale of the operations. The precise nature of the operations has, of course, to be carefully defined. I use the word " operations " intentionally to cover the widest possible area of economic activity, for standard costing is certainly not restricted in its usefulness to the field of factory production. In Holland it has been applied to railway and omnibus operation; B.O.A.C. in this country are using it most successfully to control their airline results; it has been used by local government authorities in connection with such activities as the school meals service; and a good deal of attention has been given recently to the possibility of using it more extensively in hospital costing. It can, in fact, be applied to any activity in which a substantial element of repetitiveness can be found. Of course, it *could* be used even for jobbing work—say, the inspection and maintenance of domestic appliances—but the variety of the work would involve a large number of standards, each used rather infrequently, so that the cost of costing in these circumstances could well be prohibitive. However, it is perhaps of interest to note that one of the earliest writers on standard costing, over forty years ago, described its use in connection with shipyard repair work, a field of application which would test the skill of any cost consultant even to-day.

Standard costs are not, of course, the product of any one man's brain. The comparison of " actual " costs with cost estimates had become a fairly common practice in the engineering industry during the closing decades of the nineteenth century, and an estimate is, of course, a rough and ready standard. Again, in the textile industries, the practice existed of comparing the cost of the various processes carried on in an integrated business with the prices charged for each process by outside specialists, and as early as 1889 the technique of achieving this comparison within the double-entry accounting records had been worked out by G. P. Norton, a Yorkshire accountant. This was a substantial step towards standard costing. F. W. Taylor's doctrine of *Scientific Management* and Hamilton Church's distinction between the "scientific" and "supplementary" rates of overhead cost also contributed to the development of the use of standards in costing. After the turn of the century, we find a number of writers describing systems which incorporate standards in the accounting records, and so rapidly does the idea seem to have developed that standard costing had become a fully-developed management tool, in pretty much its present-day form, by the end of the 1914–18 war.

Budgets, used as aids to planning rather than as instruments of control, are much older than standard costing. The British Government has used them for over two hundred years. In business, it is difficult to say where planning ends and budgeting begins, but I once reproduced, elsewhere, an illustration of a budget drawn up for a French farm as long ago as 1825. Dunlops have been using budgets for about fifty years.

How have these developments influenced management during the last half-century? The question would be easier to answer if management were set to do the same things now as it had to do fifty years ago. But of course its tasks have grown altogether bigger and more complex, as the business unit has grown larger, the size of the individual plant has increased, and new materials, new processes, and new products have emerged. It is reasonable to doubt whether the modern giant industrial corporation could ever have evolved, or having evolved could have survived, without some such mechanism of control as standard costs and budgets provide. For the control of a large undertaking, if it is not to employ an altogether top-heavy hierarchy of controllers, must rely very largely on what F. W. Taylor called the "Exception Principle," that is, the principle that it is only the exceptional performance which should be brought to the attention of management and make demands on its time, whether the exceptionally bad which needs to be remedied or the exceptionally good which needs to be studied and profited by. And this is precisely what standard costing is designed to secure, for only when standard and actual costs substantially diverge is the attention of management claimed by the appearance of a variance in the firm's operating statements.

The control statements which emerge from a standard costing system are the large business's substitute for the detailed personal supervision which the proprietor of a very small business can exercise on the spot. Like personal supervision, they soon cease to exert even a moral influence if the detection of any unsatisfactory performance is not promptly followed by remedial action. Unlike personal supervision, which at the best will detect failure, call for explanation and apply the remedy almost simultaneously, a control statement will often not go beyond detection, and at the best will combine detection and explanation. Remedial action must be a management, not an accounting, function. I have sometimes wondered whether the quiet efficiency with which figures were churned out by many accounting departments did not leave management unaware of this simple truth.

Value of Budgets

Budgeting, which is quite practicable without standard costs but which will be easier and more accurate where budgets are prepared in conjunction with them, is *not* merely a device for providing the large business with a substitute for the personal direction of a working proprietor, for even the smallest of businesses will probably be better run with the help of budgets than without them. There are few private individuals, even, who have not found the drawing up of a cash forecast or an income and expenditure budget a salutary experience on occasion, and when one turns from private affairs to business (even small-scale business), the need for budgeting in some form is obvious. I am not, of course, suggesting that in the typical nineteenth-century business that did not go in for normal budgeting or in the present-day business which still does not do so, such matters as future cash requirements or sales and stock policy receive no attention. The business in which these were no-one's concern would soon be on the highway to extinction. But I am equally certain that the mere discipline of putting informed guesses and rough plans down on paper tends to make these guesses and plans more realistic and therefore more useful as a guide to conduct; and this is, in part at least, essentially what budgeting is and does.

But this is not the whole story. In the small business run by one or two working proprietors, no elaborate machinery is required to co-ordinate its various activities because, in any case, these are probably few in number and adequate co-ordination is effected by informal methods. Within the large business, however, to say nothing of the giant corporation, it is *not* certain that without such formalized procedures as budgeting entails the sales department will not build up an organization to sell substantially more than the factory can produce, or that two or more departments will not, between them, be proposing to use more of a scarce material than the purchasing department can make available. Without the improvement and extension of budget procedures which have gone arm in arm with the development of standard costs, therefore, it is doubtful whether very large business organizations could function successfully for more than a very short time.

What Does the Future Hold?

How might costing and budgeting develop, and what impact might their probable development have on management in the foreseeable future? I wish I had any ground for hoping that my answer would be found, forty years from now, to correspond to the actual developments of the intervening years half as well as W. E. McHenry's prediction, made in the *Engineering Magazine* in 1914 that " 'What it costs to *do* things' and 'What it costs per HOUR' may some day supplant much present detail, laboriously worked out 'per ton' "; for in this sentence McHenry tersely summed up the whole trend of costing, as we can now see it since his time. Where do we go from here?

One line of development which I foresee is the progressive simplification of costing procedures and the elimination of superfluous work. The swing away from historical costing and towards standard costing has in itself effected a vast simplification and reduction in the volume of work in recording costs. Already simpler methods of stock control are superseding those cumbersome systems which require every receipt and every issue of material to be recorded in both quantity and value terms. There is room, certainly, for a simplification of the bases of wages calculation, to say nothing of P.A.Y.E., with which wages offices are now plagued. Further inroads into the volume of work at present done by costing departments will, I suspect, be made by the widespread use of statistical sampling methods, so that, just as already the work involved in quality control in the factory is greatly reduced by scientific sampling, so such *quantitative* controls as the measurement of output, the checking of invoices, and the like will be similarly simplified. The years ahead should see a continuous erosion of costing records which will make much of the paper work of to-day seem as cumbersome to our electronically-minded descendants as the job cost systems of fifty years ago now seem to us.

The widespread adoption of standard costing in recent years has resulted, perhaps, in an excessive emphasis on cost *control* and a relative neglect of the development of costing as an aid to management in choosing between alternative courses of action; but cost control methods are now so much more effective than formerly that there is no reason why this other important aspect of costing should not receive more attention. This is the second possible development which I foresee. Perhaps I might give one illustration of the kind of development I have in mind. The break-even chart has for many years been one of the principal instruments of what is sometimes called " marginal control." It is virtually the same device now as it was fifty years ago. On a two-dimensional diagram it plots costs and revenue against output. It can make no allowance for changes in product-mix. Neither can it allow for any influences other than output on costs and revenue. It is therefore an instrument of very limited usefulness I shall be surprised if it is the last word that can be said on the multifarious problems of marginal adjustment. It may be that cost accountants, unless they can equip themselves mathematically much better than they have needed to do hitherto, will have to cede this ground to the statisticians. Current developments in the field of linear programming also point to a need for adaptation by cost accountants to new possibilities and new techniques of business planning.

I can here mention only one other development in the field of costing which I foresee as having an important influence on management practices and policies, and that is the widespread application to the distribution function of costing methods for so long confined to production. The possibilities of such application were seen at least forty years ago in America, and a good deal of progress has been made there since, but there is little evidence in this country of any general awareness that it might be possible for a business to analyse its distribution costs between products, or between different methods or distribution, or between different types of customers, or between different sizes of order, and to profit from the information gained. The crude allocation of distribution costs between products in proportion to their production costs is still all too common. There is certainly room for development here.

COSTS, PLANS AND PRICES

The last half-century of development in cost accounting has seen notable advances in several directions. Most notable have been those in the techniques and understanding of cost control. Not that cost control is simply a matter of accounting : it involves much more than that. But the accountant's contribution to the tasks of managerial control has been a major one. The main advances have been two in number. First, standard costing and budgetary control have provided us with techniques greatly superior (for control purposes, and for most others) to the historical cost methods they are now rapidly ousting. Second, mechanisation of accounting methods has brought with it a speed and accuracy of control which are certainly destined to be carried much further, but which even now are sufficiently impressive. Together, these two forces have transformed the scene so far as the accounting aspects of cost control are concerned.

In the management accountant's other main sphere, that of the provision of data for planning and pricing purposes, the picture, I feel, is somewhat less impressive. The use of budgets (for planning as distinct from control purposes) has, to be sure, become more formalised and more widespread in business than it formerly was, and this is a development the importance of which must not be underestimated. But nor must we take too much credit for it. Let us remember that the practice of budgetting has been in use by government in this country for some two centuries, so that it is no new thing. Moreover, budgets were doubtless to be found in many businesses long before they became a subject for lecturers to discourse on.

ACCOUNTANTS AND MARGINALISM

There is another aspect of the planning problem which has received a good deal of attention from accountants in recent years, and that is the variability of costs with output or volume. It is to this that I propose to devote my attention in this paper, for in the realm of planning and pricing it is perhaps one of the most important relationships on which management has a right to look to the accountant for enlightenment. Whether the problem is one of determining selling prices, developing a new product line, entering new markets or closing a department or a plant, it is information about *incremental* costs which is relevant, and which the accountant should be able to provide. There is plenty of evidence, both in America and in Britain, that he is anxious to do what he can to provide it. The literature is full of discussions of marginal costing, cost-volume relationships, flexible budgets and break-even charts, and there are other signs that accountants have become thoroughly indoctrinated with marginalism. It is a curious fact that a few economists should have chosen just this time to advocate the abandonment of the marginal principle as a means of explaining a large sector of business behaviour, precisely when accountants are seemingly becoming converted to it in large numbers.

It must perhaps be added that it is not altogether easy to say just what it is they are being converted to ; for the discussion of marginal or variable or direct costing has been carried on at many different levels of sophistication. I propose, therefore, to attempt to distinguish between some of the different forms which accounting marginalism takes, in the hope that this may clarify subsequent discussion.

FIXED AND VARIABLE COSTS

At the lowest level of sophistication must be put all attempts to classify items in a manufacturing or profit and loss account, be it for a month or a year, into "fixed" and "variable" categories, thereby implying that a modest change in the volume of business would cause costs to vary or to remain fixed according to their classification. Such attempts may sometimes have some value. But they would appear to imply that the fixity or variability of particular kinds of cost is an inherent quality of those costs, whereas it is in reality a quality of a cost only in relation to a specific business decision. Thus most costs are fixed in relation to changes of output in the very short run, but variable if time is allowed for adaptation. Some costs are fixed in relation to one area of operations (e.g. a departmental manager's salary in relation to the operation of his department) and variable in relation to another (e.g. the departmental manager's salary in relation to the whole undertaking, if his department is closed down). Again, some costs are variable when output is expanded and yet are fixed (at least for a time) when output contracts again. Further, the degree of fixity in a fixed cost (i.e. the extent to which output can vary without the fixed cost ceasing to be fixed) may differ enormously as between one item of cost and another. It is difficult to see what questions of importance could be answered by a simple "once for all" division of costs into fixed and variable categories. Moreover, there must always be some doubt about the validity of judgments about future policy which are based on information drawn wholly from the past.

At least one of the above objections is met when figures of revenue, direct cost and margin are presented separately for each of a number of departments or product divisions, the total margin being shown as available to meet non-allocatable expenses and toprovide a profit. For this method of presenting the figures does not purport to tell us anything about the way they will behave in the face of small variations of volume, but only what costs will be avoided if the whole of a department or product division is eliminated. Such costs might be "fixed" in the face of small changes in the size of the department, but at least there is nothing arbitrary about having them charged direct to the department.

THE BREAK-EVEN CHART

I put the break-even chart next, without being too sure that it really does represent a more sophisticated approach. In some respects, of course, the break-even chart embodies a more advanced technique, since it presents a cost-profit-volume relationship as a static function, from which all extraneous disturbing factors, such as price changes, are supposed to have been eliminated. Moreover, the information it presents is budgetary in nature, not historical. A good deal more can be read from it, therefore, so far as future policy is concerned, than can be read from any account relating to a past period.

At the same time, as has been increasingly recognised in recent years, the break-even chart, and the kind of analysis which lies behind it, is subject to very serious limitations, for a number of reasons. To see these limitations at their most serious, let us suppose, first, that the break-even chart is constructed by means of the simplest techniques. This implies that expenses are categorised as fixed or variable by mere inspection of a code of accounts. Any expenses which are recognised as being semi-variable are broken down into their fixed and variable portions by the exceedingly simple device of plotting each of the semi-variables at two levels of output, and connecting the points by a straight line, the vertical intercept of this line giving the fixed portion of the expense, the slope of the line giving the variable portion. The objections to this simple approach are obvious. In categorising expenses as fixed or variable by inspection, the accountant is assuming the very knowledge he should be trying to acquire, i.e. knowledge as to the behaviour of costs with changes of output. Furthermore, in this and in his treatment of semi-variable expenses, he excludes the possibility of getting anything but a linear cost function. This result has the merit of simplicity, but little else.

It is true, as has often been claimed, that this simple approach may, by accident, give a not too unrealistic picture of the cost function. Thus, a number of different expenses, each of them varying with output in a curvilinear or irregular manner, might *in total* exhibit a linear relationship with it because the curvatures or irregularities cancelled out. Again, over the most significant range of output (say between 60 per cent. and 90 per cent. of capacity) the curvilinearity of the cost function might be so slight, or its irregularities so unimportant, that for all practical purposes it could be safely represented by a straight line. Or alternatively, the output levels at which additional fixed equipment and other resources (such as supervisory labour) have to be brought into use, and the fixed costs encountered at these output levels might, when plotted as points on a chart, form a straight line, thus suggesting that, *effectively*, the cost-function was linear after all. All these arguments can be used to support the use, for planning purposes, of a cost line derived from a simple fixed-variable classification of costs. But I do not think that we, as students and practitioners of accounting techniques, are entitled to derive much satisfaction from the fact that by a combination of happy accidents, a defective technique may give a not too misleading result.

REGRESSION ANALYSIS

So far, in my discussion of the break-even chart, I have assumed the use of only the simplest techniques in tracing the variation of costs with volume. Of course we can, and many firms do, do better than this, at the cost of bringing in some statistical assistance. And here we advance to a yet higher level of sophistication. Now we endeavour to derive from the recorded data of past periods, a more or less accurate statistical function, by which we can compute the level of costs, which can be expected to be associated with any specified scale of operation. This technique has been described in detail many times, and I do not propose to go all over this ground again. Briefly, it involves the construction of a series of scatter charts, one for each expense, or class of expenses, for which it is desired to obtain a separate cost function. Each point on the scatter chart represents the level of expense incurred at the scale of operations indicated by the distance of the point from the vertical axis. Each point therefore relates to a different moment of time. The period covered by the chart needs to be chosen carefully, of course, since ideally it should be one in which considerable fluctuations of output occurred, but in which no other disturbing factors affecting costs (e.g. changes in technique, type of production or price levels) were present. In practice, such disturbances will never have been entirely absent, however carefully the period has been chosen ; and since the period has to be a recent one if the results are to be at all relevant for future policy, the choice of time-span is in any case severely restricted. Consequently, the crude accounting data will usually have to be corrected so as to eliminate the effect of these disturbances before the data can be used, since it is the relationship of costs to scale of operations, unaffected by the influence of other factors, which we are trying to establish.

Now suppose that the scatter charts have been prepared, one for each expense or class of expense. We still have to deduce from them the regression lines which express the rate of change of each expense with changes in volume. Anyone who has done this or seen it done must have been beset by doubts as to the unique rightness of the line drawn. Of course, if the scatter charts were to present neat rows of points in straight lines, we should have no problem. But they never do so, and so the best fit possible has to be made. With luck, any error in the fit for one expense may cancel out an opposite error in another ; but the errors could conceivably be cumulative. There is, of course, no reason *a priori* why the regression line should be a straight line, though in practice it is usually drawn so.

In spite of justified doubts as to the validity of these regression lines, let us for the purposes of subsequent discussion accept them as being what they purport to be. What, then, do they purport to be? They represent nothing more nor less than an expression of the rate of change of processing costs (either individually or in the aggregate) with changes in "volume". And if we then ask what is meant by "volume", the answer must be that it is whatever it is defined to be.

This brings us to the heart of the problem of measuring incremental costs. For we find that, only in the rare instance of the firm which makes a single homogeneous product, can we, with certainty, derive from our regression lines information about the cost of increasing the output of a *specific product* by a specified number of units. In the much more typical case (we might almost say in the only case found in practice) of the firm which makes a variety of products by a variety of processes, since physical quantities of different products cannot be added together, a single figure for "output" or "volume" has to be arrived at by using some unit of input (e.g. man-hours or machine-hours) or of value (e.g. sales value or standard cost of each product) in terms of which an aggregation of different products can be expressed. It follows from this that the incremental process cost of, say, 1,000 units of each product will appear to depend on some one characteristic of the product—either the total machine hours needed to make it, or its sales value, or its standard cost, or whatever other characteristic was chosen to express its contribution to total output. So two products, each requiring the same total number of machine hours, say, or having the same standard cost will appear to have the same incremental cost at any given level of total output. There is, unfortunately, no compelling reason why these appearances need correspond with the facts.

A word about the treatment of materials is in place here. The incidence of materials costs will not usually be even approximately in line with the incidence of processing costs, as between one product and another. Nothing but harm, therefore, could be done by lumping materials in with other costs when establishing the regression lines. Materials, fortunately, are probably the one truly variable cost which can be associated with specific products (at least within the limits of any chosen flow convention—FIFO, LIFO or some other), so that their separate treatment does not present great difficulty.

Let me now sum up the dissatisfaction I feel with regression analysis, break-even charts and all that. While I do not deny that they provide useful information for some purposes, they do not provide information about the incremental cost of expanding the output of a specific product by a specific amount, taking into account the level of output of other products which are being made at the same time. Yet nothing less than this will enable management to set product selling prices in an entirely rational way. By rationality, I do not, of course, mean that the price of each product should be set so as to equate its short run marginal cost and marginal revenue. I do mean that prices should be set in the light of as much information as can be made available about these magnitudes, so that due regard can be had to them and to such other factors as management thinks relevant. Motives other than the maximisation of profit may be predominant, or long-run considerations may outweigh those of a short-run character. These are questions for management to decide. But I do not see how the best judgment about these matters can be made in the absence of accounting information about short-run marginal product costs.

DIRECT COSTING

What is variously known as direct or variable or marginal costing does, of course, present information of the so-called variable cost of each product, by computing the cost per unit of product of direct materials, direct labour and variable overheads. Usually, the variable overheads for which one unit of product "A" is held to be responsible, will be calculated by taking the departmental variable overhead rates per man-hour, or per machine-hour, established by regression analysis, or, more crudely, by the inspection of past accounts, and multiplying them by the number of man-hours or machine-hours spent by the product in each department. The aggregation of these departmental variable overheads and direct materials and labour on the product will give its total "variable cost".

Much the same doubts as I have already expressed must be raised about the claim of such a figure to represent the incremental cost of producing a unit of product "A". First, the amount of variable overhead per unit of product "A" will commonly be regarded as constant over a considerable range of output of the product, and this may (though it is not inevitable that it will) constitute a serious over-simplification. Second, it involves treating two products requiring, say, the same number of hours of processing in a department as necessarily being responsible for the same amount of variable overhead. Third, and more fundamentally, the variable overhead per unit of product "A" is regarded as dependent only on the quantity of output of product "A", regardless of the output of products "B", "C", "D", etc. ; whereas in fact, it must often be true that it costs more to increase the output of "A" by, say, 1,000 units when production of "B", "C" and "D" is at a high level than when it is low. In other words, the incremental cost of product "A" is not only a function of the level of production of "A" but also of "B", "C" and "D."

THE CRITERIA OF EFFECTIVE MARGINAL COSTING

Most of this paper, to this point, has been devoted to a somewhat destructive criticism of the manifestations of accounting marginalism which are most in evidence today. This does not mean that I think the accountant has nothing to offer in this field. But what he offers, if it is not to run the risk of ultimate rejection at the hands of management (in favour, possibly, of some alternative offering by the statisticians or engineers) must be able to stand up to careful scrutiny. I would suggest four requirements which must be met by any technique for the measurement of marginal or incremental cost before it has a right to be accepted as effective for managerial purposes :

1. If the technique purports to give us figures of short-run marginal cost, the nature and length of the short-run should be carefully specified.
2. The marginal cost data provided should be in respect of quantities of the products which the firm is making or is proposing to make, rather than in respect of amounts of a nebulous substance called "output" or "volume".
3. It should be possible fully to recognise that some costs do not change smoothly and evenly when output changes, but rather increase in jumps at critical production levels.

4. The technique should be able to take into account the quantities currently being produced not only of the product under enquiry, but also of all the other products being made as well.

It should hardly be necessary to add a fifth requirement—that the method used must not be so costly that the value of the information obtained falls short of the cost of getting it.

A SUGGESTED APPROACH

I cannot do more here than sketch in outline a method which seems to me to satisfy these requirements. It uses what is often called "the engineering approach", because so far as possible it works in terms of physical data, i.e. data as to the quantities of resources of materials, man-power, horse-power, space, etc. necessary to carry on the production of various combinations of products at various levels of output. In other respects, it resembles methods currently used for allocating overheads in certain trades, notably laundries, but with a significant difference which I shall explain.

In essence, it calls for the choice of some product characteristic which can be said to control the incidence of some one expense or more. For each expense, a different product characteristic might be chosen, though some, like weight or volume, might control the incidence of a number of expenses. In the case of some expenses, some combination of characteristics might have to be used, e.g. size-and-complexity. One unit of one product may then be chosen as a basis of measurement of this composite characteristic, units of other products being expressed as multiples or fractions thereof. Thus, in a laundry, the cost of water consumed, over and above a certain minimum cost, might vary with the weight of articles washed. The cost of calendering might vary with the superficial size of articles. Finishing costs might vary with the complexity of the articles handled, and since there is no simple unit in which to measure complexity, some basic article could be chosen and defined as being one finishing-unit, other articles being compared with this and defined as more or less than one finishing unit.

As I have said, some such method is already used by laundries to allocate costs to the great variety of articles which they handle. But there is an important difference between their practice and my suggestion : for they are concerned to allocate costs in such a way that the amounts allocated to each type of article will, at normal levels of operation, exactly absorb the total costs. My suggestion is not at all concerned with the *absorption* of costs but rather with the prediction of *variations* in cost when the size and composition of the work-load varies. The objective is therefore to build up a table of which the following might be a small extract. It shows the total cost, under a number of heads, of laundering varying numbers and assortments of articles per week.

Expense	*Product Unit*	3000	4000	5000	6000	7000
		£	£	£	£	£
Sorting	Number of articles	10	10	15	15	20
Washing	Lbs. weight	35	38	41	44	47
Drying	A space-time unit based on size and texture of material	4	6	10	12	16
Calendering	Sq. ins. area	7	8	9	10	11

In practice, of course, each"expense" above would be a whole group of expenses, for each of which the controlling product unit might have to be different.

Two important things should be noted about this table. First, the columns cannot be added up, for the totals would be without meaning. You cannot add the cost of sorting 3,000 articles to the cost of washing 3,000 lbs. weight of clothes, and come up with a meaningful total. Second, the figures need not and would not increase evenly as the number of units handled increases. At different points for different costs, additional equipment or additional labour has to be brought into use, and costs jump suddenly at these points. The above extract from the table shows this happening.

PUTTING THE TECHNIQUE TO USE

The kind of question the table is designed to answer is : "by how much might total costs be expected to increase if, at a time when existing weekly production is of a specified amount and composition, the production of article "X" is stepped up by 2,000 a week?" The answer is obtained, broadly, in two steps. First, the quantities of products already being made have to be converted into the various units used for "controlling" the different kinds of expense. Second, the production increase of 2,000 of article "X" has similarly to be converted. If, now, to revert to my earlier laundry example, the proposed production increase took the form of the laundering of 2,000 assorted articles, the foregoing calculations might show that this involved an increase in the weight of linen washed from 3,000 lbs. to 6,000 lbs., an increase in the number of drying units from 4,000 to 5,000 and so on. The incremental cost under each head could then be read off the table and aggregated to give total incremental cost.

QUESTIONS FOR DISCUSSION

The arguments used in this paper, and such constructive suggestions as it has contained, have been put forward somewhat tentatively, and it does not seem appropriate, therefore, to attempt to draw any conclusions, though some may emerge from discussion. I would, however, like to suggest a few points to which discussion might usefully be directed.

1. Can business planning in general, and price determination in particular, be effectively carried on if incremental cost data is not available ?

2. Does the group accept all the claims commonly made for the break-even chart ?

3. Do the break-even chart and other incremental cost data generally supplied to management meet all the practical needs of those exercising managerial functions ?

4. Would the proposals made at the end of this paper, if practicable, make a useful addition to the foregoing information ?

Controlling Costs in Small Businesses

By
DAVID SOLOMONS
PROFESSOR OF ACCOUNTING, UNIVERSITY OF BRISTOL

THERE can be no question but that, in all that pertains to the control of operations, small businesses start with a marked advantage over their larger competitors. In a really small business, the proprietor can exercise personal supervision of almost all that goes on; his dependence on subordinates is reduced to a minimum. Even in a business of medium size, the chain of command can still be short, with only one or two links between the boardroom and the shop or factory floor, and it is still possible to imbue employees, at least in the supervisory grades, with a sense of personal responsibility for the firm's fortunes. There can be less paperwork and more scope for individual initiative than in the large concern. Yet it is remarkable how often the small firm throws these advantages away. It throws them away because it is apt to try to operate in the dark. It so often neglects the means of keeping itself adequately informed about its costs. It is like a highly manoeuvrable vessel without good charts; in consequence, its manoeuvrability is wasted.

Information from annual accounts:

There is, nevertheless, a minimum amount of cost information which no business will be without. There will always be an annual Profit and Loss Account. The information about costs to be gleaned from this is not to be too lightly esteemed, for all its deficiencies. At the very least, it will be possible to compare expenses, suitably classified, from year to year, and therefore to detect exceptional changes. If the business is growing, so that all expenses are tending to increase, such simple comparisons will be less informative. In these circumstances, it becomes necessary to express each expense as a percentage of total expenses before unusual movements can be brought to light.

Sometimes, a cost per unit of output can be computed quite simply from the annual accounts and this provides quite a good starting point for cost comparisons. In a small distillery it might be cost per gallon, in a road haulage business it will be cost per mile or per ten-mile. In a retail shop or store, cost per customer served (the number of sales being counted on the cash register) may be a useful figure to know. But if the business's activities become more diverse, the unit of output which has been selected to be costed can less and less adequately represent all the different kinds of output which the firm produces, so that simple figures of the "cost per ton" type will no longer do. The next step, therefore, is to prepare accounts in which the results of each department or division of the business are kept separate.

A further aid to cost control can be provided by separating the fixed and variable costs—or, more precisely, the "period" costs and the "product" costs—in the accounts. When "product" costs are deducted from product revenue, the contribution towards period costs and profit which is being made by each product (if these are few in number) or each group of products is clearly shown. If conditions experienced in the immediate past can be expected to continue into the future, then it is possible to determine the level of business which has to be achieved in order that any desired level of profit shall be reached or in order that the firm as a whole shall break even.

Short-period accounts:

In what has been said about the use of figures from the annual accounts, it can hardly be a matter for argument that the same kind of information produced at intervals of less than a year will be more valuable still. Just how short the interval should be—whether one month, three, or six—must be a matter for managerial judgment in each case. You cannot increase the frequency of accounting without increasing its cost somewhat. How many more figures is it worth the small business's money to buy? All one can say is that, in too many cases, proprietors and managers of such businesses under-invest rather than over-invest in accounting information.

The limitations of accounting comparisons:

A progressive business will not be content, however, to look to the past as a means of controlling costs; and in any case, a comparison of the costs of one period with those of another may be vitiated by several disturbing factors. In the first place, the general level of prices may have changed so that what, for instance, may appear to be a serious rise in costs, reflecting adversely on the efficiency of the firm, may be no more than the inevitable result of economic factors quite outside the firm's control. Again, the character of the firm's activities or the quality of its products may have changed during the period covered by the cost comparison. This, too, will upset the comparison. Or a change in the percentage of total capacity which is being used will lead to a change in unit costs of production, simply because the fixed costs, unchanged in total, bear less heavily or more heavily on each unit of output when capacity usage goes up or down. Here are three reasons why simple cost comparisons over a period may not provide a reliable guide to the *efficiency* with which the firm is using its resources.

A different approach:

In seeking a more effective means of cost control, it is necessary to make a separate approach to the control of what I have earlier called "product costs" on the one hand, and "period costs" on the other. The classification of costs into these two categories will differ from one type of business to another; it can be seen most clearly in manufacturing businesses, where the costs of materials that go into the product and of labour that works directly on the product are the main elements of product costs, while fixed overheads typically relate to a period of production rather than to any particular product. In a distributing business, a larger part of the costs will be period costs, though some important items like packing materials and variable transport costs will constitute product costs.

Now whereas period costs in total do not vary in the face of moderate changes in the level of the firm's activity, the total of product costs is directly linked with output. These costs cannot be controlled, therefore, except by reference to the volume and assortment of products which they have generated. Management has to look at the month's production, whether before or after the event and ask itself: "what ought this output to cost?". The answer to this question can then be compared with what it actually did cost.

The need for standards:

Before the question "what ought the output to cost?" can be answered, a standard cost for each product will have to be set. This involves a good deal of detailed investigation about the materials which go into each product, the processes through which it passes, the time required in each process by each product, and the grade of labour employed on each operation. A standard cost for a product can only be built up after the process of producing it has been painstakingly analysed into fragments, and each fragment has been separately costed. There is no need to set standards for any but the direct costs: overheads can be controlled differently, as I shall explain shortly. And as material and labour costs *per unit of each product* (as distinct from overheads) will not depend, to any substantial extent, on the quantity of each product made, it is not necessary, when setting standards, to make any assumption about the volume and composition of output during the period ahead for which the standards are being set.

The setting of standards, it may be added, is itself a valuable discipline, quite apart from their subsequent use as a means of control, for it forces management to think systematically about methods of production, the choice and use of materials, sources of supply, the kind of labour employed and the way it is employed, product design, and many other aspects of the firm's operations. Of course, all these matters could be brought under review periodically by any firm, whether it used standard costing or not. The fact remains that many firms have found, when introducing standards for the first time, that there were many possible economies which might have been effected long before, but which it had been no one's specific job to ferret out.

What standards can do:

Standards, once set, can be put to work in several different ways. They can make planning easier, for the resources necessary to carry out any production programme can be worked out by building upwards from the standard requirements of materials, labour and plant capacity of individual products. They can make control more immediate, for a standard can be used as an authority for the incurrence of cost. As an example, when a production order is placed on the factory, the predetermined standard quantities—no more and no less—of the materials it calls for can be issued from store without special authorisation. Any wastage of material will immediately be brought to light by the need for a supplementary issue to complete the order.

For the accountant, the main function of standards is to give him something against which to compare actual costs, as soon as these have been ascertained. The differences between actual and standard costs can then be analysed, so as to separate out those savings or excess costs for which management can be held responsible from those which are really outside its control. A simple illustration of this use of standards should dispel the idea that all this is too complicated for the small business. We shall admittedly have to postulate conditions simpler than are usually encountered in real life, because of limitations of space; but the illustration will, perhaps, serve to explain the basic idea behind standard costing.

An illustration of standard costing for direct costs:

A firm makes two products, A and B, each of which pass through two processes, I and II. The basic information about standards so far as direct costs are concerned, can be set out in the following table:

PROCESS	Standard Process Times		Standard Wage Rates per hour	Standard Materials Cost	
	Prod. A	Prod. B.		Prod. A.	Prod. B.
I ...	30 mins.	10 mins.	4/-	10/-	6/-
II ...	45 mins.	15 mins.	5/-	—	2/-

At the end of a particular month, the actual results for each process are found to have been:

	Process I	Process II
Man-hours worked	820	1,100
Wages paid	£180	£290
Materials used (at standard prices)	£1,000	£160
,, ,, (at actual prices)	£1,075	£180

The actual output for the month was 1,000 of product A and 1,500 of product B.

We can summarise all this information and analyse the differences between actual and standard costs for the month at one and the same time. Tables I and II show the results of the analysis for direct labour costs and direct materials costs respectively. The notes to the tables show how the basic information has been derived where this is not itself original data; the ascertainment of the total variance between actual and standard costs and the way the total variance is analysed into its component parts is shown by the column numbers.

TABLE I—DIRECT LABOUR COSTS

PROCESS	Standard Labour Cost	Actual Hours @ Standard Wage Rates	Actual Wages Paid	Total Variance	Rates of Pay Variance	Efficiency Variance
	(1)	(2)	(3)	(4) = (3)—(1)	(5) = (3)—(2)	(6) = (2)—(1)
	£	£	£	£	£	£
I ...	150	164	180	30 Dr.	16 Dr.	14 Dr.
II ...	281	275	290	9 Dr.	15 Dr.	6 Cr.

		Standard Time Product A	Standard Time Product B	Total Standard Time	Std. Wage Rate	Standard Labour Cost
		(a)	(b)	(c) = (a) + (b)	(d)	(e) = (c) (d)
COL. (1):	Process I	1000 30 mins. = 500 hrs.	1500 10 mins. = 250 hrs.	750 hrs.	4/-	£150
	Process II	1000 45 mins. = 750 hrs.	1500 15 mins. = 375 hrs.	1125 hrs.	5/-	£281
COL. (2):	Process I	820 hrs. @ 4/- = £164				
	Process II	1100 hrs. @ 5/- = £275				

TABLE II—DIRECT MATERIALS COSTS

PROCESS	Standard Materials Cost	Actual Quantity used, at Standard Prices	Actual Quantity used, at actual Prices	Total Variance	Price Variance	Quantity Variance
	(1)	(2)	(3)	(4) = (3)—(1)	(5) = (3)—(2)	(6) = (2)—(1)
	£	£	£	£	£	£
I ...	950	1,000	1,075	125 Dr.	75 Dr.	50 Dr.
II ...	150	160	180	30 Dr.	20 Dr.	10 Dr.

	Standard Materials Cost of Product A	Standard Materials Cost of Product B	Total Standard Materials Cost
	(a)	(b)	(c) = (a) + (b)
COL. (1): Process I	1000 @ 10/- = £500	1500 @ 6/- = £450	£950
Process II	—	1500 @ 2/- = £150	£150

COL. (2): Given. In practice the data is derived from materials issue requisitons, priced at standard and at actual buying prices.

The significance of the information provided:

It would take too long to discuss the variances fully. Broadly, the total variance indicates how far process costs have exceeded (if a debit) or fallen short of (if a credit) the norm which has been set. Column (5), in each table, shows how much of the total variance can be explained by *price* changes (which are largely outside management's control) and column (6) shows how far it is attributable to variations in the *quantity* of materials or labour used, a matter for which management can reasonably be held responsible. Of course, the information obtainable can be greatly elaborated with a more complex system. Here I am concentrating on essentials only.

One other aspect of this method of cost control calls for comment. The emphasis is placed on the process rather than the product. Sometimes, of course, a process will be peculiar to one product; but more commonly it will be applied to a number of different products. In this case, managerial responsibility will probably be divided between processes rather than between products, and it is, therefore, appropriate that actual and standard costs should be compared and the variances investigated process by process, not product by product, so as to follow the lines of responsibility. Moreover, as most businesses have far fewer processes than they have products, the effort involved both in preparing and in interpreting the figures thrown up by standard costing is much reduced as compared with a system which month after month purports to show the "actual" unit cost of each product. This is a point which should appeal particularly to the small business.

Budgetary control of overheads:

So much for what I have called product costs, as distinct from period costs. When we turn to period costs, or overheads, we find that broadly speaking they do not fluctuate to anything like the same extent with output. They can, of course, be handled by methods similar to those just discussed for direct or product costs, but it is much less certain that for overheads the effort is worthwhile. The preparation of a simple expenditure budget, showing planned overhead expense month by month, and the comparison of actual expenditure with the budget at the end of each month, is probably all that a small business will find it useful to do. Here again, it is in the preparation and approval of the budget as much as in its subsequent use that its value lies. The preparation of the overhead budget should cause every important item of expenditure to be looked at and made to justify itself.

By far the most important item of overheads will be salaries. Not only will they in most businesses constitute a large proportion of the total overhead. They carry with them other consequential expenditure. Every time you add a man to the payroll, you also add the cost of the travelling he does, the stationery he uses, the secretary he keeps busy, and so on. Cut the administrative staff by one, and you save much more than the man's salary. Because the addition of one name to the payroll of a small firm will bring a larger proportionate addition to overheads than for a large firm, it is the small firm for which this point has special importance.

Conclusion:

There is always a danger of giving the impression, in any description of an accounting or budgetary system designed to aid control, that there is some *deus ex machina* which automatically exercises control once the system is installed. Perhaps one day we will have an "automatic pilot" which will keep a business, like an aeroplane, on its course. But that is still a very long way off, especially for the small business. A well-planned system can at present provide something like automatic control only over a small area of operations. For the rest, it can give warning of danger. It remains for management to react suitably. The reaction is much more likely to be the right one if the warning is timely and gives an indication of the nature and location of the trouble to be rectified.

OVERCOMING PROBLEMS OF NON-UNIFORM ACCOUNTING

by David Solomons
University of Bristol

I do not propose in the course of these remarks to say anything about the standardised accounting systems covering the whole of an economy, which have been adopted in a number of European countries. These systems have no counterpart, so far as I am aware, anywhere in the English-speaking world. Nor is there any important body of accounting opinion there which would favour their introduction. Perhaps we still have the old-fashioned idea that accounts should be kept primarily in the interests of the business unit and not in the interests of the State; and although, of course, a completely standardised system does have some advantages to individual businesses, insofar as comparisons of accounting information are made easier, we retain a strong suspicion that their principal value is to officials concerned with the control of industry and we have, rightly in my opinion, made their interests take second place.

In any case, it is difficult to see that there can be very much value to an individual business concern in a comparison of its own accounting data with that of widely dissimilar types of enterprise. The important problem, therefore, is to secure the highest degree of uniformity in accounting within an industry without too greatly restricting the scope for initiative by individual firms. This question of initiative is important. The introduction of a uniform system may raise the standard of accounting of backward concerns only at the cost of discouraging new developments in more go-ahead concerns. This argument weighs particularly strongly, I think, against the standardised systems already referred to.

KINDS OF NON-UNIFORMITY

Non-uniformity in accounting is of two kinds: there is, first, non-uniformity of definition and classification. In different industries and in different firms within the same industry, words mean different things and even when a particular kind of expenditure is called by the same name, it may be grouped with one set of expenses in one firm and with a different set in another, e.g. what is called "packing material" by one concern may be called "direct materials" by another. This type of non-uniformity can be dealt with comparatively simply by the introduction of a uniform vocabulary and a uniform accounting code to ensure the uniform classification of expenditure. The introduction of a uniform vocabulary need not be a highly controversial matter, and although a uniform classification of expenditure may be somewhat more controversial, the working out of the details is not likely to give rise to serious disputes.

The second type of non-uniformity concerns accounting method. Even when all the firms in an industry have agreed on what they mean by such a term as "depreciation", they may not agree on the method of calculating depreciation. The securing of uniform methods of accounting as distinct from uniform terminology and classification is a more contentious matter. It is perhaps important to realise that it may be possible to secure the first type of uniformity even where the second type is not available.

COST COMPARISONS WITHOUT UNIFORM ACCOUNTING

Even when accounting is not uniform in either of the two respects I have mentioned, cost comparisons are not entirely ruled out. Differences in the detailed classification of expenditure may cancel out if we compare expense totals or sub-totals only. And even when different firms put a particular kind of expenditure into different main groups of expenditure, so that even a comparison of expense totals is not possible, it may still be possible to compare total costs per unit of output or total costs per operating hour. Again, in a good many industries, differences between products make it useless to compare product costs, but although the products may differ, often the nature of the processes used do not. Costs per process-hour, therefore, may be comparable even though costs per unit of product are not.

It is, of course, always an essential requirement for the good presentation of accounting information, whether we are talking about uniform systems or not, that unusual items of revenue and expenditure should be fully disclosed to the reader, that they should not be hidden by being merged with more normal items, and that even the normal items should be accurately described in non-technical language so far as possible. Where these requirements are met,it may be possible to achieve something in the way of useful comparisons of figures even in the absence of uniformity of definition, classification and accounting method.

ABSENCE OF GOVERNMENT INTERVENTION IN GREAT BRITAIN

In Great Britain, the government has given very little direct impetus to uniform accounting. Of course, in those industries which have been nationalised since the end of the war, uniform accounting has gradually been introduced, but this only covers a small part of the economy. Even in the matter of financial accounting, except in a few industries such as insurance, private businesses are left with a very wide measure of freedom as to the methods they use and the information they choose to make public. Corporations are, of course, required by the Companies Act to observe a minimum degree of disclosure in the accounts which they present to their shareholders and which, except in the case of "exempt" companies, are available to the public. From time to time investigating committees, set up by the government to enquire into the working of particular industries, have advocated a greater degree of uniformity in accounting within the industry. The recommendation has usually stemmed from the difficulty which the committee ran into as soon as it began to try to collect information from firms in the industry for the purpose of its own enquiries. Either the information it wanted was not readily available or it was provided by the various firms in the industry in so many diverse forms that it was difficult to draw generalisations from it. However, even when government committees recommend more uniformity of accounting, any action required to bring this uniformity about is left to trade associations and there has never as yet been any attempt to get action by legislation.

THE ESSENTIALS OF A UNIFORM SYSTEM

Although a uniform accounting system may be prepared in great detail and may be embodied in a large publication, most of the important matters dealt with in it can be considered under seven heads. These cover the essential matters which cannot be neglected if the system is to be at all effective.

1. There should be a general description of the system which is being introduced

This should make it clear what particular range of products and processes is intended to be covered by the system ; in other words, how the "industry" for which the system is being prepared is being defined. The general description of the system should also cover such matters as the relationship and the degree of integration between the financial accounts and the cost accounts, whether standards are being used in connection with the cost accounts, and other general matters of a similar nature.

There have been references by previous speakers to the importance in certain circumstances, of having cost information in terms of opportunity costs. Uniform accounting systems are devised to give uniform accounting costs only, though as I shall mention later, there is one respect in which these systems do recognise opportunity costs. It is important to realise that a uniformity of accounting cost, when this does not represent a uniformity of opportunity cost, may be a spurious and not a significant kind of uniformity.

2. A standard vocabulary of all terms used in the accounting system and a standard classification of accounts

So far as terminology is concerned, in Great Britain the Institute of Cost and Works Accountants has published a standard cost accounting terminology for use throughout industry, and even though this terminology, like any others which may be produced from time to time, is open to criticism, there is a good deal to be said for making the terminologies adopted by particular industries consistent, so far as possible, with the general terminology. The value of a general terminology is greatest if it does not attempt to provide brief definitions of very broad concepts, e.g. "cost" or "value". These terms cannot adequately be dealt with in anything less than an extended discussion, and this is hardly appropriate for inclusion in a uniform accounting system.

The classification of assets, liabilities, expenditures and incomes can be incorporated into a code of accounts in which all items are listed and given a code number. The meaning and content of each item is best dealt with in the terminology and not in the code of accounts itself.

Not only does there need to be a standard classification of expenditures and incomes, etc. on a subjective basis. In addition, there needs to be a standard list of cost centres to which costs are to be allocated and from which costs are to be further allocated to products. Similarity of processes and of their organisation into cost centres within the firms in an industry is more important from the point of view of uniform accounting than whether they produce identical products. Where processes in an industry vary considerably from firm to firm, it is desirable to split the industry up into sub-industries. This has been done in the British plastics industry, and there are separate but related uniform accounting systems for moulders, injection moulders and fabricators.

3. Bases of valuation of inputs in the calculation of cost

We are here concerned mainly with the valuation of materials used and with the calculation of the depreciation of fixed assets. As regards materials, the problem arises because a particular type of material will come into store at different prices according to the date of purchase. This will be so even in a period when the value of money is stable, but of course the fluctuations in price are greater still in conditions of inflation or deflation. Quite different evaluations of materials used will be arrived at according as first-in-last-out, last-in-first-out, or average cost bases are adopted, and of course this does not exhaust the range of methods available. Comparability of materials costs will not be possible unless a uniform method of valuation is agreed on.

As regards the calculation of the depreciation of fixed assets, there are two different problems to be settled. There is first the choice of method of spreading the asset costs over the years of the asset's life, i.e. the familiar problem of choosing between straight line, diminishing balance, service unit or compound interest methods of depreciation. There is also what is really a much more difficult problem, that is the problem of overcoming the non-uniformity of depreciation measurement which arises from the changes in the value of money over a period of years. Suppose we are comparing the depreciation costs of two firms in respect of some important asset which one firm bought a few years ago for £1,000 and which the other firm has recently bought for £1,500. Even though they both agree to charge depreciation by the same method (e.g. the straight line method), if they both calculate depreciation on the basis of historical cost, their depreciation figures will not really be comparable because one will be expressing the cost in pounds of recent date and the other in pounds of a past date. Although these monetary units go by the same name, they are not the same thing. Non-uniformity resulting from this cause can only be dealt with by an index number technique, of which in Great Britain we still have little more than a theoretical knowledge, for accounting opinion has not yet progressed far enough to give rise to a demand for accounts expressed in pounds of constant value. Ideally, a uniform accounting system ought to provide for uniformity in the value of the monetary unit as well as for the other kinds of uniformity I have referred to.

4. Methods of allocating indirect costs to processes and products

We have here to presuppose that there is a considerable degree of uniformity in the processes adopted by the firms in the industry. If there is, it becomes relatively easy to lay down agreed methods of allocating overhead expenses to processes and hence to products. Agreement has to be reached, too, on how the costs of service departments, e.g. power or steam generation, personnel administration, plant maintenance, etc. are to be charged to production departments.

5. Treatment of idle capacity

The existence of idle capacity has not been a serious problem in most industries in recent years. But uniform accounting systems should nevertheless provide for the way in which costs should be dealt with when excess capacity exists. The problem arises, of course, because not all costs diminish when output diminishes. The use of normal overhead rates based on normal output will, therefore, leave some part of the relatively fixed overhead expenses unabsorbed if output falls below normal. The treatment of these unabsorbed overheads must be provided for in the uniform system. The system may recommend that they should be written off as special losses not to be included in product costs, or they may be absorbed by a supplementary charge to product costs. A slightly different problem arises where some part of a firm's equipment becomes surplus to requirements for a considerable period of time but yet calls for some expenditure on maintenance. The method of dealing with such maintenance expenditure must also be covered by the uniform system.

6. Treatment of imputed costs

The treatment of imputed costs has also to be dealt with in a uniform accounting system. Some firms own their premises, others rent them. Some firms are financed largely by loan capital, others by share capital only. Some proprietors may manage their own businesses, others may have salaried managers. Comparisons between such firms will be upset if costs are not imputed to the resources which are owned and not hired. The correct basis of such imputation is, of course, their opportunity cost, their value in their best alternative use.

7. Accounting for by-products

Where the industry produces by-products, a uniform treatment of costs and revenues attributable to them must be laid down. Otherwise the results shown both for the by-product and for the main products will be non-comparable.

CONCLUSION

Experience shows that it is usually not easy to get firms to adopt uniform methods and even where, in some countries, legislation has made them compulsory, firms have been known to continue their individual systems side by side with the uniform system. This points to the importance of flexibility in uniform systems so that real individual needs can be catered for within the framework of the system. Sometimes a fairly complex system may be provided for large firms in an industry, with a separate simplified system for the smaller firms. Alternatively, within a single system, it is possible to provide more detailed information for some firms than for others. These are two ways of securing flexibility.

Uniform accounting meets resistance from both large and small firms. The large ones usually have good systems of their own already and will not want to change them, while the small firms will often be content to carry on with no system at all. Any trade association which advocates uniform accounting for the purpose of getting uniformly determined selling prices, without providing the bait of organised cost comparisons for its members, is, therefore, probably beating the air. This has been a fairly common experience in Great Britain in the past.

Session 1957-58
No. 16
Joint Syllabus A.76

LECTURE

Management Accounting

By PROFESSOR D. SOLOMONS, B.Com., A.C.A.,
Professor of Accounting, Bristol University.

Delivered to the West of England Students' Society at Bristol on 7th December, 1957

You have asked me to talk about Management Accounting, and I assume from the fact that you have asked *me,* rather than someone who has a more intimate knowledge of municipal affairs, that you want me to place the emphasis on Management Accounting in business; indeed, I am not competent to do anything else. Nevertheless, we shall do well to keep before us the aim of comparing what business does with what local government either does, or might do. There is obviously room for greater cross-fertilization, I suggest, between these two interests.

THE DISTINCTIVE FEATURES OF MANAGEMENT ACCOUNTING

Why Management Accounting? What is there different between Management Accounting and other kinds of accounting, for example Professional Accounting?

I think one can pick out three or four distinguishing features of the work of the Management Accountant. The first is that it is impossible for him to take up the detached attitude of the Professional Accountant. He is very much in the thick of things—he does not come along at the end of the year or six months' period and take a detached historical view of what has taken place. He is, in fact, part of current operations and cannot sit back and look at them with detachment. In the second place, he is forced to take a very detailed view of current events for he is concerned with the relative health or sickness of different parts of the business in a way in which the Professional Accountant is not. The Professional Accountant takes a general view of the whole, whereas the Management Accountant is concerned with the health of each of the parts. It is his job among other things to try to give advice which will stimulate the growth of the prosperous parts of the business, and rectify mistakes in the less prosperous parts.

That brings me to the third distinguishing feature of the Management Accountant; that he is very much involved in the formulation of business plans in a way in which the Professional Accountant is not. It is true, of course, that Professional Accountants are sometimes called in to give advice on the way a business should be run, but this on the whole, I would say, was the exception rather than the rule, and certainly the exception in the case of businesses large enough to employ their own well qualified accounting staff. This role of the Management Accountant, his role in connection with the formulation of plans, is very much concerned with asking this question above all others—"What differences will it make?" "What difference will it make if the firm does this rather than that or does something in this way rather than that?" This question, "What difference will it make?", is one to which I shall return later on in relation to a particular business problem and I shall then suggest how I at least would solve it.

Then, finally, there is the control aspect of Management Accounting. Here, of course, there is a certain amount of common ground between the Management Accountant and the Professional Auditor.

It is, I think, worth having a look at this word "control", to see what it means, because, as accountants, we use the word in all sorts of different senses, sometimes without realising that we *are* using it in different senses. It seems to me to have at least three or four different meanings. Sometimes it is used simply to indicate custody. One talks about the cashier having "control" of the cash, or storekeepers having "control" of the stores when we simply mean they have custody of the cash or the stores. The word, again, is used in a different sense when it is used to show that one wants to maintain the total value of some asset, maybe stores again, or outstanding debts, between some predetermined upper and lower limit. This is what is meant when one talks about "stock control" or "credit control", and here it means a good deal more than merely custody. I suppose that the word "control" is applied in pretty much this sense when one talks of budgetary control, about which I shall have more to say later on.

Then, when we talk about a control statement, control here seems to mean not much more than detection, because a control statement obviously does not control anything, it simply detects certain areas in which real control ought to be exercised. It would detect, for instance, that there was excessive idle time in the factory or that the cost of defective work or scrap was perhaps more than could be tolerated, or that the total amount of extra allowances paid to workers was more than was expected. A typical statement would show up these things, it would detect them, but it would not control them. Finally, of course, control is sometimes used to mean simply audit, although perhaps it would be better if it were called audit when that is what is meant.

THE LIMITATIONS OF HISTORICAL COSTS

It is convenient to divide Management Accounting into its planning functions and its control functions and that is, in fact, how I shall deal with it. We no longer think that the same kind of accounting information will always, or even usually, serve both these purposes. Yet, for a good many years, people were content to accept some kind of cost figure as the accountant's main contribution both in the field of planning and control. In the iron and steel industry, for instance, cost per ton of pig iron, or cost per ton of steel billets is the basic cost figure which is ascertained. One can try to use this kind of figure for a good many planning purposes and for control purposes. Whether it is suitable or not, will, I hope, appear from some of my later remarks. These cost figures, as you know—for you have the same kind of costing in local government—are really average costs, the result of aggregating materials allocated to particular units of output, labour costs and overheads allocated in some way usually described as "equitable" or "reasonable". They are simply the results of applying generally accepted costing techniques.

The question that the cost accountant has throughout most of his historically traceable career been trying to answer is: "What did the product cost?" Here I am talking, of course, about industry rather than government. Costing techniques, over the years, have become more and more refined, and the cost accountant can throw up with some show of accuracy an answer to this question—"What did the product cost?" But when one looks at the answers closely one finds that the accuracy is to some extent spurious. It has been an accuracy gained by applying certain conventions all of which are open to question, all of which involve some degree of arbitrariness. If I try to be more specific, you will see what I mean.

In the field of materials costing for instance, the cost accountant tries to attach a value to the cost of materials used on a particular unit of a product made on a particular day, but a difficulty at once arises because materials taken from store are being taken from an aggregation of materials which have come into the store at different prices. One does not have a position in which each bit of material has, so to speak, a price ticket attached to it. Some convention has to be adopted, e.g.—first-in first-out, or last-in, first-out—before a figure of materials cost can be attached to the output of any one product on some particular day. Since different conventions give different figures, none of these figures can claim to be uniquely correct.

The biggest problem, of course, in the costing field, is the problem of allocating overheads. It is difficult to attach much meaning to the question "What is the overhead cost of a particular unit of product in a firm making a considerable variety of products?" There are intractable questions such as, for instance, whether to include interest on capital in ascertaining these costs. Another difficult question also would be how to deal with the cost of idle capacity. One of the awkward things about overheads, as you know, is that in general they do not contract when the use of capacity contracts. If a plant is working only at 60% capacity, some of the overheads are probably not very much less than they were when it was working at 100% capacity. Are we to have unit cost figures, therefore, which go down when the use of capacity goes up, and which go up when the use of capacity goes down, or are we to say that the overhead cost per unit of output in a factory working only at 60% capacity has, in fact, been the same as it was in a factory working at 100% capacity, and that a considerable proportion of the overheads should be written off as a special kind of loss, a kind of cost of surplus capacity? Obviously, according to the way in which this question is answered we shall get quite different unit cost figures in a factory which has been, in fact, working at only 60% capacity.

I simply raise these difficulties to raise doubts in your minds. Probably there will be doubts already, as to the merit of figures of the "cost per ton" type which I mentioned earlier in connection with iron and steel, though as a matter of fact in that industry the seriousness of some of the difficulties I have referred to is less than in good many other industries. Yet, broadly speaking, I think we must conclude that it is not possible, except in an arbitrary kind of way, to ascertain cost per unit of output with anything like the degree of accuracy that cost accountants would like. But suppose it were possible? Would figures of that kind be particularly useful? What could they be used for?

FIXING A SELLING PRICE

In business, of course, one of the main uses would be to fix a selling price for the product. This is a problem which is not a major one in local government, so I will not dwell on it. Even you, however, have to fix the selling prices for some products. You run Civic Restaurants, and some Municipalities operate Transport Undertakings, so that it is not a problem which Municipal Accountants can neglect, even though it would be true to say that it is not one of their major problems.

Nevertheless, in a business where price determination is a major problem, it is natural, I suppose, to start by thinking that once a unit cost for the product has been ascertained one would be well on the way to fixing a selling price. You might say to someone "Find what the product costs, then add on 10% and that will be our selling price." On further examination, however, it would turn out to be a very unsatisfactory way of fixing selling prices. In the first place, as I have said, there is not really any one answer to the question—"What did the product cost?" For this, the incidence of fixed overheads to which I have already referred is mainly responsible. What the product costs per unit of output depends upon how much of it is produced, because the more one makes the more one can spread the fixed overheads. The cost per unit of output does therefore to a considerable extent depend on the amount produced and the amount produced depends on the amount sold, and the amount of the product sold will depend on the price charged for it. It is therefore as true to say that the cost per unit of output depends on the price, as it would be to say that the price should depend on the cost. The two things are obviously interdependent and one does not really get a rational answer to the problem of price-determination simply by calculating figures of average cost per unit of output. However, I had better resist the temptation to go on and say how I think prices ought to be determined in a rational way since, as I have said, this is not really one of your major problems.

Now this question of determination of selling prices is one aspect of the planning problem which besets all businesses and is perhaps one of the most important, but it is not the only one. It is one, however, in which the accountant has a great deal to contribute so long as he is prepared to be a little more subtle than simply to "find what the product costs and add on 10%."

MAKE OR BUY?

Now, let us take a different kind of problem. Should a business, or a local government authority—because this problem could be at least as important for a local authority as for a business working in a competitive economy—continue to provide some service for itself, or should it go out and buy it from an independent contractor? Or putting the question the other way round, should you continue to buy a service from outside or should you set up a department for yourself to provide the service required? It is convenient to refer to this kind of problem as the "make or buy" problem, in which guise I expect it is already familiar to a good many of you. Should one make or should one buy?

This is another problem in which cost data of the conventional kind which I very briefly described above would not, I suggest, usually be very suitable. A different kind of cost data is needed to settle this question. For this purpose you need a notion of cost which economists call opportunity cost. The economists' idea of opportunity costs is simply that what it costs to use resources now depends on their alternative uses; if one is using up resources, whatever they may have cost in the past, and they have no alternative use, either in the present or future, and they cannot be sold, then it does not cost anything to use them. The opportunity cost of a particular operation depends on what might have been done instead with the same resources.

This idea is familiar enough in a domestic setting although one would never dream of calling it anything as pretentious as opportunity cost. Let me take a simple example. Suppose we have two men both owning identical houses in different parts of the city, and both running identical motor cars. Both houses have garages attached to them, but one house is in a part of the city where all the other houses in the road also have attached garages and so everybody is adequately garaged, so to speak, and the other house is in a part of the city where garages are very difficult to come by; most of the houses are terraced houses without garages. The two houses are identical but the districts are not, and the motor cars run by these two gentlemen are also identical. Now does it cost the two men the same amount per week or per year to run their cars? In terms of money outlay the answer is probably that it does cost them exactly the same—same outlay for petrol, repairs and so on—assuming they do the same mileage, and neither of them has to pay any garage rent for both have their own garages. But in terms of opportunity cost it is highly probable that the cost of running these cars will not be the same because, taking the man with the house in the adequately garaged area, if I may call it that, if he did not use his own garage for his own car he could not do anything else with it. No-one would pay rent for a garage in an area where everybody has his own. No amount need be included in his motoring costs, therefore, in respect of garage rent. The other man, on the other hand, by using his own garage for his own car will, in fact, be foregoing the rent which he could get by sub-letting his garage. You will remember he lives in an area where garages are difficult to come by and could therefore probably command a substantial rent. His motoring costs, although they would include no actual cash outlay for garage rent, should certainly include a figure for garage rent foregone, in the sense that he is deprived of an income by using the garage himself. Some accountants would include a notional figure of the rent of that garage in the calculation of costs, but if we keep our eyes glued to cash outlays the differences between the two men will not emerge.

Rather than continuing to talk in general terms, I should like now to take a look at a specific problem of the "make or buy" type.

A food-canning firm makes its own containers, in a department whose annual costs have been set out thus:—

	£	£	£
Direct material		4000	
Direct labour		3000	
Department overheads:			
Foreman	500		
Depreciation of machinery	1500		
Rent, etc.	800		
Miscellaneous	700		
	——	3500	
		——	10500
General overheads at 10%			1050
Total cost			£11550

As an independent maker of containers is willing to supply the same quantity for £10,000 p.a., the firm asks you to report on whether this offer should be accepted (and the firm's own container department given up). You find:—

(*a*) All the workmen could be transferred, without any pay changes, etc., to other departments, except for the foreman. He is due to retire in about four years, and is too old to learn a new job; nor would the firm like to dismiss him now.

(*b*) If the department's buildings were freed, there would be some gain in convenience. They would be used as a warehouse, in place of one at present rented at £920 per annum.

(*c*) Depreciation (i.e. the £1,500 shown above) is the charge of one large machine, which originally cost £15,000; it had a ten year life, of which half has so far passed. A similar machine (new) would now cost £25,000. Saleable value is nil.

(*d*) Miscellaneous expenses would fall to zero. General overheads are administrative costs, etc., that would be unaffected.

What conclusion do you reach?*

In deciding what advice to give to the firm, I should start by comparing the opportunity cost of continuing the container department with the cost of buying the containers outside. As is usually the case, we find that existing commitments bind us more in the immediate future than they do in the more remote future. There are expenditures which cannot be avoided immediately, even if the department is shut down, and these are therefore not properly included in a list of the "costs" of keeping it open. The further into the future we go, the more these present commitments are worked off and the more expenditures we can avoid by closing down. Hence, if we could assume (as in practice we certainly could not) that all the facts given would remain unchanged for at least six years ahead, we

* The foregoing problem was set as an examination question in the B.Sc.(Econ.) (London) Part II Examination in 1952, and is reprinted with the kind permission of the University of London. The University is in no way responsible for my suggested solution to the problem.

could draw up a table like the following one, from which it would appear that it will pay us to keep the department open until the existing machinery wears out, but that it will not pay us to continue to make our own containers after that because of the high capital cost of new equipment.

COMPARATIVE STATEMENT OF AVOIDABLE COST OF MAKING AND BUYING CONTAINERS

	Years 1—4	*Year* 5	*Year* 6 *onwards*
	£	£	£
Avoidable annual cost of *buying* containers	10000	10000	10000
Avoidable annual cost of *making* containers:			
Direct material	4000	4000	4000
Direct labour	3000	3000	3000
Departmental overheads:			
Foreman	—	500	500
Depreciation of machinery... ...	—	—	2500
Rent	920	920	920
Miscellaneous expenses	700	700	700
	£8620	£9120	£11620
Annual gain or *loss* from continuing production	+£1380	+£880	−*£1620*

On the facts given, assuming that the present machine has no saleable value if discarded now, it will pay to continue production until the machine has to be replaced in five years' time. Then, if all the facts are still the same, it will pay to discontinue production, as the avoidable costs of production will, from then on, exceed the cost of buying containers by £1,620.

Note that the occupation of the building must be included in the cost comparison at its "opportunity cost", which in this case exceeds the annual rent paid for it.

BUDGET OR NO BUDGET?

I have mentioned the pricing problem and the "make or buy" problem simply as illustrations of the kind of planning problems which may be put to the Management Accountant for his advice. The decisions which are taken with regard to these matters must then be incorporated in the firm's budget. When we come to the subject of budgetting, we find much more common ground between business practice and municipal practice than in the area which I have been discussing hitherto.

A firm's budget constitutes a synthesis of all the planning decisions applicable to, let us say, the next twelve months, if that is the planning period. It also provides some mechanism for control, because it provides a standard against which the firm can measure its success in carrying out its chosen plans. In the absence of a budget, for control purposes, the firm would probably try to use figures of the "cost per ton" type which I mentioned earlier. Without a budget against which to compare its actual performance, the best a business can do is to compare what it costs to produce a unit of product this month with what it cost to make it last month or in the corresponding month last year.

This kind of cost comparison will be very familiar to you in the municipal field, not only cost comparisons between different periods, but also between different authorities. As you know, these comparisons have very serious limitations, particularly comparisons between periods. In the first place they are affected by price changes. The fact that the cost of producing a ton of steel this month was more than it was last month or last year might simply mean that the prices of the things purchased, which were quite beyond one's control, had gone up. Again, as I have already mentioned, "cost per ton" will be affected by the volume of output and this again may be outside anyone's control. The incidence of fixed overheads will bear more heavily per ton in months of low output than in months of high output. Third, and perhaps most important, the mere fact that cost performance this month is better than it was last month may simply mean that one has improved on a very inefficient performance in the previous month. The improvement may, in fact, represent no ground for satisfaction or complacency whatever. The yardstick used, i.e. last month's cost is, in fact, one of very doubtful value.

THE USE OF BUDGETS IN BUSINESS

This brings me to the use of budgets as a much more satisfactory yardstick. The uses that business firms make of budgets can be listed under four headings. In the first place a firm's budget will embody its strategic or long-term plan so far as capital expenditure and research and development expenditure, at least, are concerned. A capital expenditure budget in very broad outline over the next 10 years is not at all uncommon in business, though, of course, one cannot go into detail when looking that far ahead. So much for the strategic plan. Secondly the firm's budget will contain its tactical plan in considerable detail for the next twelve months, in much the same way as local authority budgets. It will serve to keep the various parts of the organisation together, to ensure, for instance, that the factory is not planning to make twice as much as the sales department is planning to sell, or that the factory and the sales department together are not planning a much larger scale of business than that for which finance can be found. Then there is the use of the budget in business, as in local government, to set limits within which subordinate officials can be given delegated powers to spend money without having to refer to higher authority every time. This, I suppose, is a general use of budgets. And finally, as I have already suggested, there is the use of the budget as a standard by which to compare actual performance, to see whether performance has exceeded or fallen short of the target.

The first step in the introduction of budgetary control in a business would be to divide the business into a number of budget centres. Each production department would be a budget centre, that is, a centre having its own separate budget. Each service department such as the power house, the personnel department, etc., probably would have its own budget; the stores department would have its own budget, and there would most likely be a separate budget for general administration. In these respects I think it is fair to say that business has followed government rather than the other way round, although in other respects business has run ahead of government in the use and refinement of budget procedure.

In a business which has a well developed budgetary system there would usually be a number of ways in which the procedure would be formalised, because it is only if it is formalised that it can be made to work in a large business. There would, for instance, be a detailed budgetary manual of procedure to which anyone could refer if they wanted to know how some question of budgetary procedure was to be dealt with. The manual would certainly include a detailed budgetary timetable, informing everybody exactly when the budget procedure must be initiated, by what dates the budget must move up to the next senior official, leading on eventually to the date by which the final overall budget must be agreed by the budget committee, if there is a budget committee, so as to become effective from, say, the following 1st January. There would, also, be a detailed account code, which I have no doubt you use too, to ensure that the comparison of actual expenditure, after the event, with the budget allowances, will not be upset by errors of analysis of expenditure.

In drawing up budgets for the different parts of a business, we naturally find that the plans of each part determine and are themselves determined by the plans of all the other parts. It is one of the great virtues of a system of formal budgets that it forces the different departments in the business—sales, production, finance—to keep in step, at least in intention. The sales department is restrained from trying to sell more than the works can make, the works is prevented from planning to use more of some scarce raw material than the purchasing department can procure, and so on. But we have to break into the circle somewhere, we have to find a starting point for the whole budgetting process, and this will be different for different businesses and at different times. The starting point will be determined by whatever is the limiting factor which is holding up expansion. This may be the finance which is available, or it may be factory space, but more often than not it is sales. Usually, if orders can be obtained, finance and productive capacity can be found too. In such a situation, the sales budget will be prepared first and the other budgets will develop from it.

This will not always be the case, however. In fact, it has only recently, I suppose, become a typical situation once more, since 1939. During most of the intervening period firms have had no difficulty in selling anything that they could make, and what they could make has been limited by supplies of raw material and labour, skilled and unskilled. An industrialist was telling me recently that during the Korean War, for instance, in his firm everything depended on the supply of copper. In that case, if you were budgetting for his business, you would have to start with the amount of copper you thought could be purchased and everything else would depend on that. It is not too difficult diagrammatically to sum up the relationship between the various budgets prepared in business, and I have attempted to do this in my diagram. It shows how the principal budgets (in practice there would be many subsidiary ones in addition) are drawn together into a profit forecast on the one hand and a cash forecast on the other.

THE RELATION BETWEEN CASH AND PROFIT FORECASTS

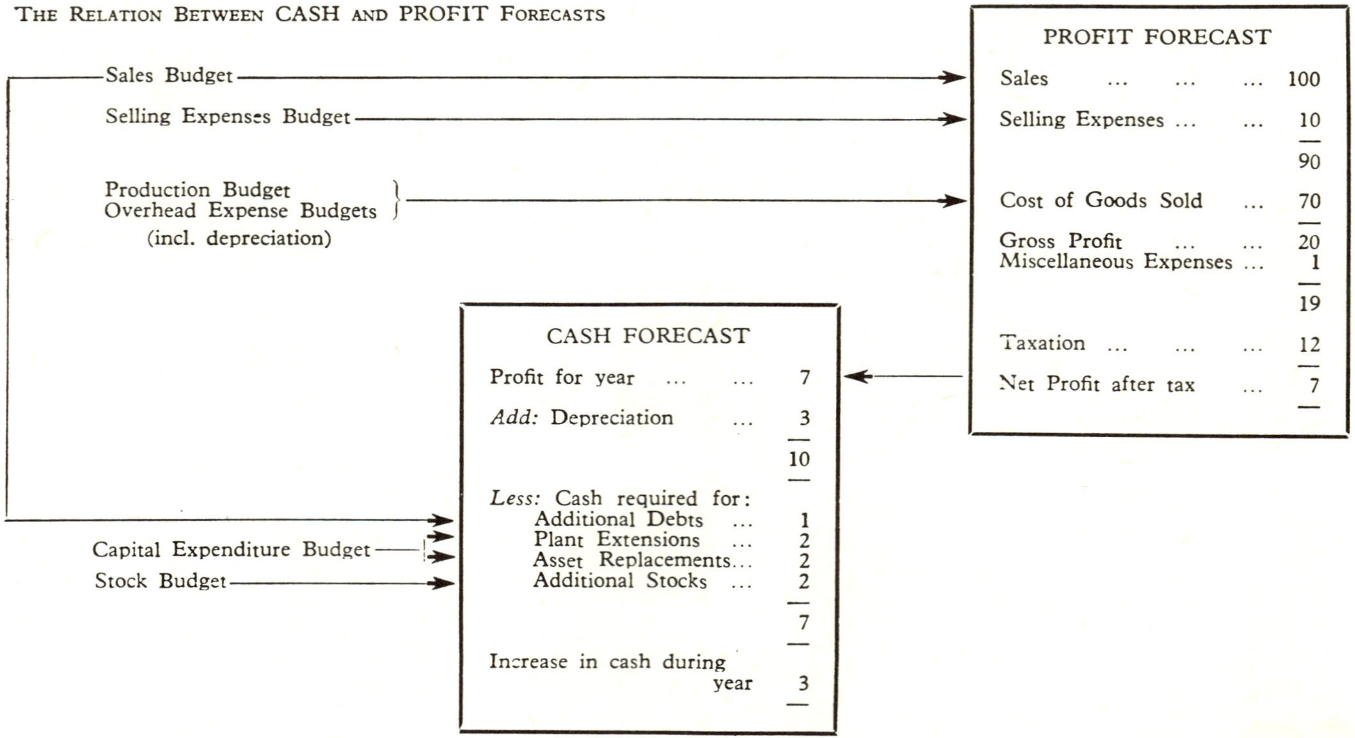

THE RELATION OF BUDGETS AND STANDARD COSTS

In a business, as in local government, or indeed in any other government service, budgetting only becomes manageable if it is worked out in great detail. One cannot budget for a business of any size or even for a small business by looking at it all at once. The problem is quite unmanageable. One has to reduce it down to its smallest components. The sales have to be budgetted product by product, area by area, salesman's territory by salesman's territory. Then taking each product, it is necessary to work out the labour and materials requirements needed per unit of each product, so that by multiplying these unit requirements by the volume of each product which is going to be made, we can budget the total expenditure on labour and materials for all the products together.

This is where standard costs come to the rescue of the business budgetter. The labour and materials budgets are built up from aggregates of unit standard costs. Someone has to decide how much material and labour is to go into making one unit of each product. The products being made may be very numerous, of course. From these unit calculations of standard direct costs, the total cost of each product and of all products together can be built up in a series of aggregates so far as labour and materials are concerned. Overheads have to be dealt with the other way round. Having settled the budgetted figures of output, someone has to estimate what facilities will be necessary to give this volume of output. From this estimate of necessary facilities, there has to be deduced an estimate of the overhead expenses, item by item, associated with the provision of those facilities. This gives the total overheads, which can then be allocated down to the product standard costs. The relationship between budgetary control and standard costs in business can thus be seen to be a two-way affair. So far as materials and labour are concerned, the standards are the building bricks from which the materials and labour budgets are built up. So far as overheads are concerned, an estimate of the facilities necessary has to be made, then an estimate of the overheads to which they give rise, and finally these overheads are allocated down to the products to get a total product standard cost, if required. I say "if required", because a great deal of useful information can be derived from a standard costing system even if it stops short of the allocation of overheads to products.

I cannot, in the time at my disposal, hope to describe how standard costs work or to assess the contribution they can make to cost control. They have, as you know, been applied in some fields of local government activity such as civic catering and, I believe, transport. Although there may be serious difficulties in the way of their further application to governmental activities, I have little doubt that we are not yet anywhere near to exploiting them fully in this field. I hope that in our ensuing discussion, we shall be able to look both at the opportunities of putting standard costs more effectively to work, and at the difficulties of doing so.

CONFLICT: an Accounting By-product

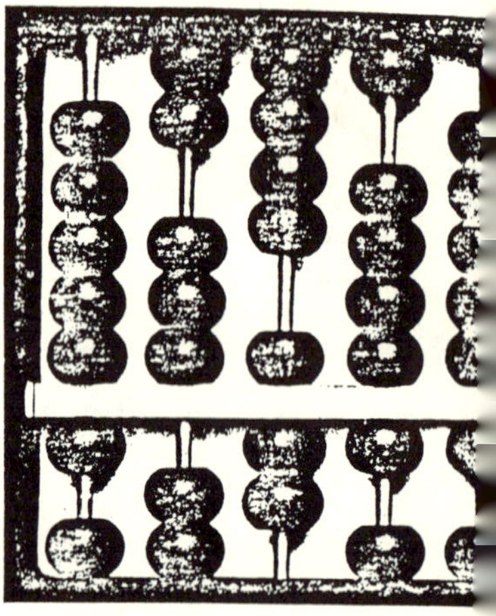

BY DAVID SOLOMONS

What is the effect of accounting methods on managerial behavior?

THE MANAGEMENT accountant is not normally thought of as having any considerable responsibility for generating conflicts within a corporation—nor for resolving them. He is generally regarded as occupying a neutral position. His job is to supply information. In that capacity, he stands on the sidelines. Departments may fight each other, but all he does is to keep score.

This is an innocent enough activity. Why blame the scorekeeper if the players sometimes do not like the way the game is played?

The fact is that to view the accountant merely as a scorekeeper is to miss much that is significant in his job. For he not only keeps the score, he also devises the rules for scoring. This is why he has more power than is generally recognized to induce harmony or conflict between the various parts of an organization.

Consider some of the methods used for measuring managerial performance. It is not difficult to formulate certain broad rules to which such methods should conform. For instance, it seems reasonable to assert that the performance of a manager of a department or other segment of a business should be so measured that it is, so far as possible, independent of decisions taken elsewhere in the company or of performance elsewhere in the company.

Again, it ought not to be possible for a manager to appear to be performing successfully when he is in fact causing the corporate performance (the only kind of performance which ultimately concerns the stockholders) to suffer. Yet there is no doubt that widely accepted accounting methods may infringe these rules. A simple illustration will explain how.

A certain company operated a de-

Exhibit I: Departmental Results for First Quarter of 1965.

	Dept. A	Dept. B	Dept. C	Store Total
	$	$	$	$
Net Sales	1,000	500	500	2,000
Cost of Sales	550	240	215	1,005
Departmental Expenses	150	60	85	295
	700	300	300	1,300
Departmental Contributions	300	200	200	700
General Store Expenses (apportioned)	200	100	100	400
Net Profit before taxes	100	100	100	300

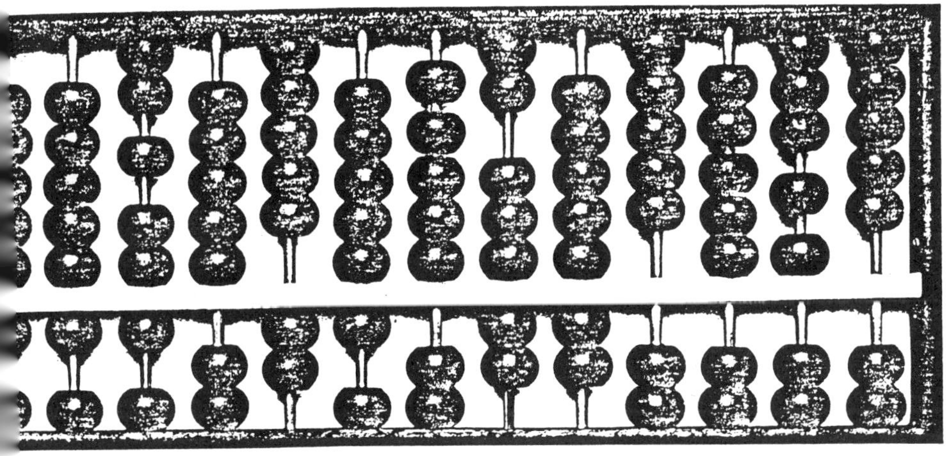

partment store. There were many departments, but for the purpose of our illustration, they can be grouped into three super-departments, A, B and C. Departments, of course, had to bear their own departmental expenses, and were also charged with a proportion of the general store expenses. These for years had been apportioned between departments on the basis of departmental sales. The results for the first quarter of 1965 (000's omitted and after rounding) are shown in Exhibit I.

When, in March 1965, a new manager was appointed to take over Department A, one of his first tasks was to look carefully at the figures for his department's operations. One thing he found was that, while more than half the department's business was quite profitable, there was a large volume of low-margin sales. When this analysis was applied to the department's figures for the first quarter of 1965, the results looked as in Exhibit II.

Two alternatives presented themselves for his consideration. One was to improve the profitability of the low-margin items. The other was to eliminate these lines.

The great attraction of the second alternative was that, with no effort on his part, his departmental performance could actually be made to look *better* than before, even though dropping the low-margin lines would, at least in the short run, reduce the total store profit *below* its previous level.

This result would be achieved essentially because, under the company's method of apportioning general store expenses, the reduction in Department A's sales would reduce the charge to his department for general expenses; but since there would be no immediate reduction in the total amount to be borne by the three departments together, any reduction in the amount borne by one would increase the burden to be carried by the others.

A reconstruction of the figures for the first quarter of 1965, had the strategy considered by the new manager of Department A been put into operation at the end of 1964, and making an

Exhibit II: Break-down of Department A's Results for First Quarter of 1965.

	Total for Dept.	High-margin Sales	Low-margin Sales
	$	$	$
Net Sales	1,000	600	400
Cost of Sales	550	240	310
Departmental Expenses	150	80	70
	700	320	380
Contribution	300	280	20

9

Exhibit III: Departmental Results for First Quarter of 1965 after eliminating Dept. A's low-margin sales and reapportioning general store expenses.

	Dept. A	Dept. B	Dept. C	Store Total
	$	$	$	$
Net Sales	600	500	500	1,600
Cost of Sales	240	240	215	695
Departmental Expenses	80	60	85	225
	320	300	300	920
Departmental Contributions	280	200	200	680
General Store Expenses (apportioned)	150	125	125	400
Net Profit	130	75	75	280

assumption of *ceteris paribus*, appears in Exhibit III.

WHEN Exhibits I and III are compared, the moral to be drawn is plain enough. As a result of eliminating his low-margin (but yet not entirely unprofitable) lines, the manager of Department A would have inflicted losses on the company in the form of a reduced total net profit for the store, while apparently improving his own performance, as measured by his departmental net profit, by no less than 30%. This could have been achieved by forcing the other two departments to carry an increased share of the general store expenses. Thus both of the rules for performance measurement which were formulated earlier would have been broken simultaneously.

Department A's manager would have turned in an improved performance while causing the corporation as a whole to perform less effectively. And the performance of the other two department managers would have appeared to deteriorate though nothing they themselves could control had changed.

At first sight, the rule that the measurement of a manager's performance should not be affected by activities outside his control may seem to contradict another rule of sound accounting, that a segment of a business should bear *all* the costs of conducting its affairs even if some of these costs are beyond the control of its manager. The simplest example is the salary of the manager himself. That is one expense which he usually does not control. Does that mean that his department should not be charged with his salary? The answer, of course, is no.

The department can only be judged when all the costs of running it have been taken into account. But judging the *department* and judging the *manager* are not the same thing. This is why the apparent contradiction noted above is not really a contradiction. Non-controllable items may be irrelevant for judging a manager and yet be relevant for judging his department. Failure to recognize this point can cause much managerial discontent.

ANOTHER sensitive area in which accounting procedures may generate friction between parts of a business is that of transfer pricing. Where a considerable volume of goods or service passes between departments, managerial behavior can be greatly affected by the way these transfers are charged, and the measurement of performance can be seriously distorted.

Ideally, a transfer pricing system ought to achieve two things. It ought to inculcate in department managers a sense that they and their departments are being treated fairly and that performance measures (specifically, department profits) are not being distorted by it. And at the same time it should motivate managers to act in ways which both optimize the results of their own departments and conduce to optimal results for the corporation.

It is easy to achieve one or other of these two objectives; and if there is a well-defined market in which the transferred goods or services can be bought and sold, then using market prices as transfer prices will secure both objectives. But in the absence of such market prices, it is by no means easy to devise a transfer pricing scheme which will hit both targets at once.

RATIOS HAVE long held a place in the accountant's kit of measuring instruments. The ratio of net earnings to sales and the ratio of net earnings to investment (the rate of

(Continued on Page 15)

a briton at wharton

A native Englishman, David Solomons is a graduate of the London School of Economics. He worked as a chartered accountant before joining the British Army, was captured in North Africa in 1942, and spent three years as a prisoner of war.

In 1946 he began teaching at the London School of Economics. He was appointed first professor of accounting at the University of Bristol in 1955, and has served as visiting professor at the University of California, Berkeley, and at I.M.E.D.E., in Lausanne.

Since 1959 he has been professor of accounting in the Wharton School.

Accounting Today

(Continued from page 10)

return on investment or ROI) are perhaps the two most widely used. Ratios of this kind need to be used with circumspection if they are not to motivate department managers to act against the true interests of the company.

Department ratios can be improved by activity which yet injures the company. When we looked at Department A of the department store earlier, we might have noted that the department's ratio of net profit to sales could have been improved from 10% to nearly 22% by dropping the low-margin sales, while leaving the company worse off than before. Similarly, departmental ROI can be raised by shedding less profitable investments: yet if these are earning more than is needed to pay for the capital employed in them, raising ROI will not necessarily be in the stockholders' interest.

There has been growing interest in accounting circles in recent years in the effect of accounting methods on managerial behavior. Behavioral scientists are beginning to add their insights in this area. Only when management accounting is seen as primarily a motivating device which can lead managers just as easily in the wrong as in the right direction can its full managerial significance be understood.

ERRATA

In "Breakeven Analysis under Absorption Costing," errors of notation occur in two places.

1. In the last sentence of the section headed "The Breakeven Equation under Absorption Costing," Q_s should read Q_c.
2. In Figure 1, the notation for the line OA should read $Q_s(p - v_s)$. The notation for the line RL should read $F_{m+s} + Qv_m$.

Reprinted from
The Accounting Review
Vol. XLIII, No. 3, July, 1968

Breakeven Analysis Under Absorption Costing

David Solomons

THE simplistic assumptions underlying the classical breakeven chart have long been recognized as unsatisfactory. Many of those who have felt this dissatisfaction have been content to apologize for the shortcomings of breakeven analysis. A few have labored to remove or minimize them.[1] The purpose of this article is to clarify these assumptions somewhat, and in particular to adapt the breakeven chart to a situation in which absorption costing is being used. It is important to recognize that, in its usual form, breakeven analysis is based on a direct costing approach to cost behavior, an approach which is by no means universally accepted.

Failure to grasp the implications of the direct cost philosophy for breakeven analysis leads to misunderstandings. For instance, it is commonly said that the classical breakeven chart assumes an identity of sales and production quantities. In fact, no such assumption is necessary, for under direct costing, all fixed costs are to be covered out of current revenue; no fixed costs are inventoriable. Once such a view has been accepted, a difference between the quantity produced and the quantity sold has no effect on the breakeven quantity or on the firm's profit, for any quantity of product put into inventory or taken out, being valued at variable cost only, has no effect on the (variable) cost of goods sold or on the fixed costs charged against current operations. It is because of this that the breakeven chart, as traditionally drawn assuming linear cost and revenue functions, has one and only one breakeven point.

As soon as adaptation of the chart to reflect conditions under absorption costing is attempted, the fact that fixed costs are no longer all non-inventoriable has to be faced. Absorption costing confines non-inventoriable fixed costs to:

(a) non-manufacturing expenses, and
(b) under-absorbed fixed manufacturing expense, i.e., any unfavorable volume variance.

I gladly acknowledge my debt to my colleague, Dr. Matthew J. Stephens, Jr., who made several suggestions which enabled me to clarify the presentation in this paper.

[1] Three notable examples are A. W. Patrick's "Some Observations on the Break-Even Chart," THE ACCOUNTING REVIEW (October 1958), pp. 573–580, about which more later; Rene Manes's "A New Dimension to Breakeven Analysis," *Journal of Accounting Research* (Spring 1966), pp. 87–100, which introduces the time-value of money into the analysis; and Jaedicke and Robichek's "Cost-Volume-Profit Analysis under Conditions of Uncertainty," THE ACCOUNTING REVIEW (October 1964), pp. 917–926.

David Solomons is Professor of Accounting at the University of Pennsylvania.

The second of these two categories is a function of actual output in relation to normal output. So, therefore, is non-inventoriable fixed cost. It follows, then, that whereas the traditional breakeven chart points to a unique breakeven point and a unique profit figure for each level of sales (including zero profit at the breakeven level), breakeven analysis adapted to absorption costing must provide many breakeven production-sales combinations; for if production is high, the firm can break even with low sales, whereas if there is a lot of idle capacity (and consequently a large unfavorable volume variance) higher sales will be needed to generate enough contribution to cover this non-inventoriable cost.

Although, under direct costing, changes in inventory during a period do not affect the breakeven point, it does turn out that, under absorption costing, a firm can break even while achieving an identity of production and sales only at the traditional breakeven sales level. This will be demonstrated later. It is enough to note here that this is probably what is meant when it is said that an identity of sales and production is assumed in the traditional breakeven chart. In fact neither under direct costing nor absorption costing does such a condition need to be satisfied, unless the breakeven point under absorption costing is required to be the same as under direct costing.

The non-uniqueness of the breakeven point under absorption costing was discussed ten years ago by A. W. Patrick, in an outstanding article which has already been referred to. However, Patrick's analysis has three deficiencies:

1. It lacks generality, based as it is on an illustrative set of figures.
2. The position of the locus of breakeven points on his diagram is computed by use of the illustrative figures, and then put on to the diagram. It is not self-evident from the diagram itself.
3. It does not distinguish as clearly as could be wished between the two different influences on the breakeven point under absorption costing, namely the relationship of sales and production quantities on the one hand and the amount of idle production capacity on the other.

It is the aim of this paper to complete Patrick's work on breakeven analysis,[2] and incidentally to present a simple pedagogic aid to explain graphically how operating results differ under direct and absorption costing.

The Breakeven Equation under Absorption Costing

Let

Q_s = Sales quantity (actual)

$Q_{sb(a)}$ = Sales quantity, at breakeven, under absorption costing

$Q_{sb(d)}$ = Sales quantity, at breakeven, under direct costing

Q_c = Production quantity at capacity[3]

Q_p = Production quantity (actual)

F_m = Total manufacturing fixed expense

F_s = Total selling and administrative fixed expense

v_m = Variable manufacturing cost per unit produced

v_s = Variable selling cost per unit sold

p = Selling price per unit.

Then, under absorption costing, at breakeven, total revenue equals total non-inventoriable cost, i.e.,

[2] This is not to say that other dimensions do not need to be added also, but only that they will not be discussed in this paper. Articles which remove two other simplifications—cost-free capital and conditions of certainty—have already been cited.

[3] This leaves capacity to be defined in any one of a number of ways, e.g., normal capacity, practical capacity etc. The use of normal capacity makes favorable volume variances possible. Although not discussed below, the analysis for them is symmetrical with that for unfavorable variances, so long as they are regarded as (negatively) inventoriable.

$$Q_{sb(a)}(p - v_s) \quad = \quad Q_{sb(a)}v_m \quad + \quad Q_{sb(a)}\frac{F_m}{Q_c} \quad + \quad (Q_c - Q_p)\frac{F_m}{Q_c} \quad + \quad F_s$$

Net revenue from sales, after variable selling costs	Variable manufacturing cost of sales	Fixed cost of sales at standard overhead rate	Volume variance	Fixed Selling and Administrative Costs

$$\therefore\ Q_{sb(a)}\left(p - v_s - v_m - \frac{F_m}{Q_c}\right) = (Q_c - Q_p)\frac{F_m}{Q_c} + F_s$$

(1)
$$\therefore\ Q_{sb(a)} = \frac{(Q_c - Q_p)\dfrac{F_m}{Q_c} + F_s}{p - v_s - v_m - \dfrac{F_m}{Q_c}}$$

What equation (1) says is that the breakeven sales quantity is determined by dividing total non-inventoriable fixed costs (made up of unabsorbed fixed manufacturing cost and all fixed non-manufacturing cost) by the net contribution per unit sold (after charging fixed costs at the standard rate). It is clear that, since the expression on the right contains Q_p, the quantity produced, there can be no unique value for $Q_{sb(a)}$, but only a set of values, one for each value of Q_p.

It is easy to see from equation (1) that if production is proceeding at capacity (i.e., if $Q_p = Q_c$), the first term in the numerator vanishes, and to break even under absorption costing it is only necessary to sell enough to generate net contribution to cover fixed selling and administrative expenses. If $Q_p = Q_s$ and F_s is zero, then, as was pointed out above, it is possible to break even with zero sales.

The Breakeven Chart under Absorption Costing

The graphical representation in Figure 1 brings out these relationships, and some additional ones besides. The $Q_s(p - v_s)$ line shows total sales revenue (quantity sold × price) net of variable selling costs. The lower horizontal line represents total fixed selling costs, F_s, and to this is added total fixed manufacturing costs to give the upper horizontal line, F_{m+s}, total fixed costs. Variable manufacturing costs are added to give the total cost line, RL $(= F_{m+s} + Qv_m)$. Capacity output is Q_c and a vertical is erected at this point. Through L, the intersection of this vertical with the total cost line, a line is drawn to T, the Y intercept of the F_s line. The slope of this line represents the *standard* rate of fixed manufacturing overhead.

Everything on the chart so far represents budgetary information. If actual production is now added, the sales required to break even can easily be pointed to; and if actual sales are added, the result of selling more or less than the breakeven quantity can be indicated.

Let actual production be Q_p, and let a vertical be erected at this point. Through B, the intersection of this vertical with RL, draw a line parallel to TL. The abscissa of the point H at which this line (drawn as a dotted line on Figure 1) cuts the net revenue line, OHA, gives the quantity of sales necessary to break even when production is equal to Q_p. The breakeven sales quantity is $OQ_{sb(a)}$. The net revenue generated, $HQ_{sb(a)}$ is just sufficient to cover the fixed selling expenses, $VQ_{sb(a)}$, the manu-

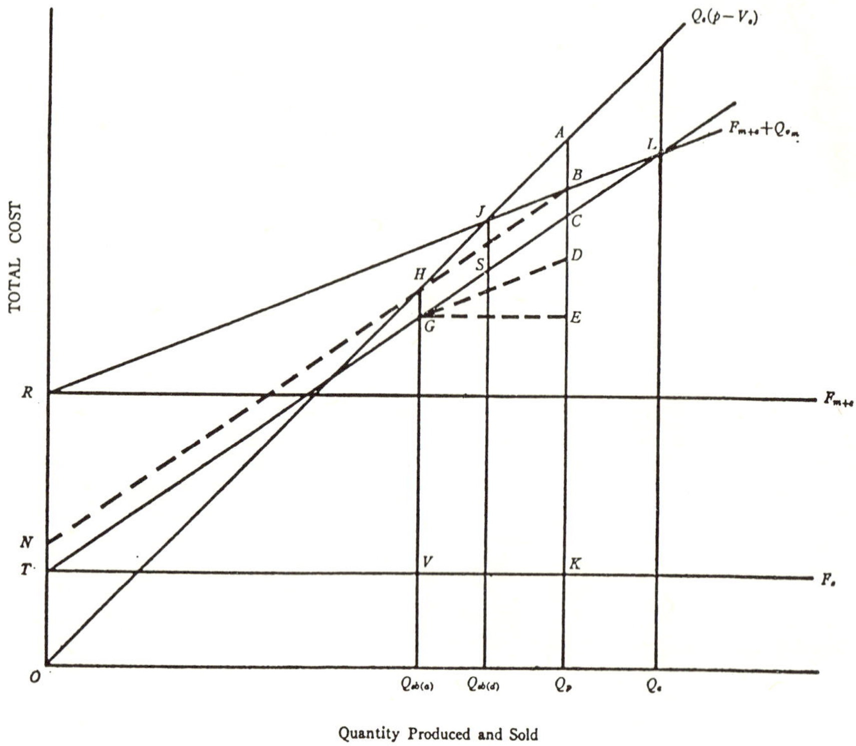

FIGURE 1

facturing cost of sales, GV, and the adverse volume variance, HG.

If a horizontal line is drawn through G to cut the Q_p vertical at E, it can be seen that, having accounted for $BC+EK+KQ_p$ $(=HG+GV+VQ_{sb(a)})$, when production is OQ_p ,the only part of total cost of production, BQ_p, not yet accounted for is CE. And this, of course, is the manufacturing cost which, under absorption costing, would go into inventory with the unsold output, $OQ_p-OQ_{sb(a)}$, if sales were at breakeven.

It is worth noting that, under absorption costing, in the limit, if actual production equalled normal capacity so that there were no volume variance, and if there were no fixed selling and administrative expenses, a firm could break even if it sold nothing at all! All its production would go into inventory, and fixed manufacturing expense would go into inventory with it.

RESULTS UNDER ABSORPTION COSTING AND DIRECT COSTING COMPARED

The chart enables all the important differences between absorption costing and direct costing to be seen. Direct costing offers a unique breakeven point, J. A sales quantity $OQ_{sb(d)}$ is required to break even under direct costing, while only $OQ_{sb(a)}$ is required under absorption costing so long as production is OQ_p. By extending the dotted line BH to intercept the Y axis at N, it can be seen that even if nothing was sold at all, under absorption costing the loss would only be ON, equal to the adverse volume variance and fixed nonmanufacturing cost, whereas under direct costing with zero sales the loss would be equal to total fixed costs, OR.

Generalizing this relationship produces an interesting result. The profitability of sales above breakeven, under direct costing, is given by the angle AJB, and under absorption costing by the angle JHB, and correspondingly for losses when sales fall short of breakeven. The difference between these two angles is equal to the angle CGD, GD having been drawn through G parallel to RL. This can easily be proved geometrically,[4] but it is also intuitively obvious as soon as it is remembered that the slope of $GC = v_m + (F_m/Q_c)$, while the slope of GD, parallel to JB, $= v_m$. The difference in slopes (angle CGD) $= F_m/Q_c$, the standard absorption rate of fixed manufacturing cost. The side opposite the angle CGD on the Q_p vertical, CD, measures the difference in profit under the two costing methods, absorption costing giving the bigger profit whenever production exceeds sales.

Quantitatively, the argument about the relative effect on profit of direct costing and absorption costing, which in the textbooks has taken so many tedious numerical illustrations to explain, can all be reduced to the triangle CGD. When production exceeds sales, absorption costing will give the greater profit by an amount equal to the fixed cost put into inventory, i.e., by $(Q_p - Q_s)(F_m/Q_c)$, and correspondingly when $Q_s > Q_p$, the profit under direct costing will be greater. It is obvious from the chart that as the gap between Q_s and Q_p closes, CD diminishes and eventually vanishes; and if the relative positions of Q_s and Q_p are transposed, CD re-appears with a changed sign.

It was pointed out at the beginning of this paper that the traditional breakeven chart, contrary to what is commonly said about it, does not need an assumption of identity between Q_s and Q_p. Referring to Figure 1, the traditional breakeven point is J. Assume that sales were $OQ_{sb(d)}$ and production OQ_p. Under direct costing, the products which are put into inventory, the excess of production over sales, go in at variable manufacturing cost, and the unique breakeven point is unaffected. Now let us ask, assuming absorption costing to be used, at what level of sales the firm would break even when a requirement is added that production must equal sales. The answer is that production and sales must both equal $OQ_{sb(d)}$. At that output, the adverse volume variance is JS, and to cover this and the other costs of production and selling, $SQ_{sb(d)}$, sales revenue must be $JQ_{sb(d)}$. This occurs only when sales are $OQ_{sb(d)}$—which is the traditional breakeven sales volume also. As Patrick pointed out,[5] the traditional breakeven point, given the use of absorption costing, is *the* breakeven point only in the special circumstance that production and sales are required to be equal.

Before concluding this discussion, two gaps in it must be noted. First, throughout, the assumption has been that $Q_p \geq Q_s$.

[4] $\angle JHB + \angle JBH = 180° - \angle HJB$

$\angle AJB = 180° - \angle HJB$

$\therefore \angle JHB + \angle JBH = \angle AJB$

$\therefore \angle JBH = \angle AJB - \angle JHB$

but, since $JB // GD$ and $HB // GC$, $\angle JBH = \angle CGD$

$\therefore \angle CGD = \angle AJB - \angle JHB$

Q.E.D.

[5] A. W. Patrick, *op. cit.*, p. 578.

Hence, reductions in inventory have been ignored. The analysis above is quite symmetrical as between increases and decreases in inventory *so long as there is no change in cost conditions from period to period.* But if the unit cost of last period's production should be different from this period's, the effect of a run-down of inventory will not be precisely the same, in the opposite direction, as an increase in inventory out of current production.

A second gap in the discussion is the neglect of variances other than volume variances. As non-inventoriable costs, these, too, need to be covered out of gross margin if the firm is to break even. But it would add little of value to the analysis to take this into account. Breakeven analysis is concerned with projections into the future, it aims to answer the question "What would happen if . . . ?" From the consideration of such a question it seems reasonable to exclude departures from budget which are not of the first importance.

THE ANALYSIS

OF STANDARD COST VARIANCES

The Analysis of Standard Cost Variances[1]

by David Solomons[2]

It was in 1911 that G. Charter Harrison designed and installed what he described as "the first complete standard cost system on record as far as I know." Several men before Charter Harrison had seen the potentialities of the use of standards as an aid to management, though their use of them was partial and fragmentary, whereas his was rounded and complete. This system has developed into an extraordinarily versatile tool; for it is perhaps the most impressive achievement of standard costing that it has gone such a long way toward providing, by means of a single integrated system, so many different kinds of cost data for so many different purposes. For the purposes of inventory valuation we can use product standard costs or, if variances from standard are too large to ignore, we can approximate product actual costs by prorating the variances over the products. For pricing purposes, either full product standard costs or product direct standard costs can be used, depending on whether absorption costing or direct costing is favored. For control purposes, costs can be allocated not to products but to responsibility centers and cost centers, with as elaborate an analysis of variances from standard as may be desired. No one can say that standard costing is not versatile.

But we have a long way to go before standard costing can be regarded as having been perfected. Though it probably represents the greatest advance in accounting since the development of double-entry bookkeeping itself, yet that does not mean, even after more than half a century, that it has reached anything like its full growth.

What Kind of Standards?

One difficulty which has beset standard costing from the earliest days is that of agreeing upon and defining the nature of the standards to be

[1]The first part of this article is adapted from "Standard Costing Needs Better Variances," published in the *N.A.A. Bulletin*, Vol. 43, No. 4, December 1961, pp. 29–39. The discussion of overhead variances is adapted from "Flexible Budgets and the Analysis of Overhead Variances," published in *Management International*, Vol. 1, No. 1, January-February 1961, pp. 84–92.

[2]Professor of Accounting, University of Pennsylvania.

used; out of the discussion has come a large measure of agreement that the most useful type of standard is one which represents "attainable good performance." However, this question cannot be regarded as closed, and indeed Stedry's work[3] forces us to look at it afresh.

Usually the effect of the standard on the level of performance has been ignored, on the assumption that as the process of measuring physical quantities does not have any effect on what is being measured, so the level at which a standard is set has no effect on the level of achievement; or, alternatively, it has been assumed that an unattainably high standard will be ignored by those who are expected to work to it and will therefore be ineffective. Stedry's experimental results cast doubt on these assumptions and suggest that setting a high standard, even if it is not attained, may significantly raise the level of performance above that achieved when standards are loose. Stedry's conclusions are not lightly to be accepted as applicable under normal working conditions. Indeed, there is room for scepticism about the relevance of his findings —based as they are on a short-term experiment on university students, even though carefully designed and executed—to the long-run behavior of people working for their living. As Stedry himself recognizes, a stimulus which is effective in the short-run may not persist or may even "backfire" and have undesirable long-term effects. The important point is that a substantial amount of research is still required to establish the facts. Accountants are apt to regard standards and budgets rather mechanically, without benefit of what the behavioral scientists can tell us or find out for us about their impact on people and on their aspirations.

Incidentally, the N.A.A.'s generally excellent *Re-Examination of Standard Costs*[4] perhaps itself needs re-examining on this point. "While it is sometimes said," it states, "that an unattainable tight standard provides an incentive to reduce costs, it seems that this use of the standard confuses the objectives of cost reduction and cost control. Cost reduction proceeds by finding ways to achieve a given result through improved design, better methods, new layouts, incentive plans, etc. Hence, cost reduction results in the establishment of new standards. On the other hand, cost control is a process of maintaining performance at as near existing standards as is possible." This surely makes the mistake which has just been discussed of ignoring the impact of standards on behavior. Cost control and cost reduction cannot be wholly separated. The results obtained are not just the result of "improved design, better methods, new layouts, incentive plans, etc." Human effort, both on the part of workers and managers, presumably still has its part to play. If the level of performance is itself a function of budget levels and standards, the methods used to control costs will directly affect the level of costs

[3] *Budget Control and Cost Behavior*, Andrew C. Stedry, Prentice Hall 1960.
[4] Research Series No. 11, *N.A.(C.)A. Bulletin*, Section 3, February 1948.

achieved. Cost control and cost reduction are inextricably mixed up with each other, and to realize this fact is not to "confuse" them, but to recognize a potentially important relationship.

What Kind of Variances?

Having raised some questions about the nature of standards, it is time to ask a few questions about the nature of variances, for if there is to be any substance in the claim that standard costing makes possible "management by exception," the significance to be attached to variances from standard cost must be clear and unambiguous; variances which go by the same name must represent the same thing, and fundamentally different kinds of "exceptions" from normal must be reflected accordingly in accounting statements. Of course normal procedures already go quite a long way in this direction and it must be recognized that further refinements may cost more than they are worth. Yet there are some directions in which perhaps further refinement would be worth its modest cost, for if a variance which masquerades as a substantially homogeneous quantity is really not so, of if a variance, because of the name given it, pretends to be one thing and is really another, then the money at present being spent on quantifying it is, at the best, being wasted and, at the worst, is causing management to be misled.

What Does Price Variance Mean?

Although a great deal has been written about the impact of rising prices on financial reporting and about its effect on the real burden of taxation, relatively little has been said about the disturbing effect it may have on accounting for managerial purposes. It may be argued, of course, that standard costing does all that needs to be done by separating out the effect of inflation as a price variance. Certainly, to the extent that it does this, standard costing represents a considerable advance over conventional historical costing, which makes no attempt to distinguish between price and quantity effects. Nevertheless, it may be doubted whether such a simple distinction is good enough, for, on closer examination, a price variance will be seen to be anything but homogeneous. In fact, it may turn out to be a mixture of at least five different things, namely:

1. The result of price fluctuations which have occurred since the standards were set.
2. The result of inefficient buying.
3. The result of quality substitutions differing from standard.
4. The result of inflationary pressures on prices in general.
5. The effect on the buying price of purchasing in more or less than the budgeted quantities.

The discussion which follows will be confined to raw material prices. Much the same considerations apply, of course, to other resources which are purchased at fluctuating prices.

Ideally, the above five causes of variance between actual and standard prices ought to be kept separate from each other. Many costing installations do separate as a cost variance the effect of the substitution of one material for another or one quality for another. Little attempt has been made, on the other hand, to reflect the other distinctions referred to above—distinctions between the effect of price fluctuations and of inefficient buying, between fluctuations in relative prices and inflation pressures on prices in general, and the incidence of quantity rebates.

The failure to make the first of these distinctions is easy enough to account for. The fact is that it is probably impossible to say whether a price variance has been caused by a movement of relative prices away from the standard or whether it was caused by inefficient buying.[5] Inefficient buying may mean many different things, some of them having nothing to do with price. Buying at a price different from standard certainly does not necessarily imply inefficiency; buying at a price higher than it need have been probably does. In any particular instance, it is impossible for anyone but the person responsible for a purchase to say whether the price was "higher than it need have been." Thus, it is impossible, as a matter of routine, to say whether an unfavorable price variance represents an uncontrollable price change or an avoidable inefficiency in purchasing. Conversely, a favorable price variance or the absence of an unfavorable price variance does not imply that the purchasing function has been carried out efficiently.

This means that the significance to be attached to a price variance is always subject to some doubt. Nevertheless, the area of doubt could be reduced somewhat if we did more than is commonly done to determine the fourth element of the price variance listed above—the effect of inflation (or deflation, of course) on prices—and to carry this to a separate variance account. There is no need to go into detail here about the technique of stabilizing accounts during period of inflation, since this has been described many times. What is called for, so far as it concerns standard costing, is simply the calculation of a "price-level price variance."[6] This can be done by comparing the actual cost of materials purchased during the period with the same figure adjusted to the price-level ruling at the beginning of the period.

Suppose that the actual purchases for a period amounted to $15,000,

[5]Here, and throughout this paper, the discussion of variances is couched mostly in terms of *favorable* variances. The reader should have no difficulty in re-phrasing the discussion in terms of favorable variances.

[6]It seems better to avoid the term "inflation price variance," since periods of inflation and deflation might one day again alternate with each other, and the term "price-level price variance" would cover both.

the wholesale price index at the beginning of the period had been 110 and the average index for the period was 112; then the price-level variance (unfavorable), in terms of average dollars of the period, would have been $\$15{,}000 \times \frac{112 - 110}{112}$ or \$268. It will be noted that this figure has been calculated by reference to the materials purchased during the period, not by reference to the materials consumed. The price-level variance makes much more sense this way (as do all price variances, probably). It would be possible to calculate it by reference to the period's consumption, but this procedure would be both more complicated and less meaningful.

THE FURTHER ANALYSIS OF PRICE VARIANCES

Before leaving the analysis of price variances, two other unsatisfactory aspects of standard costing which are of some theoretical interest should be faced. One of these is the failure to distinguish the fifth element of price variance which has been listed above, namely increments or decrements in price which are the result of purchasing larger or smaller quantities of material than budgeted. The other is the difficulty, perhaps the impossibility, of satisfactorily dividing the total difference between the actual and standard cost of materials into price effects (however analysed) and the quantity effect in a uniquely correct and unambiguous manner.

Diagram I makes it possible to consider both of these matters together. For simplicity, suppose that a single basic material is used, say pulp of some kind, and suppose, further, that there is no change in raw materials inventory during the period, *i.e.* that purchases equal consumption. The lower curve OCB represents the budgeted cost of buying varying quantities of pulp. Because the price is expected to fall as the quantity bought increases, the curve rises at a diminishing rate.[7] The expected usage at standard is the quantity OQ, and through Q we draw the vertical SQ (for standard quantity). Suppose the actual quantity used, OQ′, exceeds the standard quantity. Through Q′ draw the vertical AQ (for actual quantity). The standard price (the originally budgeted price) is represented by the slope of the line OC drawn from the origin through C (the intersection of the budget curve with the vertical SQ) and extended on to D, where it cuts AQ. The budgeted cost for the actual quantity used is given by the point B, the intersection of the budget curve with the vertical AQ. The actual prices ruling during the period, supposing they turned out to be above what was expected, for some reason unconnected with quantity rebates, are represented by the

[7]It would no doubt be more realistic to represent the function by a series of line segments rather than a smooth curve; but, while not affecting the principle at all, this would be both less pleasing aesthetically and less tractable mathematically.

upper curve OEF, E and F being its points of intersection with SQ and AQ respectively. This curve will be of roughly the same shape as the budget curve, no doubt, but on the assumption that actual prices were above those budgeted, it had to be drawn at a higher level.

It can now be seen that what would usually be regarded as the unfavorable price variance FD, the excess (in this case) of the actual quantity of purchases evaluated at the actual price (FQ′) over the actual quantity evaluated at the standard price (DQ′), is really made up of two elements. One of these is the excess of the actual quantity at the actual price (again FQ′) over the actual quantity at the budgeted price (BQ′). This excess is the amount FB and it represents, it may be argued, the true price variance—unfavorable in this case. The other part of what would usually be called the price variance is the difference between the actual quantity of purchases evaluated at the standard price and the actual quantity evaluated at the budgeted price. This is the favorable variance BD and it represents the saving which results from the lower prices obtained because of the greater-than-standard purchases. It can perhaps be called a quantity rebate variance, and it arises because the standard price is constant for all levels of quantity purchased, whereas budgeted prices are not. It is closely related to the capacity variance encountered in the analysis of overhead variances, in that this also arises because the standard overhead rate, once set, is constant for all levels of capacity, with the result that standard cost varies directly with the level of activity whereas the budgeted cost, which we read off the flexible budget and which usually contains some fixed costs, does not.

Here, then, is another instance where standard costing presents as a homogeneous variance something that actually comprises two or more different elements. In the case illustrated, the true price variance would be substantially understated by the conventional method and, as an incidental consequence, so would the price-level variance advocated earlier in this article. Since, for control purposes, the effectiveness of standard costing depends on our ability to recognize the true significance of variances when they appear, their correct analysis is of no little importance. To say this is not to lose sight of the fact that, in practice, some of the distinctions which have been drawn here may involve quite small sums of money and, thus, may not be worth worrying about. Yet, if the calculations are not made, it may be impossible to say whether the amounts are big enough to be important or not.

Diagram I can also be used to illustrate another ambiguity which surrounds price and quantity variances, and perhaps always will. A second look at the diagram will show that there is an alternative way of analyzing the total variance between the price and quantity effects. On this alternative view, the quantity variance, *i.e.*, the cost of using more than the standard quantity of material, is to be determined by evaluating the excess quantity at the actual price, not at the standard price. The

15

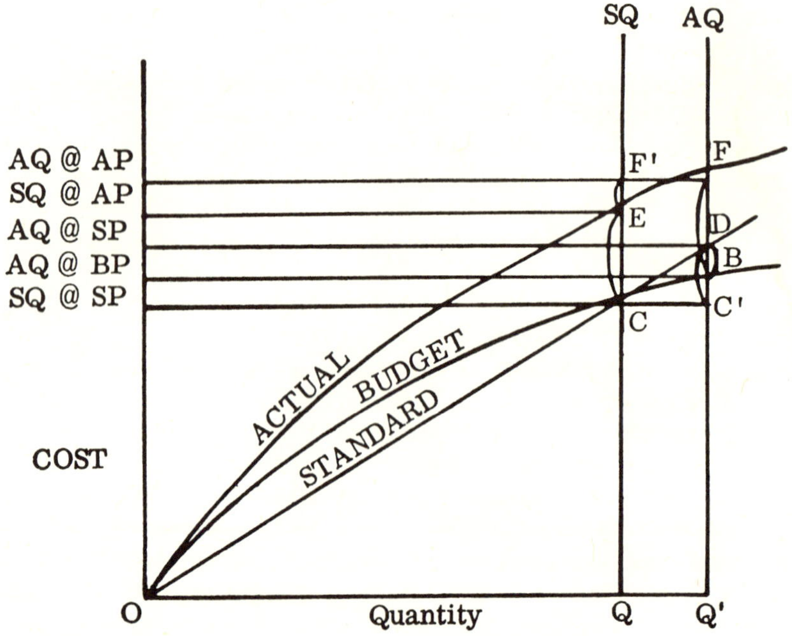

Key
SQ = Standard Quantity
AQ = Actual Quantity
SP = Standard Price
AP = Actual Price
BP = Budget Price

View (1)
True Price Variance = FB(unfav.)
Quantity Rebate Variance = BD(fav.)
Quantity Variance = DC′(unfav.)

View (2)
Price Variance = EC(unfav.)
Quantity Variance = F′E(unfav.)

DIAGRAM I

price variance is arrived at by applying the excess price (excess of actual over standard) to the standard quantity of material, not to the actual quantity. The difference between the two contrasting views can be briefly summed up as follows:

Let P = Standard price.
Q = Standard quantity.
$\triangle P$ = Excess of actual price over standard.
$\triangle Q$ = Excess of actual quantity over standard.

Then standard cost is QP and actual cost is $(Q + \triangle Q)\ (P + \triangle P)$. Multiplying out this expression for actual cost we get $QP + Q\triangle P + P\triangle Q + \triangle Q\triangle P$. The last three terms in this expression make up the total variance. Both of the views under discussion allocate the first of these terms to the price variance and the second to the quantity variance. The argument is about what to do with the last term, $\triangle Q\triangle P$.

The first view regards it as part of the price variance, the second as part of the quantity variance. Diagram I makes it easy to compare the two alternative sets of variances. The total variance is, of course, the same in both cases.

This is not by any means an empty argument, for it is concerned with the allocation of responsibility for the incurrence of cost. Suppose both price and quantity variances are unfavorable. Are the people in the plant who waste or spoil material to be held responsible for its actual cost or its standard cost? They will probably argue that any extra price paid was due to bad purchasing. Are the purchasing people responsible for the extra cost of all material used or only the standard quantity? They will argue that, if the material had not been wasted in the plant, it would not have to be bought at the extra price. I do not know how to answer these questions, any more than I know whether, when I drop a glass on the floor and it breaks, this is because of the hardness of the floor or the fragility of the glass. The answer usually given in theoretical discussion is that $\triangle P \triangle Q$, which is what we are talking about, ought to be assigned to a special "composite variance" account and excluded from both price and quantity variances; but this does not seem often to be done in practice.

Incidentally, what happens to the quantity rebate variance if we adopt what may be called the "second view" of price and quantity variances? The answer is that it vanishes. The formula for the quantity rebate variance is, on the first view, AQ(BP—SP). In relation to the actual quantity, BP and SP need not be equal to each other, and so the quantity rebate variance will not usually be zero. On the second view, however, the quantity rebate variance is SQ (BP-SP). In relation to the standard quantity, BP will normally equal SP, so BP – SP = O and the quantity rebate variance vanishes.

Overhead Variances

Turning now to overhead variances, again there are reasons for thinking that while the conventional methods of variance analysis are often too complex to be easily understood by laymen, they are at the same time too simple to have the significance which they purport to have.

The conventional analysis of overhead variances is illustrated in diagram II. Diagram II(*a*) shows the analysis of variance into two parts, a controllable variance, as it is usually called, and a volume variance. In the situation illustrated, the actual man-hours worked fell seriously short of the man-hours budgeted, and the actual efficiency of the work done was also substantially below 100 per cent, so that the output produced (expressed in standard hours) was less than it should have been in the man-hours actually worked. These three quantities, budgeted hours, actual hours and achieved standard hours (*i.e.*, actual output) are

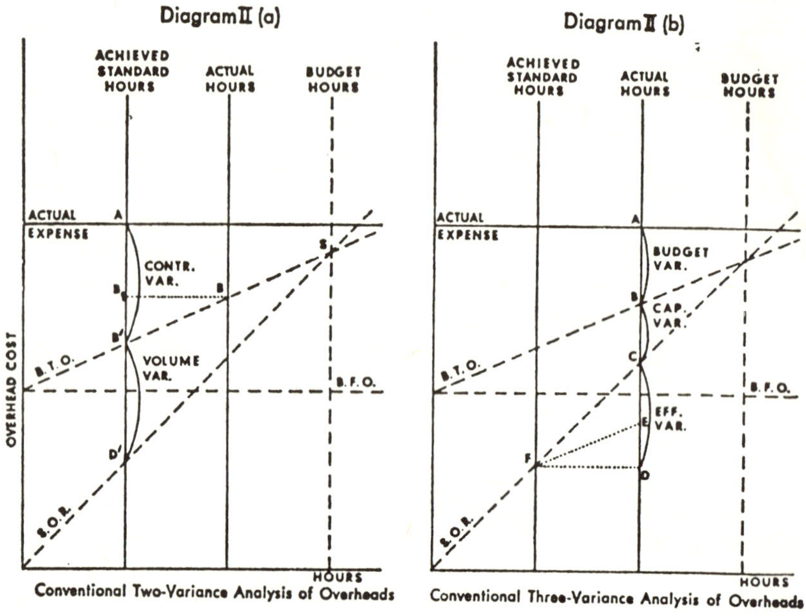

DIAGRAM II

represented by the three vertical lines. Budgeted fixed overheads are represented by the horizontal line BFO and on top of this the variable expenses budgeted for varying levels of output are superimposed to, give the line BTO, representing budgeted total overheads. This line represents the flexible budget, and shows at each level of activity the total overhead expenditure allowed by the budget. While this is shown as a straight line in the diagram, it might like, the materials cost line in diagram I, have been shown as curved instead of straight, or even as rising in discontinuous jumps.[8]

The standard overhead rate is computed by dividing the total overhead budget allowance appropriate to the budgeted level of activity by the number of man-hours to be worked. This gives the standard hourly rate of overheads, and is represented by a straight line joining the point S (the point where the budget expense line BTO cuts the "budget hours" vertical) to the origin. This line cannot be anything but straight, since the standard rate, once fixed, cannot vary during the period, whatever fluctuations of output or expenditure may occur. Only when there is a revision of standards will the standard overhead rate change.

The actual expenditure on overheads during the period under

[8]To enable a clear distinction between the budgetary data in the diagram and the information about actual results to be kept in mind, budget data is represented by broken lines and "actual" data by unbroken lines.

examination is shown by the horizontal line passing through the point A.

With the two-variance system,[9] the flexible budget allowance is regarded as being set by the level of output achieved, and in diagram II(*a*) it is represented by the point B′, allowed expense, the point at which the vertical for actual output cuts the flexible budget line. The excess of actual expense over allowed expense, represented by the vertical distance AB′, is the controllable variance, the excess expenditure (in this case) for which the departmental officials and foreman can be held responsible. The difference between the allowed expense and the overheads absorbed into actual production at the standard overhead rate—the absorbed expense—is the non-controllable or volume variance. It represents the fixed overheads which are left unabsorbed because production (expressed in standard hours) fell short of budgeted production. As can be seen from the diagram, if output had been as budgeted, the volume variance would have been nil. If output had been zero, then the volume variance would have been equal to—it would in fact have consisted of—the total fixed overheads. The diagram makes it quite clear that there would be no volume variance if there were no fixed costs. It can further be seen that if the achieved standard hours were to exceed the budgeted hours either because of intensive use of capacity or because of high productivity per hour, then the standard overhead recovery line would have crossed and been above the budget line, and the volume variance would be favorable, *i.e.*, it would represent an over-absorption of fixed costs.

Substituting figures for the diagram, suppose that the budget for the month calls for 2,000 standard hours of output in 2,000 man-hours. At this level of activity, budgeted expenses are $1,000 fixed expense and $1,000 variable expense for the month. At the end of the month, it is found that only 1,800 man-hours were worked and only 1,600 standard hours were produced, while actual overhead expenditure was $2,150.

Then we have:	$	
Actual expense	2,150	
Allowed expense:		$350 (unfav.) controllable variance
$\$1{,}000 + \left(\$1{,}000 \times \dfrac{1{,}600}{2{,}000}\right)$	= 1,800	
Fixed Variable		$200 (unfav.) non-controllable variance
Absorbed expense		
1,600 standard hours at $1 an hour	= 1,600	
Total variance		$550 (unfav.)

[9]In the diagrams, the variances have been exaggerated to make the demonstrations more effective. The diagrams are therefore not drawn on a scale corresponding to the numerical illustrations. It need hardly be pointed out that the method of analysis used is equally applicable, whether any or all of the variances are favorable or unfavorable.

Turning to diagram II(*b*), we have an illustration of the conventional three-variance system. The data is the same as in diagram II(*a*), and the notation is almost the same. As can be seen from the diagram, with this system the budget allowance for overheads is determined by reference to the actual man-hours worked, at point B.

The three variances can now be identified. The vertical distance AB, the excess of actual overheads over the budget allowance, represents the budget variance. This variance will usually be in part a price variance, due to differences between the standard and actual prices of overhead services or indirect materials, and in part a spending variance, due to divergences between actual and budget expenditures unrelated to price variations. There is no technical difficulty whatever in making this division between the price element and the "spending" element in the budget variance, for all that needs to be done is to have all overhead services, indirect materials and indirect labor priced at both actual and standard prices in the same way as is done for direct materials and direct labor. But in practice it is not often thought worthwhile to go to these lengths.

The vertical distance BC is the capacity variance. As can be seen, it is the difference between the budget allowance for the hours actually worked, and the cost which would have been absorbed, at the standard overhead rate, if every hour worked had been 100 per cent effective in producing output. This latter amount, the actual hours worked evaluated at the standard overhead rate per hour, which we might appropriately call the time-absorbed expense, is represented by point C. Like the volume variance of diagram II(*a*), the capacity variance can be seen to be equal to the full fixed costs when output is zero, falling to a nil variance when actual hours are equal to budget hours, and then reversing its sign and becoming a favorable variance when actual hours exceed budget hours.

The third member of the trinity is the efficiency variance. This is the vertical distance CD. The point D is merely a projection on to the "actual hours" vertical of the point F, which represents the standard cost recovered or absorbed by actual output.

It will be seen that the efficiency variance, so measured, is the difference between the standard overhead cost absorbed by actual output and what we have called the time-absorbed expense—the standard overhead cost which would have been absorbed if the actual hours worked had been fully effective in producing output.

Using the same figures as previously, the total variance of $550 is the same as before: its analysis, however, would look like this:

	$	
Actual expense	2,150	
		$250 (unfav.) budget variance
Allowed expense $\$1{,}000 + \left(\$1{,}000 \times \frac{1{,}800}{2{,}000}\right)$ Fixed Variable	= 1,900	
		$100 (unfav.) capacity variance
Time-absorbed expense 1,800 hours at $1 (Actual hours at standard overhead rate)	= 1,800	
		$200 (unfav.) efficiency variance
Absorbed expense 1,600 standard hours at $1 (Actual output at standard overhead rate)	= 1,600	
Total variance		$550 (unfav.)

As may be supposed, the two methods of variance analysis just explained are not unrelated to each other. The controllable variance of the two-variance method is equal to the budget variance plus part of the efficiency variance of the other method—a part equal to the difference between the budget allowance for actual hours and the budget allowance for achieved standard hours, represented on diagram II(*a*) by the vertical distance B_1B'. The same quantity is shown on diagram II(*b*) as the vertical distance ED, a part of the efficiency variance. The position of E is determined by drawing a straight line from F, the absorbed expense, parallel to the flexible budget line until it cuts the "actual hours" vertical. The slope of EF represents the variable overhead rate per hour, and ED therefore represents the extra variable cost incurred because it took more actual hours to get the output achieved than it would have done had efficiency been 100 per cent. Since diagrams II(*a*) and II(*b*) are basically identical, it is easy to prove that ED is equal to B_1B', since the triangles FED and BB_1B' are congruent.

This relationship is significant in any assessment of the relative merits of the two systems. The chief defect of the two-variance system is that it does not distinguish between the "spending" element and the "efficiency" element of the controllable variance; it does not, that is to say, distinguish between excessive expenditure due to loose control of spending or price increases and excessive expenditure arising from man-hours wasted through inefficiency.[10] The three-variance system, on the other hand, does yield a separate efficiency variance, but it does so in a very questionable manner; for the efficiency variance, as conventionally determined, does not represent the true extra cost which results from inefficiency or the cost saving which results from high efficiency, but rather the difference between two hypothetical figures of "absorbed" expense.

[10]What is said here in terms of unfavorable variances of course applies, *mutatis mutandis*, to cost savings which give rise to favorable variances.

Another criticism, which can be levelled at both methods, is that the budget allowance for overheads, as set by the flexible budget, is regarded as a function of a single variable. All expenses are regarded as varying, if they vary at all, either with the number of man-hours worked (as in the three-variance system) or with the level of output produced (as in the two variance system), whereas the facts of cost behavior clearly make any such simple assumption unrealistic.

Realism demands that we recognize at least three types of expense:

(*a*) those that vary with the volume of output, *e.g.*, manufacturing supplies, certain costs of materials handling and maintenance of equipment, royalties, inspection costs.[11]

(*b*) those that vary with the number of man-hours worked, *e.g.*, welfare expenditure, supervision, heating and lighting.

(*c*) those that vary only with the length of the period, and not with the amount of work done or the output obtained, *e.g.*, rent, fire insurance.

This points to the need to make the flexible budget flexible in more than one direction, taking each expense separately and making appropriate adjustments to the original budget figures in the light of what is known, at the end of the period, about the number of man-hours worked and the level of output achieved.[12]

Recognition of the fact that at least two independent variables control the level of overheads suggests that many more variables could be introduced into the function, bringing greater realism but also, unfortunately, greater complexity. For the more or less routine purpose of expenditure control, it is doubtful whether the greater complexity would be worthwhile.

An Improved Method of Overhead Variance Analysis—Four Variances

The shortcomings of the conventional methods of variance analysis which were pointed out above can be met, while retaining their virtues, by recognizing at least four separate variances, viz:

[11]The assertion of a functional relationship between cost and volume or cost and any other independent variable does not imply that the relationship is necessarily a simple one, and certainly not that it is one of direct proportionality. This point will be emphasized again below.

[12]Professor W. J. Vatter gave a pointer in the same direction some years ago: "Rate of activity is often (and I think wrongly) taken as output or capacity or some related concept. Costs for planning and control purposes are related to decisions. Decisions have to do with inputs, not output. It would be better to talk and think about break-even charts, budgets, and other planning devices in terms of the input factors which must be controlled, rather than the output bases on which we can write up our post-mortems." (N.A.C.A. Conference Proceedings, August 1954, p. 1700.) I would rather say that we have to have regard to both inputs and outputs.

1. A budget variance. This is, as normally, the difference between actual expenditure on overheads and the allowance set by the flexible budget; but by making the flexible budget more flexible, as has already been suggested, the budget variance can be made much more meaningful than it commonly is. The flexible budget must be made to register the allowance for overheads appropriate to the actual number of hours worked *and* the actual level of output achieved.

Nothing that is said here precludes more detailed analysis of the budget variance such as, for instance, the separation of the effects of price and quantity variations, although nothing more will be said about such further analysis. Again, it may be presumed that in practice the budget variance will be examined item by item rather than in terms of total overhead or of broad categories of overhead, as is done here.

2. A true efficiency variance—true, because it really measures the gain or loss in overhead expenditure attributable to variations away from the level of efficiency stipulated in the budget. One of the figures necessary in this calculation is the flexible budget allowance just mentioned. The other figure, which can easily be derived from the flexible budget, is the budget allowance appropriate to the production of the achieved output in the standard number of man-hours, as distinct from the actual number of man-hours. Clearly, those expenses which vary with output and not with working time (and also, of course, those which are fixed in relation to both) will be unaffected by excess man-hours or savings in man-hours as compared with the standard time required to produce the actual output. Such expenses are determined by the actual output, not by the time it takes to produce it. The expenses linked to man-hours, on the other hand, will be directly affected by excesses or savings in man-hours. It is these expenses, and these alone, which should enter into the overhead efficiency variance, which now becomes the difference between the flexible budget allowance for the actual output obtained in the actual man-hours worked and the budget allowance which would have been set if the actual output had been obtained in the standard number of man-hours.[13]

3. A volume (capacity) variance. This is one part of the unabsorbed (or over-absorbed) fixed costs—the part attributable to the loss or gain in output resulting from the difference between the budgeted number of man-hours and the actual man-hours worked.

4. A volume (efficiency) variance, being the remaining part of the unabsorbed or overabsorbed fixed costs. This part is attributable to the difference between actual output and the output which would have

[13]The standard number of man-hours is not to be confused with budgeted man-hours. The standard man-hours are arrived at by multiplying actual output by the standard time per unit of output. Budget man-hours are the result of multiplying budgeted output by the standard time per unit of output.

been obtainable from the actual number of man-hours worked if these had all been worked at standard efficiency.

This system combines the advantages of the two-variance and the three-variance systems, without their shortcomings. All that is needed is to build into the system a capacity to distinguish between the two types of variable expense just discussed—the time-variable expenses, as they might be called, and the output-variable expenses. This is not a difficult thing to do. The method is perhaps best explained by means of an illustration, using the same basic data as in the earlier illustrations, but making the further assumptions that (1) the original overhead budget allowance of $1,000 for variable expenses is divisible into $600 for output-variable items and $400 for the time-variables, while (2) the actual expenditure of $2,150 is made up of $1,050 in fixed expenses, $675 in output-variables and $425 in time-variable items.

Using these data, we can see from the table below how the variances would be arrived at.[14]

Type of expense	*Original overhead budget for 2,000 standard hours of output obtained in 2,000 man-hours*	*Actual overhead expenditure for period*	*Expense allowance for actual output (1,600 standard hours) in actual time (1,800 man-hours)*	*Expense allowance for actual output (1,600 standard hours) in standard time (1,600 man-hours)*	*Absorbed Expense (1,600 standard hours at standard rate of $1*
	(1)	(2)	(3)	(4)	(5)
	$	$	$	$	$
Fixed	1,000	1,050	1,000	1,000	
Output-variable	600	675	480	480	1,600
Time-variable	400	425	360	320	
	2,000	2,150	1,840	1,800	1,600

$310 *Budget Variance (unfav.)* — between (2) and (3)

$40 *Efficiency Variance (unfav.)* — between (3) and (4)

$200 *Volume Variance (unfav.)* — between (4) and (5)

[14]In this illustration, the variable expenses (of both types) are regarded as being *proportionately* variable with man-hours or output. As was noted above in connection with Diagram II, it is not really necessary to take any such simple assumption. The variations might be continuous but disproportional, or they might be discontinuous. In either case, the flexible budget would be embodied in a table, only a little more complex than the kind commonly used at present, and the figures could be read off quite simply.

Column (1) of the table sets out the original budget figures, classified under types of expense, and based on a plan to produce 2,000 standard hours of output in 2,000 man-hours. The actual expenditure for the period, as ascertained at the end of the period, and following the same classification of expenses, is shown in column (2). Column (3) shows how the original budget is adjusted to take account of the actual time worked and the actual output produced in that time. Fixed expenses call for no adjustment. The expenses which vary with output are reduced to 1,600/2,000 of the original budget figure, and the expenses which vary with man-hours worked are reduced to 1,800/2,000 of the original budget. The total adjusted budget for the actual output in the actual time is therefore $1,840. Column (4) shows what the budget allowance would have been if the actual output had been produced in the standard time. Fixed expenses and those that vary with output would have been as shown in column (3) but the allowance for expenses varying with time has to be reduced to only 1,600/2,000 of the original budget. The total adjusted budget for the actual output in the standard time is therefore $1,800. Finally, column (5) shows the absorbed overheads as $1,600, *i.e.*, 1,600 standard hours of output at the standard rate of $1 an hour.

The determination of the budget and efficiency variances from the table is sufficiently obvious to need no comment. The budget variance of $310 is the excess of column (2) over column (3) and the efficiency variance of $40 is the excess of column (3) over column (4). The treatment of the volume variance of $200 is not so obvious, however, and calls for explanation.

There is really only one difference between column (4) and column (5), and that is in the fixed expenses. In column (4) only the fixed expenses are unchanged from the original budget in column (1). The other types of expense have shrunk to 1,600/2,000 of the original figures. In column (5), *all* the figures in effect, have shrunk to 1,600/2,000 of the original budget. The difference between column (4) and column (5), therefore, consists of the 400/2,000 of $1,000, or $200, by which the fixed expenses have failed to shrink with the shortfall of output below the quantity originally budgeted, and this $200 is the volume variance. But we can go further than this. Using the *fixed* overhead rate of $1,000/2,000 or $0.50 per standard hour, we can say that $0.50 × (2,000–1,800) or $100 of fixed expenses remain unabsorbed because less capacity was used than was expected, and that $0.50 × (1,800–1,600) or a further $100 are left unabsorbed because the capacity that was used was used with less than standard efficiency. Thus the volume variance of $200 can be split into a volume (capacity) variance of $100 and a volume (efficiency) variance of a further $100.

Diagrammatic Representation of the Revised System

As overheads now have to be regarded as a function of two independent variables—man-hours *and* output—instead of one—man-hours *or* output—this system cannot be represented on a simple two-dimensional diagram. But it may be illuminating to compare it diagrammatically in a partial way with the conventional systems, and this can be done if we concentrate our attention on those costs which are fixed and those which vary with the number of man-hours worked, ignoring those costs which vary with output. By so doing, we can represent the system on a two-dimensional diagram.

Diagram III (a)

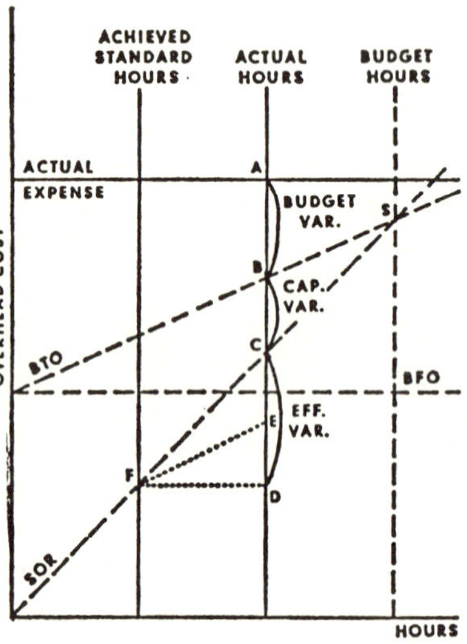

Conventional Three-Variance Analysis of Overheads

Diagram III (b)

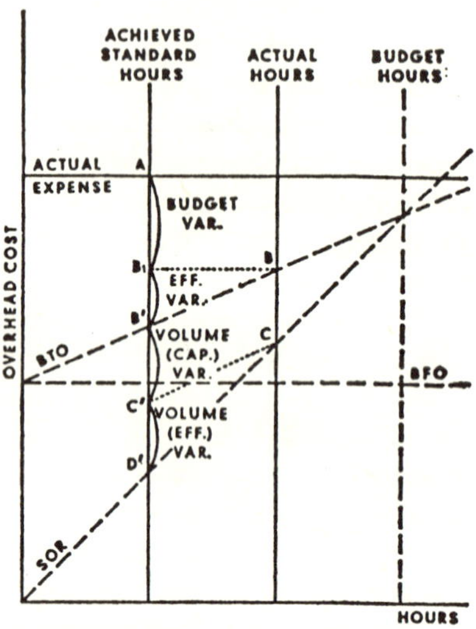

Four-Variance Analysis of Overheads
(All expenses assumed to vary with hours worked)

Diagram III(*a*) merely repeats diagram II(*b*), to facilitate comparison between the three-variance system there shown and the four-variance system represented in diagram III(*b*). The underlying data are again the same as before, so that all the lines have the same slope as in the previous diagram, and the actual overhead expenditure for the period is the same as before also.

Since in diagram III(*b*) we are dealing only with expenses which are fixed or which vary with the man-hours worked, the flexible budget allowance for the period is indicated by the point B, where the budget line is cut by the "actual hours" vertical. Point B is projected across to the left to give B_1, and the vertical distance AB is the budget variance. It is, of course, equal to AB, the budget variance in diagram III(*a*).

The second of the four variances in diagram III(*b*) is the efficiency variance. This is the vertical distance B_1B'; for B_1 (equal to B) is the budget expense allowance for the man-hours actually worked, and B′ is the allowance for the hours which the output achieved ought to have taken. B_1B' is therefore the cost increment resulting from wasted hours, and is truly an efficient variance. As already noted when we were discussing diagram II above, B_1B' in diagram III(*b*) is equal to ED, a part of the efficiency variance, in diagram III(*a*).

The distance B′C′ is the volume (capacity) variance. It is, by construction, equal to BC, since the point C′ is determined by the intersection of the "achieved standard hours" vertical with a line through C drawn parallel to the budget line, so that B′BCC′ is a parallelogram, the opposite sides of which are equal. B′C′, because it is equal to BC on diagram III(*b*), is also equal to BC on diagram III(*a*). It represents the fixed overheads which are unabsorbed by reason of the fact that the actual man-hours worked fell short of the budgeted hours by reference to which the standard overhead rate was fixed.

The fourth variance is the volume (efficiency) variance. It is the balance of the unabsorbed fixed costs, the portion which is unabsorbed because the actual output (which can alone really absorb costs) fell short of the output which the actual man-hours worked would have achieved if the standard level of efficiency had been maintained. It is represented by the vertical distance C′D′.

Shortcomings Provide an Opportunity

Standard costing is the victim of its own pretensions. Job costs and process costs of the old-fashioned historical kind offer little or no information which is directly relevant to the control of costs and, therefore, are not subject to criticism for failures in this field. But with standard costing it is different. Though, as was said earlier, it is a versatile tool, with many uses, its greatest contribution is in the field of cost control. Its shortcomings are liable to criticism, simply because it has such tremendous potentialities. These potentialities have really only just begun to be explored. In the development of concepts, in accounting as in other fields, half a century is not a long period. So if, as has been suggested here, standard costing in its present form is still too simple an instrument to provide more than a part of the information which cost control demands if it is to be really effective, we are entitled to regard this as an opportunity, not a failure.

I

INTRACORPORATE CONFLICT IN INTERNATIONAL BUSINESS *

DAVID SOLOMONS

I do not know whether I should feel called upon to defend my choice of subject. If I do, it is because this is primarily an accounting occasion; and a talk bearing the above-stated title does not sound as if it is particularly relevant to an accounting audience. I hope you will feel at the end of my presentation that it is.

Let me proceed with the defense of my choice of subject. It stems rather naturally from my interest in the subject of divisionalization and divisional performance. After working on the book that Dr. Mattessich referred to when he was introducing me,[1] I then had the opportunity of spending a year teaching in Lausanne in Switzerland, a superb center for the study of international business. It was rather natural that my interest in intracorporate conflicts within a domestic business should be carried over into the international field. Second, this seemed to me *par excellence* an international occasion. Here am I, an Englishman, resident in the United States, lecturing in Canada — I guess that makes it international. And third, I was interested to learn yesterday afternoon, when we were being shown around Vancouver, that this is in fact, contrary to what most Americans think at least, the most important port on the West Coast of North America. It seems to me therefore a natural center for the study of international business. I hope you will agree before I sit down that these considerations, together with the fact that the problems of the relations between the parts of an international business present the accountant with a very difficult problem of measurement, in fact make this a perfectly appropriate subject. Moreover I understand that in the audience there may well be some students of international business as well as students of accounting. Of course on top of all that there has been the enormous growth in the importance of

* I wish to express my gratitude to IMEDE, Lausanne, Switzerland for the support which, during the year I was on its faculty, made the collection of much of the material in this lecture possible.

1 *Divisional Performance: Measurement and Control* (New York: Financial Executives Research Foundation, 1965).

international business, certainly in the United States, and I am sure in Canada also, in recent years. As the international interests of a large domestic business, or a business which was formerly domestically oriented, increased, there soon developed new possibilities of conflict between corporate headquarters and the subsidiaries which are usually formed to carry on the business of an international company in foreign markets; and also, of course there are increasing possibilities of conflict between the subsidiaries themselves, between one subsidiary and another. These conflicts are in fact my subject. The problem of measurement arises when you give each subsidiary in an international area the goal to optimize its results, and you hope that the sum total of all these optima will add up to a corporate optimum, and of course there is a very fair chance that it will not. The more self-contained each national affiliate or subsidiary is, the more likely it is that when it optimizes its results, its contribution to the corporate result will also be optimized. I shall be at some pains to point out before I am through that in fact you do not usually find these self-contained national subsidiaries, and the problem of sub-optimization then becomes an important one.

Now the problems that you meet with in international business are not fundamentally different from those that you meet in a large segmented domestic business. However, for the reasons which I shall mention shortly, although they are fundamentally the same problems they seem to be accentuated by national differences, they are more difficult to resolve, and of course they very often have political implications.

The problem arises because no one has yet really come up with a much better measurement of performance than operating profit. And when a subsidiary in a foreign country is judged by its profit results, then naturally the management in that particular country becomes sensitive about anything which appears to inhibit its own profit maximization. It becomes sensitive about conflicts with other parts of the organization, whether the corporate headquarters or other subsidiary companies, which prevent it from going all out to make the biggest profit it can for itself. And if these subsidiaries weren't being judged by their superiors on the basis of profit, they probably would be evaluating their own performance in those terms anyway.

INTRACORPORATE RELATIONS

Now there are several reasons for saying that you cannot really isolate a subsidiary's contribution to corporate results and look at it in isolation. First of all in its national area — incidentally, it would not do any great harm if you think of a Canadian subsidiary to an American affiliate, a common enough situation — the subsidiary both helps to create the corporate name, (it usually uses the corporate name, of course), and build its reputation, but it also trades on its reputation. As a matter of fact, in talking to executives in European subsidiary companies, I found that some of them felt that the use of an American name was an advantage. Others felt that it was a distinct disadvantage; they did not want to be tarred with the American brush. So it works both ways. This is one reason for saying that the national subsidiary, however self-contained it would like to be, is known to be associated with a corporate headquarter located in another country. The second point is that the national affiliate will almost always use some of the results of centralized research and development. It will be making products which have been developed elsewhere. It may occasionally contribute to the product line something which can be sold in other parts of the corporate empire. But more commonly it will be using research results developed at the corporate headquarters, wherever that may be. It may be using materials which have been bought centrally. One of the European companies I had a chance to study particularly was the Nestlé Co. which has its headquarters only a few miles from Lausanne in Switzerland. It is a company which uses a vast amount of cocoa beans and coffee beans in making chocolate and Nescafé. These were purchased centrally for subsidiary companies all over the world, so that this was another factor which affected the profits directly of those subsidiary companies. Again, the national subsidiaries usually will be subject to orders from headquarters as to what they will make and what they will spend. For instance what they are to spend on advertising may well be something not left to decision at the national level. There will almost always be some degree of guidance from corporate executives; and there will usually be some degree of transfer of products or materials from one national area to another. Of course the prices at which these transfers are valued will have an immediate direct effect on national profitability.

STAGES IN THE GROWTH OF INTERNATIONAL BUSINESSES

International businesses, I suggest, go through three stages in their development, and perhaps only in the second stage is the profit of a national subsidiary even an approximately good measure of company performance. The first of these three stages is where the international side of the domestic business's operations is largely an export operation from the home country. In that case the overseas branches are simply selling outlets, sales offices. In a case like that no one would suggest that the profit shown by the sales outlet really represents the total contribution made by that sales outlet to corporate performance, since everything depends on the cost and prices at which the products are transferred to the sales outlet for sale. Then in the second stage, the stage perhaps at which national subsidiary profits do come closest to being a useful measure of performance, the national subsidiary becomes a full fledged production and marketing unit with its own manufacturing organization. Of course there may still be transfers between it and other parts of the corporate organization, but these may be at a minimum, so that we are dealing with something approximately like a self-contained business entity; and profit here does have its uses as a measure of performance. This is a stage into which many international businesses have moved and out of which the bigger ones are now moving into a third stage, where more and more the tendency is for the whole company to take a world view; hence production will be specialized, as far as possible, in those countries which are particularly well fitted to produce certain products. Production becomes specialized in certain centres from which other markets are supplied. Transfers multiply, personnel moves around so that the president of an American company with international operations no longer has to be an American, he may be drawn from any part of the world where the company is doing business. In these circumstances, it becomes increasingly difficult to say where the profit on a sale for that company is made. I shall have more to say about that shortly.

In this advanced stage separate national profits really totally lose their significance as a measure of the performance of any particular affiliate of a company. You see this perhaps most clearly if you look at the organization of a world wide oil company. I had a chance to visit two regional headquarters in Europe of one of the large American companies, one in Geneva and one in Paris. One of these offices was responsible for Europe, north of the Mediterranean, the other one was responsible for the Mediterranean area and North Africa. It is really very difficult, if not impossible, to separate the regional profits of these regions from what the company is doing in other parts of the world. If it is difficult to do it on a regional basis, it is certainly impossible to do it on a national basis. For instance, take one of the national companies in a part of one of these regions which happens to have a refinery. Of course not all national affiliates of oil companies have their own refinery, but let us take one that does. Then the refinery program is externally controlled, not in the local region but either in New York or in Houston, for instance. And it is controlled that way to meet demands not only in that region but in other regions in which the company is doing business. Stocks of crude oil are switched around the world by New York or Houston to meet corporate needs. The refinery is told what price it will have to pay for the crude oil it takes, it will even be told within limits what kind of crude oil it is going to get. New York or Houston fixes the transfer prices of refined products in the light of fiscal and tax considerations. Then so far as the selling prices at which the products will be marketed are concerned, in some countries these are controlled by government action, in others they are fixed by agreement among the producers (and certainly the corporate head office expects to be consulted about that), so that the affiliates have relatively little control over the prices at which they sell their products. And then finally, some affiliates have the minimum amount of control over the amount of capital investment. They have to call on corporate sources of capital anyway for the most part, and in some countries the amount of capital expenditure which they are free to make without approval from higher echelons of management is minute — in one country, as they told me, not enough to open a gas station. In the total world view of a world-wide oil company, that does not amount to very much.

That is not quite the total list of reasons why a national affiliate of an oil company is not really free to do much to control its own profitability, but it will be enough to make my point. The affiliate, as you can see, does not control its buying prices, it does not control its selling prices, it does not control what it will make or what it will invest. That is true in a country in which the company under discussion has an oil refinery. Most of the countries in Europe, or many of them at least, do not have oil refineries or at least do not have an oil refinery owned by that particular company, and therefore what I have said about the lack of control by a single subsidiary of its own performance is even more true.

CAUSES OF CONFLICT

As a result of my study of this problem, both in Europe and in the United States, I have put together quite a lengthy list of causes of conflict within an international business, based on actual cases, some of which I want to discuss with you. I think you will see at the end that the moral is quite clear, that in business as elsewhere, the whole is more than the sum of its parts. That is true of a domestic business; it is even more true of an international business. I shall have a word to say later why I think these problems are more severe in the international field than in the domestic field.

One kind of cause of conflict concerned sources of supply. Subsidiary A may be able to buy from outside sources of supply in its country or elsewhere more cheaply than it can buy from a fellow subsidiary. But although it may be cheaper to the subsidiary to buy from outside, it may not be cheaper to the total corporation, because of course there is an absorption of overhead in the selling subsidiary when A buys from subsidiary B in another country. Subsidiary B may have idle capacity which corporate headquarters is anxious to find work for, so subsidiary A is told it must take high cost supplies from B rather than low cost supplies from an outside supplier. That is an obvious and fruitful source of conflict. Why should A's profits suffer in order to help the profits of a subsidiary in another country? As a matter of fact an example of this concerned a large Canadian company which helped me with my work in this field; a Canadian company which had subsidiaries in the United Kingdom and in France. They were making agricultural machinery. One particular machine was being made in both countries, but there was surplus capacity in France, and the United Kingdom company was told to stop making that machine and to buy, at what they thought was a high price, from the French subsidiary. On top of having to pay the high price they had to pay an import duty as well. They were not very happy about it. But from the corporate point of view this made sense.

Another kind of conflict arose in another company where a subsidiary in Denmark was making a product both for its home market and for sale to another subsidiary of the corporation, and they had some freedom in the methods they used to allocate cost among products. As you can guess, they did not stint the amount of cost allocated to the proportion of their product which was charged to their fellow subsidiary. By charging more cost there, they were able to charge less cost to the home market and show a good profit in the home market.

Another cause of conflict, quite a different kind of conflict, arose in another company when one subsidiary which had an undertaking to supply products to a sister subsidiary reneged on its contract because it was able to sell those products more profitably to another customer. It may well, by its default, have inflicted long-run damage, even short-run damage, on the other subsidiary which suffered from this violation of contract. It may well be that the whole corporation suffered long-run damage. But there was a short-run advantage in terms of profitability to the subsidiary which was able to sell more profitably to an outside customer rather than to the other subsidiary. The two countries concerned in this case were France and Italy. In the same company there was a different kind of conflict, as to the direction in which the corporation's research funds should be used. In one country they wanted research activity to be stepped up in the field of cast iron products. In another country they wanted research activity to be extended in the production of steel products, and an argument went on as to how the corporation should allocate its research funds. Nothing that the corporation could do would be likely to please both of these national affiliates. One thought that its particular market called for steel products, the other for cast iron products. Both wanted development to serve their special interests.

Here is a different kind of conflict — the conflict that arises where a corporation has an affiliate in a country which is subject to very serious inflation. Brazil is the country in question in this case, the Brazilian affiliate of a European parent company. From the point of view of the affiliate they would like funds to be made available cheaply by corporate headquarters. Corporate headquarters of course sees that investing outside money in a country which is suffering from galloping inflation, as Brazil was, is unwise. Local borrowing at almost any kind of interest rate at which you could get money made much more sense, because the purchasing power of your debt was being wiped out month by month as the price-level rose. So these very high interest rates did not suit the national affiliate, but they suited European headquarters very well. Local borrowing provided a hedge against inflation. The same kind of situation gives rise to a slightly different kind of problem, a problem which should be of interest to us as accountants in connection with profit measurement. We talk about business maximizing profits, but whose profits and what profits? Maximizing profits in the local currency of a country where there is a serious inflation is one thing, and that is of course all the local management is interested in. But it is not what the corporate management desires. They are interested in maximizing the profits they can take out. They wish to maximize profit in their external currency, American dollars or Swiss francs. And as I have already said, this will certainly tend to inhibit investment in the national subsidiary, giving rise to discontent and frustrations there.

You will expect that any list of these causes of conflict should mention taxation at some stage. And of course the incidence of taxation which varies from country to country may turn high profits before tax in one country into low profits after tax when corporate headquarters gets its hand on them, because of the differences between tax rates in different countries. So it may pay corporate headquarters to squeeze one subsidiary for the benefit of another for a number of tax reasons. For instance one subsidiary may have accumulated tax losses. Obviously it pays the corporation to pump as much profit as it can, for a time, into the country where there are accumulated tax losses, and it may do this by requiring other national subsidiaries to ship goods to that country at as low a transfer price as the authorities will allow. Of course the authorities have some say on this for reasons relating to customs duties and other factors. But subject to that, other companies may feel that they are being sacrificed to the company which is receiving low cost transfers of products, yet it may pay the corporation very well to do just that.

Another kind of situation arose during the period I am talking about in connection with the Italian subsidary of one of the companies I studied, which had set up an establishment in the Mezzogiorno, a southern part of Italy which at that time enjoyed very special tax privileges because it was a part of Italy which the Italian government was trying hard to develop, and into which they were trying to introduce new businesses. New businesses in that area enjoyed a tax holiday, I think for as much as ten years. It would pay a corporation to push as much profit as possible to a subsidiary located there to enjoy this tax holiday to the full. That means of course that other subsidiaries would have to suffer, with all the frustrations that would follow from that.

Here is a different kind of situation, which international companies try hard to avoid. A French subsidiary was making a product which the German subsidiary did not make. The French company accepted an order for these products from a German customer. This meant that another German company lost the order, and the other German company outside the corporate family which lost the order was itself a customer of the German affiliate. To recapitulate, the French affiliate takes an order from a German customer, another German company loses the order. The other German company is a customer of the German affiliate and becomes hostile to the whole corporation. The German affiliate suffers, the French affiliate enjoys the profits of the order from its German customer. This is a very direct example of an intracorporate conflict, and generally international businesses do have rules about this kind of thing. They are usually rules which require consultation, there is not much else you can do about it. No company is likely to make absolutely rigid rules that in no circumstances will a French company take an order from a German customer; that would not make much sense. There are rules which require consultation, and in the particular case I am citing they had not worked very well, or maybe there were no rules at that time, I am not sure.

Whenever a subsidiary in a foreign country is required to pay a dividend to corporate headquarters, that very fact gives rise to an intracorporate conflict. Subsidiaries do not like paying dividends; they prefer to plow back their earnings. They like reinvesting them in their own national area, especially if it happens to be short of capacity and needs capital for expansion. The requirement that a subsidary pays out even a proportion of its profits does not add to the popularity of the corporate headquarters located in another country.

Political considerations give rise to yet another kind of conflict and I suspect Canada could provide us with examples of this. A Canadian subsidiary of an American parent company — I am not thinking of a specific case — may have opportunities for doing profitable business with Cuba. I do not know whether American parents exert pressure on Canadian companies not to do business with Cuba in so-called strategic products, but whether it happens or not, it is obviously a stiuation that could happen. Another striking example, which I know of, occurred when one subsidiary of a corporation was doing business with Israel, and caused problems for other subsidiaries doing business with Arab countries. There is an obvious conflict of interest here since the Israeli business may be very profitable to the affiliate which does business with Israel, but may inflict greater losses on the corporation because of the loss of Arab business.

Conflict may obviously result when there is direct competition between subsidiary companies in a neutral market. In the case of a company which I have already referred to, there was a French affiliate and a German affiliate, but the corporation did not have a company in Holland, and both the French and German companies were free to do business in Holland and competed with each other in the Dutch market. I suppose there could have been rules to avoid that but there were none.

On top of all the problems I have talked about, an additional dimension is introduced where a subsidiary in one of these countries has outside shareholders. Where it is not a wholly-owned subsidiary, even more than in the case of the wholly-owned subsidiary it ceases to be a matter of indifference as to where profits are made. Obviously the corporation would like to put as much profit as it can into its wholly-owned subsidiary and as little as it can into the subsidiary which has outside shareholders. So, for instance, if there is a possibility of exporting to a neutral market from country A or country B, and subsidiary A is wholly-owned and subsidiary B has outside shareholders, clearly it would pay a corporation to supply the neutral market from the subsidiary which is wholly-owned, other things being equal. Of course there are some limits imposed by considerations of equity as to how far a corporation can go in neglecting or damaging the interest of outside stockholders, but you can see that there would be a temptation to arrange matters to put as much profit as possible into the wholly-owned subsidiary.

DOMESTIC AND INTERNATIONAL CONFLICT COMPARED

Nearly everything that I have said could be found to have an analogue within a wholly domestic divisionalized company, if there is such a thing. Probably there is no important company in the United States that does not have some international business. But almost everything that I have said could be matched by something very similar in a domestic setting. Nevertheless, as I indicated earlier, there are two or three reasons for saying that these intracorporate conflicts become more severe in an international business. For one thing, communication problems are more severe. Problems are generated by distance, differences of language, differences of custom and culture. All this makes communication somewhat more difficult, and misunderstanding somewhat easier. And of course there are usually more stages in the reporting process between the subordinate managers in a foreign subsidiary and top management in the corporate head office; so that, quite apart from differences of language and culture, this proliferation of stages in the reporting process is likely to make communication more difficult rather than less. In addition, there are questions of national pride that intervene. This obviously makes for added sensitivity to the particular method of performance measurement which the company uses. It is not just a question that division A made more profit than B, or division A increased its profit by 25% and division B only increased it by 10%. It now becomes a question that Frenchmen increased their profit by 25% and the Germans only increased it by 10%. That makes for great sensitivity. As a third reason for saying that these international differences are more serious than they would be in a purely domestic setting, there are the differences in legal systems and tax systems which become so important that a corporation is not free to arrange its affairs in a way that might appear to be theoretically best. It is not free to organize itself in what might seem to it to be an ideal manner.

For instance, an American company had important operations in Germany but also in many other countries of Europe. It had its main European production facilities in Germany. The sensible arrangement would be for this production facility not to be part of any national affiliate at all, as it was serving many national affiliates in different parts of the continent. But German law required that it had to be part of the German affiliate and it had to pay German taxes on its profits. And its profits had to be reasonable profits within the definition laid down by the German tax authority. By that was meant that the prices at which this facility transferred its manufactured products to other subsidiaries in other countries of Europe could not be dictated by purely economic considerations, could not be those prices which would maximize corporate profits. They had to be prices which would allow a reasonable degree of profit within Germany to be taxed under German law.

INTERNATIONAL TRANSFER PRICES

I wanted to say something more than I have said about international transfer prices. Let me just mention one or two considerations which make the setting of international transfer prices more difficult and somewhat different from the exceedingly difficult problem of setting domestic transfer prices. Some of the points here, which I am going to make very briefly, have in fact really been implied by what I have already said. There is the desire, for instance, in setting international transfer prices, to minimize the burden of taxation. The whole international corporation would like to transfer products at low transfer prices to low tax countries, to pump as much profit as possible into these countries. The extreme case was to invoice transfers at a low price to tax havens like Nassau. This is not so popular now, since the 1962 U.S. Revenue Act appeared, as it used to be. Another factor which complicates the transfer pricing problem over international frontiers is that setting low prices provides a means of remitting earnings from one country to another where this remittance of earnings is hindered by foreign exchange regulation, for instance. There have been times when you could not get money out of Britain very easily, so you want to keep profits low in Britain. You therefore transfer products to Britain at high prices. This really eliminates the profit that you cannot get out, and makes them appear in the country from which Britain is supplied by the international corporation.

Another thing an international business wants to do is to minimize the burden of tariffs. This makes it want to import into high tariff countries as cheaply as possible. So it sets low transfer prices on goods shipped to high tariff countries. Of course tariff authorities are alive to that and will usually introduce some kind of uplift system to avoid this kind of tariff evasion. But at least the international corporation is likely to go as far as it can to evade tariffs by the manipulation of its transfer prices. Yet another reason for manipulating transfer prices is to provide finance for expansion of a subsidiary in a country which for some reason restricts the importation of capital. I suppose that Canada might one day become so nationally conscious as to restrict capital imports from the United States.

I believe there are restrictions on the importation of capital into Ireland from foreign countries; 50% of Irish companies have to be owned by Irish nationals. Well, transfer pricing may allow you to get around that a bit, for by transferring products at low transfer prices to a national affiliate in a country which restricts importation of capital, you allow the affiliate to make substantial profits, profits substantial enough to provide for self-financing of expansion. That is another consideration which enters into international transfer prices, which is not present when you are considering purely domestic transfer prices.

PERFORMANCE MEASUREMENT AND REPORTING SYSTEMS

Finally let me say a word about what all this adds up to so far as accounting reporting systems are concerned. What we are likely to finish up with, if we do nothing about it, is a series of profits of national subsidiaries which are the result of all these manipulations; all these considerations, anyway, which put business where it pays the corporation to put it. We finish up with a lot of national profit figures which really mean very little if we are looking for a measurement of managerial performance in each national affiliate. Therefore, what we need to do is some reshuffling. We need to have some means of translating these fiscal profits into management profits to give us at least a first approximation to a measure of performance of each of these affiliates. We would like to know how much each national affiliate really is contributing to the success of the corporation.

It seems to me that there are probably three different approaches. I do not suggest that any of these approaches provides us with a complete answer to this problem. There is still room for plenty of work in this field. What a few companies do is to determine the profits of their subsidiaries in two different ways. Fiscal considerations, such as those I have just been mentioning, require them to use "reasonable" transfer prices because tax authorities and customs authorities do not like it otherwise. This does not mean that for managerial purposes this is what one should do. You can have a separate system of transfer prices at marginal cost; for instance, a set of marginal cost transfer prices which would, subject to some reservations, cause the full profitability of a national market to show up in the accounts of the national affiliate. I am not suggesting that this is what you would do for official tax accounting purposes. It might be the last thing you would want to do in a high tax country. But for managerial purposes, if you want to see what that particular market is contributing to corporate success, you would arrange transfers at marginal cost in this dual set of accounting records. I frankly do not know many companies, or more than one company to my knowledge, that do it, but it is a possible approach. A different kind of approach is to assert, more or less honestly, that no one can say how much corporate profit is being generated in each country.

Incidentally, when I look at the glossy financial reports that international oil companies publish, usually with a breakdown as to where profits have come from, so much from Asia, so much from Europe and so on, I wonder how they have solved this really insoluble problem of saying where the profits have come from. Of course you can have arbitrary accounting rules which provide you with figures, but it makes me a little uneasy to have these figures presented to the public with all the authority that the nicely printed document carries with it.

Even if we accept that it is impossible to determine where profits have been generated, it should be possible to report how variations from planned profit have been generated. This would require that each affiliate analyzes variations from planned or budgeted profit depending on how these variations resulted from actions which have been taken freely within that subsidiary, or from actions which have been taken elsewhere (for instance, a request by corporate headquarters that a product should be transferred to another affiliate at a price which the first affiliate would not have chosen itself but which it is charging because it was told to do so). Changes of that kind occurring during the year will obviously give rise to a variation of actual profit at the end of the year as compared with the planned profit. If the extent to which the change in transfer prices had affected profits could be picked up as a variation generated from outside the country, that would be useful information. Or, for instance, corporate headquarters may require one affiliate to give extended credit to another affiliate. That might give rise to a variation of profit which could be separated out as something caused by corporate considerations, not national considerations.

Another suggestion was made by Butler and Dearden a few years ago.[2] I do not think that they made their point very clear in that article, but what they seem to be arguing for is really an unscrambling of the omelet, so to speak. Whatever is done for fiscal purposes in the accounts, they suggest that once a year all the divisions and affiliates of a company should be required to assign all the costs in those affiliates and divisions, and the capital employed, to major product groups. So you would come up with a sort of full cost of all the products made all over the corporation. These product costs and the investments which generated the products are then charged to the divisions which are responsible for sales in a particular area. This information is used to produce what they call realistic product-stream profit and loss statements and figures of return on investment for major customer groups by product or product groups. I have already said that I do not think they make their point clearly, and I am making it even less clear by trying to paraphrase it in a few words.

This is an unsatisfactory point at which to stop. There is a challenge here for accountants, or for anyone concerned with performance measure-

---

[2] W. Jack Butler and J.W. Dearden, "Managing a World-wide Business", *Harvard Business Review*, May-June, 1965, pp. 93-102.

ment. Maybe, we have not done a superb job of solving these problems in the domestic field, although a lot of progress has been made there. There is still quite a challenge in the international field. It is a field in which accountants, students of international business, international finance, management science and a lot of other disciplines can usefully come together. I hope you think that that makes it a fairly suitable topic for discussion in this seminar.

* * * * * *

List of Titles

Accounting History and the Development of a Profession

Management Accounting Research: A Review and Annotated Bibliography.
Charles F. Klemstine and Michael W. Maher. New York, 1984.

Accounting Literature in Non-Accounting Journals: An Annotated Bibliography.
Panadda Tantral. New York, 1984.

The Evolution of Behavioral Accounting Research: An Overview.
Robert H. Ashton, editor. New York, 1984.

Some Early Contributions to the Study of Audit Judgment.
Robert H. Ashton, editor. New York, 1984.

Depreciation and Capital Maintenance.
Richard P. Brief, editor. New York, 1984.

The Case for Continuously Contemporary Accounting.
G. W. Dean and M. C. Wells, editors. New York, 1984.

Studies of Company Records: 1830–1974.
J. R. Edwards, editor. New York, 1984.

European Equity Markets: Risk, Return, and Efficiency.
Gabriel Hawawini and Pierre Michel, editors. New York, 1984.

Transactions of the Chartered Accountants Students' Societies of Edinburgh and Glasgow: A Selection of Writings, 1886–1958.
Thomas A. Lee, editor. New York, 1984.

The Development of Double Entry: Selected Essays.
Christopher Nobes, editor. New York, 1984.

Papers on Accounting History.
R. H. Parker. New York, 1984.

Collected Papers on Accounting and Accounting Education.
David Solomons. New York, 1984.

The General Principles of the Science of Accounts and the Accountancy of Investment.
Charles E. Sprague. New York, 1984.

Selected Papers on Accounting, Auditing, and Professional Problems.
Edward Stamp. New York, 1984.

Factory Accounts.
John Whitmore. New York, 1984.

Sourcebook on Accounting Principles and Auditing Procedures: 1917–1953 (in two volumes).
Stephen A. Zeff and Maurice Moonitz, editors. New York, 1984.

The First Fifty Years 1913–1963.
Arthur Andersen Company. Chicago, 1963.

Paciolo on Accounting.
R. Gene Brown and Kenneth S. Johnston. New York, 1963.

The Early History of Coopers & Lybrand.
Coopers & Lybrand. New York, 1984.

Report of the Trial . . . Against the Directors and the Manager of the City of Glasgow Bank.
Charles Tennant Couper. Edinburgh, 1879.

Development of Accounting Thought.
Harvey T. Deinzer. New York, 1965.

The Principles of Auditing.
F.R.M. De Paula. London, 1915.

The Accountant, or, the Method of Bookkeeping Deduced from Clear Principles, and Illustrated by a Variety of Examples.
James Dodson. London, 1750.

A Common Sense Method of Double Entry Bookkeeping, on First Principles, as Suggested by De Morgan. Part I, Theoretical.
S. Dyer. London, 1897.

Economics of Fatigue and Unrest and the Efficiency of Labour in English and American Industry.
P. Sargant Florence. London, 1923.

Haskins & Sells: Our First Seventy-Five Years.
Arthur B. Foye. New York, 1970.

The History of the Society of Incorporated Accountants, 1885–1957.
A. A. Garrett. Oxford, 1961.

The Game of Budget Control.
Geert Hofstede. Assen, 1967.

The History of The Institute of Chartered Accountants in England and Wales 1880–1965, and of Its Founder Accountancy Bodies 1870–1880.
Sir Harold Howitt. London, 1966.

History of the Chartered Accountants of Scotland from the Earliest Times to 1954.
Institute of Chartered Accountants of Scotland. Edinburgh, 1954.

Accounting Thought and Education: Six English Pioneers.
J. Kitchen and R. H. Parker. London, 1980.

The Evolution of Corporate Financial Reporting.
T. A. Lee and R. H. Parker. Middlesex, 1979.

Accounting in Scotland: A Historical Bibliography.
Janet E. Pryce-Jones and R. H. Parker. Edinburgh, 1976.

A History of Accountants in Ireland.
H. W. Robinson. Dublin, 1964.

The Sixth International Congress on Accounting.
London, 1952.

The Accomptant's Oracle: or, Key to Science, Being a Compleat Practical System of Book-keeping.
Wardbaugh Thompson. York, 1777.

Accountancy in Transition

The Tangled Web of Price Variation Accounting: The Development of Ideas Underlying Professional Prescriptions in Six Countries.
F. L. Clarke. New York, 1982.

Beta Alpha Psi, From Alpha to Omega: Pursuing a Vision of Professional Education for Accountants, 1919–1945.
Terry K. Sheldahl. New York, 1982.

Four Classics on the Theory of Double-Entry Bookkeeping.
Richard P. Brief, editor. New York, 1982.

Forerunners of Realizable Values Accounting in Financial Reporting.
G. W. Dean and M. C. Wells, editors. New York, 1982.

Accounting Queries.
Harold C. Edey. New York, 1982.

The Development of Accounting Theory: Significant Contributors to Accounting Thought in the 20th Century.
Michael Gaffikin and Michael Aitken, editors. New York, 1982.

Studies in Social and Private Accounting.
Solomon Fabricant. New York, 1982.

Bond Duration and Immunization: Early Developments and Recent Contributions.
Gabriel A. Hawawini, editor. New York, 1982.

Further Essays on the History of Accounting.
Basil S. Yamey. New York, 1982.

Accounting Principles Through The Years: The Views of Professional and Academic Leaders 1938–1954.
Stephen A. Zeff, editor. New York, 1982.

The Accounting Postulates and Principles Controversy of the 1960s.
Stephen A. Zeff, editor. New York, 1982.

Fiftieth Anniversary Celebration.
American Institute of Accountants. New York, 1937.

Library Catalogue.
American Institute of Accountants. New York, 1919.

Four Essays in Accounting Theory.
F. Sewell Bray. London, 1953. *bound with*
Some Accounting Terms and Concepts.
Institute of Chartered Accountants in England and Wales and The National Institute of Economic and Social Research. Cambridge, 1951.

Accounting in Disarray.
R. J. Chambers. Melbourne, 1973.

The Balance-Sheet.
Charles B. Couchman. New York, 1924.

Audits.
Arthur E. Cutforth. London, 1906.

Methods of Amalgamation.
Arthur E. Cutforth. London, 1926.

Deloitte & Co. 1845–1956.
Sir Russell Kettle. Oxford, 1958. *bound with*
Fifty-seven Years in an Accountant's Office.
Ernest Cooper. London, 1921.

Accountants and the Law of Negligence.
R. W. Dickerson. Toronto, 1966.

Consolidated Statements.
H. A. Finney. New York, 1922.

The Rate of Interest.
Irving Fisher. New York, 1907.

Holding Companies and Their Published Accounts.
Sir Gilbert Garnsey. London, 1923. *bound with*
Limitations of a Balance Sheet.
Sir Gilbert Garnsey. London, 1928.

Accounting Concepts of Profit.
Stephen Gilman. New York, 1939.

An Introduction to Merchandise, Parts IV and V (Italian Bookkeeping and Practical Bookkeeping).
Robert Hamilton. Edinburgh, 1788.

The Merchant's Magazine: or, Trades-man's Treasury.
Edward Hatton. London, 1695.

The Law of Accounting and Financial Statements.
George S. Hills. Boston, 1957.

International Congress on Accounting 1929.
New York, 1930.

Fourth International Congress on Accounting 1933.
London, 1933.

Magnificent Masquerade.
Charles Keats. New York, 1964.

Profit Measurement and Price Changes.
Kenneth Lacey. London, 1952.

The American Accomptant.
Chauncey Lee. Lansingburgh, 1797.

Consolidated Balance Sheets.
George Hills Newlove. New York, 1926.

Consolidated and Other Group Accounts.
T. B. Robson. London, 1950.

Accounting Method.
C. Rufus Rorem. Chicago, 1928.

Shareholder's Money.
Horace B. Samuel. London, 1933.

Standardized Accountancy in Germany. (With a new appendix.)
H. W. Singer. Cambridge, 1943.

The Securities and Exchange Commission in the Matter of McKesson & Robbins, Inc. Report on Investigation.
Washington, D. C., 1940.

The Securities and Exchange Commission in the Matter of McKesson & Robbins, Inc. Testimony of Expert Witnesses.
Washington, D. C., 1939.

Accounting in England and Scotland: 1543–1800.
B. S. Yamey, H. C. Edey, Hugh W. Thomson. London, 1963.